Evaluating Quality in Services
for Disabled and Older People

Jб

Disability and Rehabilitation series

Approaches to Case Management for People with Disabilities
Doria Pilling
ISBN 1 85302 099 0
Disability and Rehabilitation 1

Managing Disability at Work
Improving Practice in Organisations
Brenda Smith, Margery Povall and Michael Floyd
ISBN 1 85302 123 7
Disability and Rehabilitation 2

Information Technology Training for People with Disabilities
Edited by Michael Floyd
ISBN 1 85302 129 6
Disability and Rehabilitation 4

Mental Health at Work
Issues and Initiatives
Edited by Michael Floyd, Margery Povall and Graham Watson
Disability and Rehabilitation 5

Evaluating Quality in Services for Disabled and Older People

Edited by Doria Pilling and Graham Watson

Disability and Rehabilitation 7

Jessica Kingsley Publishers • London and Bristol, Pennsylvania *and*
The Rehabilitation Resource Centre, City University, London

Figure 14.5 originally published in 'Rest Assured: New Moves in Quality Assurance for Residential Care' by Leonie Kellaher and Sheila Peace. In J. Johnson and R. Slater (eds) *Ageing and Later Life*, Open University Press/Sage, 1993. Reproduced by permission.

First published in the United Kingdom in 1995 by
Jessica Kingsley Publishers Ltd
116 Pentonville Road
London N1 9JB, England
and
1900 Frost Road, Suite 101
Bristol, PA 19007, U S A

Copyright © 1995 The contributors and the publisher

Library of Congress Cataloging in Publication Data
Evaluating quality in services for disabled and older people / edited
by Doria Pilling and Graham Watson.
p. cm. -- (Disability and rehabilitation : 7)
Includes bibliographical references and index.
ISBN 1-85302-289-6
1. Handicapped--Services for--Evaluation. 2. Quality assurance.
I. Pilling, Doria. II. Watson, Graham, 1926– . III. City
University (London, England). Rehabilitation Resource Centre.
IV. Series: Disability and rehabilitation series : 7.
IN PROCESS
362.4'0685--dc20   95-7249
                                                         CIP

British Library Cataloguing in Publication Data
A CIP catalogue record for this book is available from the British Library

ISBN 1-85302-289-6

Printed and Bound in Great Britain by
Cromwell Press, Melksham, Wiltshire

Contents

Acknowledgements   vii

Introduction   1
Doria Pilling

Part 1. Evaluating PASS and PASSING as Quality Measures

Chairman's Introduction – PASS and PASSING in the Context of their Time   11
David Felce

1. The PASS and PASSING Evaluation Instruments   13
   Paul Williams

2. What Have We Been Learning from PASS and PASSING in Workshops
   and Real Evaluations?   25
   Alan Tyne

3. Evaluation and Change in Service Systems for People with Disabilities   33
   Gerald Midgley

4. Do PASS and PASSING Pass? A Critique of PASS/ING   50
   Doria Pilling

5. The Results from PASS and PASSING Evaluations   61
   Paul Williams

6. ACE – An Assessment of Care Environments   78
   Paul Wolfson

7. PASS/ING and ACE in Action – Similarities and Differences in Evaluating
   Services   84
   Doria Pilling and Gerald Midgley

Part 2. Workshops: Is a Consensus on Quality Standards Possible?

8. Evaluating Quality   107
   Peter Allen

9. Exploring Quality of Life and its Relationship to PASS: Looking
   for Agreement   114
   David Felce

10. Quality Measurement in the All-Wales Strategy   126
    Judy Renshaw

Part 3. Perspectives on Quality

11. QUARTZ, PASSING and User Involvement: Meeting Points
    and Departure Points   135
    Stephen Pilling

12. What Do Users Think About Quality?   148
    *Peter Lindley, Jim Band, Bill Gorf, Margaret Guerrero, Dale Walker
    and Kath Gillespie Sells*

13. Quality for People – Learning from Service Users About Quality   158
    Alison Kerruish

14. IQA: Inside Quality Assurance – Its Rationale and Use in Residential
    and Non-Residential Settings   164
    Leonie Kellaher

15. Framework for Accomplishment   180
    Alan Tyne

Part 4. Workshops: What Are Evaluations for, and How Should they be Carried Out?

16. Service Evaluation by People with Learning Difficulties   191
    Simon Gardner and Andrea Whittaker

17. Aiming for Objectivity and Balance in the Evaluation of the Quality of
    Life Experienced by Service Users with Learning Disabilities   201
    David Hughes

18. Who Should Evaluations be Carried Out for?   207
    Charles Ritchie

Part 5. Towards Quality

19. Summing Up – Safeguarding Quality   213
    David Felce

Contributors   217

Index   221

Acknowledgements

Thanks must go first of all to the King Edward's Hospital Fund for London, and in particular to Dr Iden Wickings, the Deputy Director who started off the whole process from which this book has emerged. They initiated the idea of an evaluation of PASS and PASSING, gave the RRC at City University the grant to carry it out, and supported the conference that grew from it, and on which this book is based. We would also like to thank, in particular, Paul Williams, the Director of Community and Mental Handicap Educational and Research Association, the main organisation promoting PASS and PASSING in this country, for his co-operation during the evaluation, which must have sometimes been an uncomfortable process. The Advisory Group, during the evaluation, of Brian McGinnis, Roger Blunden and Peter Lindley was very helpful in many ways. It is quite impossible to thank all the people to whom we talked, or who helped in some way during the evaluation of PASS and PASSING. We must, though, give special thanks to those who agreed to our evaluating their services. One person who must be mentioned by name is Don Braisby, without whom the comparison we made of PASS and PASSING with another method of assessing service quality would have been impossible. We are also very grateful to Mike Floyd for his support in organising the conference, to David Felce for chairing it so well, pulling the diverse threads together, and to Brian McGinnis for standing in as chairman for a couple of sessions so that David could keep a prior commitment. Finally, we would like to thank everyone who agreed to contribute to the conference and the book.

Acknowledgements

Introduction

Doria Pilling

This book is based on contributions to a conference on *Evaluating Quality* in services for disabled and older people. One of the central debates running through the conference was the role of service users in defining 'quality'. Should they be the final arbiters, or because of the devaluation and disempowerment that many service users experience, are the expectations of some service users likely to be limited, are they unlikely to demand radical changes? Should 'quality' be more concerned about redressing the devalued position of disabled and disadvantaged people in society.

The *Evaluating Quality* Conference

The conference had five main, and overlapping, aims:

- To present to a wider audience some of the findings from an evaluation of a method of assessing service quality that has had an extremely influential role in changing service provision, particularly in the learning disabilities area, and the thinking of service planners and providers since the early 1980s – PASS and its updated version PASSING. Quality criteria are derived from the normalisation/social role valorisation theory of its main author (Wolfensberger and Glenn 1975, Wolfensberger and Thomas 1983), and aimed at revaluing people who are devalued in society. Evaluation is carried out by a team trained and experienced in the method.
- To present contrasting methods of assessing service quality that have recently been developed, particularly those that give 'insiders' in services a major role in defining what quality is and in carrying out service evaluation.
- To provide a forum for debate of some of the problems involved in determining what quality in services is, who should define it, whether a consensus on quality is possible, whose interests should be taken into account, and whether standards should be 'idealistic' or realistic.
- To present service users' perspectives on what quality is and how it should be assessed.

- To inform people who are concerned with improving services of the role that evaluation can play in this, of the uses, strengths and limitations of different methods.

PASS, PASSING and the Evaluation of These Measures

The conference itself stemmed from an evaluation of PASS (Program Analysis of Service Systems, Wolfensberger and Glenn 1975) and its updated version PASS-ING (Program Analysis of Service Systems' Implementation of Normalization Goals, Wolfensberger and Thomas 1983), that the RRC at City University had carried out, on the initiative of, and with a grant from, the King's Fund (see Chapter 4 for how this came about). PASS and PASSING are quantitative methods for evaluating the quality of services for any group of people with disabilities or disadvantages. The essence of the normalisation principle on which they are based (Wolfensberger 1972, 1980) is that people with disabilities or disadvantages should have as culturally valued a life as possible, or, in a more recent formulation (in which Wolfensberger, 1983, suggests that a preferable term is 'social role valorisation') that they should be enabled to attain/maintain valued roles in society. Services are rated on the extent to which they promote these objectives. The overall aim is a long-term one, to redress society's attitude to people who are devalued, to open up opportunities and experiences, rather than simply to improve people's quality of life in the short term (see Williams, Chapter 1, and Pilling, Chapter 4, for accounts of these ideas).

Although there have been a number of commissioned evaluations using PASS in this country, carried out by a trained and experienced team, the instruments have been used most extensively, and have achieved most of their influence, in normalisation training workshops, during which practice evaluations are carried out (Lindley and Wainwright 1992).

How to evaluate complex measures like PASS and PASSING, based on a controversial theory, posed considerable methodological problems (see Pilling and Midgley, Chapter 7, for some discussion of these). Much time was spent discussing with those experienced in the use of the methods and with researchers knowledgeable about evaluation. Eventually, the centre of our investigation became a comparison of the way PASS/ING and ACE (Clifford and Wolfson 1989), a measure recently devised to assess overall service quality, evaluated services (Chapter 7 reports on this). Other aspects included: a review of the available literature on PASS and PASSING, and normalisation/social role valorisation theory, which from a relatively thin start grew quite rapidly during the period of the evaluation (see Pilling, Chapter 4); a theoretical analysis by Gerald Midgley, of the appropriate context for using PASS and PASSING and of how other methods can complement them (see Chapter 3); and interviews with those whose service had had a commissioned PASS evaluation to find out its impact.

How the Conference Came About

The King's Fund had suggested holding a seminar to disseminate the findings of the evaluation of PASS and PASSING. The idea of the conference grew out of this. It seemed to us at the RRC that the issues that had arisen on how quality in services should be defined, who should define it, and who should carry out evaluations were of far wider interest than to people who already knew something about PASS and PASSING. This was particularly so in the new era of community care, following the National Health Service and Community Care Act (1990), with the emphasis on contracting for service provision bringing the need to safeguard standards and improve the fit to users' needs to the foreground. It was decided to extend the theme of the conference to bring in presentations from those who were developing other methods of evaluating service quality, and to set up a debate between those with contrasting views.

The Structure and Content of the Book

The book keeps the same structure as the conference. Discussion is included, summarised at the end of the presentation at which it took place, but covering more than one presentation in some cases. Contributors were given the opportunity to review their presentations if they wished. The workshops are summarised, but problems with recording meant that the discussion could not always be included.

Part 1 focuses on PASS and PASSING, the ideas behind them, and the main aspects of the RRC's evaluation. Part 2 comprises the first set of workshops, broadly around the theme of whether there can be a consensus on quality standards. Part 3 presents a number of different methods of evaluating service quality, and the views of service users on what quality is and how it should be assessed. Part 4 comprises the second set of workshops, around the theme of who and what evaluations are for, and who should carry them out. In Part 5, the conference chairman, David Felce, sums up the issues covered and examines the role of the three concepts, normalisation/social role valorisation, user empowerment and quality of life in safeguarding quality standards for people with disabilities or at a disadvantage.

Part 1 starts off with the chairman's Introduction to the conference, in which David Felce indicates how PASS immensely broadened the scope of what constitutes service quality.

Paul Williams, in Chapter 1, especially written for this book, provides the most comprehensive description of and background to PASS and PASSING that has been written so far. He details the ratings in the measures and the rationale for including them. He goes on to discuss the influences on their main author, Wolfensberger, which led him to devise his principles of normalisation, and a measure of service quality based upon them, including: the research carried out in the 1950s and 1960s in this country indicating the work potential of many people with severe learning disabilities; the Scandinavian concept of 'normalisation'; Wolfensberger's own historical work showing how negative perceptions of people with learning disabilities affected the behaviour of the public and service planners towards them; the opportunity to take part in establishing a pioneer community service for people with learning disabilities in Canada, and need for an instrument to evaluate its quality.

Wolfensberger's experiences led him to emphasise in the instrument not only the lifestyle of service users, but whether the service's practices were likely to lead to more helpful public perceptions of the users. Paul Williams also gives his answer, in this chapter, to one of the most common criticisms of the measures, that they do not take account of ethnic or gender identities of service users, by describing a lesser-known aspect of a PASS or PASSING evaluation, the 'foundation discussion', which he considers can incorporate recognition of, and respect for, the values of any section of the community from which a person may come.

Alan Tyne's contribution, Chapter 2, was the first presentation at the conference. He explains the context of services in the 1970s into which he introduced PASS, having chanced upon it in a workshop in Wisconsin, and how the time was right to explore the underlying ideology of service provision. He sees the theory of devaluation of service users, from which PASS and PASSING are derived, as being based on three key values of our society – justice, stewardship and community. He views the disabled people's movement as being based on the same values, but looking at the problem rather differently – as one of disempowerment or exclusion. He looks at what has been learned from PASS and PASSING workshops and evaluations, and ends by describing the care that needs to be taken in presenting feedback, for it is likely to involve telling people who have invited you to evaluate their service that they have been doing things wrong.

Gerald Midgley, in Chapter 3, starts with the assumption that no single evaluation method, or method of directing organisational change, can cope with every single issue that has to be faced in evaluating or trying to change service systems for people with disabilities. Writing from the theoretical perspective of Critical Systems Thinking he identifies the context in which he thinks PASS and PASSING can most profitably be employed – one where the issues are relatively clear and there is general (though not necessarily complete) agreement with its ideology of normalisation. He goes on to examine three methods which he sees as being able to complement PASS/ING: a method of diagnosing problems of communication and control in the management of services; a method of establishing structured debate when there are different interest groups with different perspectives on issues; and a method of increasing understanding, and beginning to move towards better ways of working in a situation where the problems are unclear. He gives a hypothetical example of how these methods might work together.

Next, in Chapter 4, Doria Pilling reviews some aspects of Wolfensberger's normalisation ideas, and some of the most commonly made criticisms of these and the measures based on them. Her own work on expectation theory, on which Wolfensberger's ideas draw heavily, suggests that most of the experimental work carried out on this issue has been inadequate, but that naturally occurring (rather than artificially induced) expectations do have an effect, especially when reinforced by the practices and opportunities provided by society. Other aspects considered are: why integration is so central to Wolfensberger's normalisation ideas; whether there is too much emphasis on image-enhancement in the ratings; what should be regarded as 'valued'; whether the need to change society's attitudes and values is emphasised enough; de-institutionalisation; the strengths of a PASS/ING evaluation, and the care needed in feedback to staff and managers when radical change is recommended.

Chapter 5 includes an account of the work that Paul Williams himself has carried out evaluating PASS/ING. He starts by detailing the scoring system, describes his own and North American work on the reliability of these instruments, and his work on their validity and consistency. Taking a series of residential services for adults with learning difficulties, evaluated by PASS3, he suggests that the order of quality in which they are placed, as measured by this instrument, is a sensible one, according with independent criteria of quality. However, he concedes that the actual scores are considerably harsher than would be obtained using other quality measures, but argues that the high standards have awakened many service planners and providers to service inadequacies. He also uses illustrative data to show how PASS and PASSING scores and subscores, i.e. scores derived by grouping together ratings – in particular areas of service practice – can be used to compare services. The chapter ends, though, with his contention that the most important aspect of an evaluation, particularly from the point of view of initiating change, is often the analysis of service users' needs in the 'foundation discussion', rather than the quantitative results.

As Paul Wolfson said at the Evaluating Quality conference, ACE is described because it was the quality measure that PASS and PASSING were compared with in the RRC evaluation. However, this should not lead to its being underestimated. It was chosen precisely because it is one of the few other measures of overall service quality, and is one that can be used in most types of setting, can be carried out in a short time and the findings are relatively easy to interpret. Devised by Paul Clifford and Paul Wolfson to measure environmental quality in the evaluation of the closure of Cane Hill hospital, ACE is particularly useful in finding differences in similar types of setting. Paul Wolfson, in Chapter 6, explains why it was needed and illustrates its use by showing how it differentiates between a ward with a rehabilitation team and a conventional long-stay ward, and how it indicates changes in a low staff home in the community over the period of a year.

In Chapter 7 Doria Pilling and Gerald Midgley discuss the methodological decisions they took in deciding that a comparison of the results of PASS/ING and ACE evaluations should be the central aspect of their investigation of the validity of PASS and PASSING. They describe how the comparisons were made and give a detailed account of the similarities and differences between PASSING and ACE ratings of a residential service for older people, investigating the reasons for differences. In particular they try to explain how it can be that, despite many similarities in the picture of the service provided by the two instruments, its relevance to its users is rated totally inadequate in PASSING, while in ACE it is seen as relatively appropriate. The chapter ends with a summary of the similarities and differences in the way which ACE and PASS/ING rate services, emerging from all four comparisons carried out, the likely reasons for the differences, and the particular strengths of the instruments.

Part 2 comprises the workshops held on the first day of the conference, based loosely around the theme of whether a consensus on quality standards is possible.

In Chapter 8, based on the first workshop, Peter Allen describes some of the experiences of a Quality Action Group in East London, and how they attempted to define quality. A major theme of the discussion around this was whether 'quality' is about the small changes that such a group can bring about, or whether it is about making much more fundamental changes in the position of service users in society.

David Felce examines quality of life measures in Chapter 9, based on the second workshop (but entirely rewritten for the book as the recording of the conference presentation was very poor). He describes four models for conceptualising quality of life, and suggests that there is considerable agreement on the aspects of life that should be included in measures of this. Although PASS is not a quality of life measure, it evaluates the extent to which services enable users to attain conditions of life that are valued in the society. An analysis of its ratings shows that they are consistent with the life domains usually found in quality of life measures.

Judy Renshaw's presentation in the third workshop, in Chapter 10, provides much useful information on how to evaluate service quality, drawing on lessons learned from a survey of the monitoring and evaluation that has been carried out of the All-Wales Strategy. Having learned from this survey, the team in the Audit Commission/Welsh Office project she is describing set out to build its own evaluation instrument, on the foundation provided by those in use. In the course of this, a comparison was made of checklists drawn from policy documents, and users' views, about how services should be run, and the four instruments that have had most influence on evaluation in Wales, including PASSING. PASSING was somewhat more in accord with the checklists than the other three instruments considered, but placed more emphasis on image enhancement and less on user–staff relationships.

Part 3 moves away from PASS/ING, with several accounts of other methods of assessing service quality that have recently been developed, presented by one of the authors of the methods. These methods all have an element of 'insider' evaluation, but the balance between 'inside' and 'external' evaluation, and the weight given to staff and users varies. Part 3 also contains the presentations of people who are service users themselves, giving their views of what quality measures should be like. In the last chapter in Part 3, Alan Tyne, who has much experience in its use, describes Framework for Accomplishment, a method compatible with normalisation ideas, but which involves a collaborative process for making changes in services, rather than being a quantitative rating method.

To start off Part 3, in Chapter 11 Stephen Pilling, one of its authors, provides an overview of the rationale, development and components of QUARTZ, a comprehensive quality assurance method, devised initially for mental health services but being used much more widely. It is based on current conceptions of good practice, and the findings of empirical research. Because of the number of factors and complexity of interaction between them in developing and maintaining quality it is suggested that a multi-dimensional approach is necessary. Schedules are provided to examine all aspects of the setting, and a number of these are selected for use by the reviewer and staff of the setting. The combination of elements of external review with the central involvement of staff, who are seen as the primary determinants of the quality of care provided, are distinguishing features of the method. This does not mean that users' views are not taken into account, and the author gives detailed examples of the consultation process with service users and the results of this, particularly its contribution to developing a dialogue between staff and users. He also gives his view of various ways in which QUARTZ differs from PASSING.

In the first part of the next chapter, Chapter 12, Peter Lindley, Jim Band, Bill Gorf, Margaret Guerrero and Dale Walker bring together the views of mental health service users and ex-users, including their contributions at the conference, and views from pre-conference preparation meetings. One of the main conference themes is epitomised in their changing the title of this presentation, from the original at the conference of 'The insiders' view of quality', to 'What do users think about quality?', because, they say, users feel that they are on the outside of the system, having to accept what is on offer. Service providers, and staff, users believe, are the real 'insiders', with power to make changes. They think, though, that the situation is improving, and users' voices are being listened to more. They say that it should be service users who set the agenda in deciding standards, and that users should also contribute to the assessment process. They consider some aspects of mental health services – abuse, protection of women, ECT, medication – that are often seen as being outside the province of quality assurance systems, but whose inclusion is essential if these are to fulfil users' requirements.

Kath Gillespie Sells was invited to present the views on quality of people with a physical disability but points out, in the second part of Chapter 12, that divisions between disabled people are unhelpful and divide the movement. Nor are there rigid divisions between who is a user and who a professional. She provides a guide for exploring whether services really are what the disabled person wants. She emphasises the need for users to be represented in all aspects of planning and providing services, including training the professionals.

Continuing the theme of listening to 'insiders' Alison Kerruish describes, in Chapter 13, the project in which she was involved, which attempted to establish what for residents constitutes a good quality residential service, and to develop user-led ways of monitoring the service. The residents involved were living in supported housing, having previously spent many years in psychiatric hospitals. She describes the process of obtaining information, through unstructured group discussions, on what residents thought was good and bad about the residential service, of categorising the information, and designing monitoring methods that would be appropriate for the issues raised. Most important, though, she says was the initial phase in which the research team got to know and establish trust between themselves and the residents, and those working in the houses. She also discusses the issue of how much users can be empowered.

Leonie Kellaher presents, in Chapter 14, another method of establishing a system of review in individual residential homes, which seeks to place the resident at the centre, IQA (Inside Quality Assurance). The rationale for this method is that the resident collectivity is 'the most fixed point in the complex entity that is residential care', and so accounts given by this group should have great weight. Views of others 'within' the home are also taken into account, including staff and relatives, and the IQA process is steered by a group made up of both insiders and outsiders. The author describes the process through which information is obtained, and gives examples of what people say. She deals with possible difficulties, such as the issue of confidentiality, and possible criticisms, for example, that the information may be too 'soft' to lead to managerial or organisational action. The impact of IQA is being evaluated. Although it has mainly been used in homes for older people, it is seen as applicable to all user groups, and potentially for domiciliary as well as residential care.

In a deliberate symmetry, Alan Tyne was asked to make the last as well as the first presentation at the conference, of Framework for Accomplishment, which he describes as neither an evaluation instrument nor training method, but a framework to use for people who want to find an effective way of improving services. Framework is quoted frequently by those attempting to assess service quality (see, for example, Chapters 13 and 16), but rarely written about in any detail. Alan Tyne provides here, in Chapter 15, the most comprehensive description so far available of its development, of what people do at a Framework workshop, and explains some differences from PASS/ING. Although entirely compatible with normalisation, he says that Framework is based on wider ideas, growing from 'the ground' rather than down from sociological theory. It focuses on 'capacity', not deficits, helping participants to suggest innovative and creative ways of using resources that would make a real difference to an individual's life. And it is a collaborative process, in which teams are encouraged to build relationships with the service they are visiting.

Part 4 comprises the second set of workshops, loosely based around the themes of who and what evaluations are for, and by whom they should be carried out.

In Chapter 16 Simon Gardner and Andrea Whittaker describe the advantages of services being evaluated by service users, in this case people with learning disabilities, particularly the increased rapport that can be achieved in the interviews. Much of this workshop was in the form of a dialogue with workshop participants, and the interesting question was raised of what the evaluator should do if service users' views conflict with their own.

In Chapter 17 David Hughes discusses the strengths and weaknesses of three methods of evaluating services for people with severe learning disabilities: non-participant observation, taking a momentary time sample; participant observation; and interviewing. Much of this workshop consisted of group discussions – of how to obtain the views of people with severe communication problems and how users might be involved more fully in the evaluation process, and summaries of these are included.

The third workshop, reported by Charles Ritchie in Chapter 18, consisted of a participatory exercise around the evaluation of a hypothetical health project. Workshop participants were split into four groups, representing different stakeholder interests: recipients; providers; funders; other vested interests. Each was asked to consider: the aims they might have for the project; the decisions they might want to take based on the evaluation findings; the information they would need to collect, and how, and by whom this should be categorised. In the final discussion 'insiders' were seen as those who best knew what was going on in projects, it was thought to be difficult to reconcile the competing needs of the different stakeholder groups in the evaluation process, and there was a wariness of external evaluation.

Part 5 contains David Felce's summing-up of the whole conference. He says that three main themes have been discussed: normalisation/social role valorisation (SRV), user empowerment and quality of life, which are distinct issues, and should be viewed as such, although they overlap. The importance of all three is more established than it was a decade or more ago, and all have a role in making sure that the quality of life and place in society of people who are vulnerable is safeguarded. All also have their weaknesses. But he sees SRV as providing a strong basis for the protection of people, because it provides an absolute standard, one of equality with the typical culture, which is a safeguard against low expectations, or lower standards for people who are vulnerable.

Terminology

PASS and PASSING are sometimes referred to, for convenience, as PASS/ING, where a distinction between them is not essential.

References

Clifford, P. and Wolfson, P. (1989) *FACE. A Functional Assessment of Care Environments, the Cane Hill Version*. London: RDP/Sainsbury Centre for Mental Health.

Lindley, P. and Wainwright, T. (1992) Normalisation training: conversion or commitment. In H. Brown and H. Smith (eds) *Normalisation: A Reader for the Nineties*. London: Routledge.

Wolfensberger, W. (1972) *The Principle of Normalization in Human Services*. Toronto: National Institute on Mental Retardation.

Wolfensberger, W. (1980) The definition of normalization: update, disagreements and misunderstandings. In R. Flynn and K. Nitsch (eds) *Normalization, Social Integration and Community Services*. Baltimore: University Park Press.

Wolfensberger, W. (1983) Social role valorisation: a proposed new term for the principle of normalization. *Mental Retardation*, Vol 21, 235–239.

Wolfensberger, W. and Glenn, L. (1975) *Programme Analysis of Service Systems: Handbook and Field Manual*, 3rd edition. Toronto: National Institute on Mental Retardation.

Wolfensberger, W. and Thomas, S. (1983) *Programme Analysis of Service Systems' Implementation of Normalization Goals: Normalization Criteria and Ratings Manual*, 2nd edition. Toronto: National Institute on Mental Retardation.

Chairman's Introduction – PASS and PASSING in the Context of their Time

David Felce

I do not want to overextend my introduction to the Conference but I thought it might be useful to put the development of PASS and PASSING in the context of their time. Most people know PASS through the third edition which was published in 1975 (Wolfensberger and Glenn 1975). This was just two years after I had started work for the first time. In 1973, I joined a research unit in Wessex looking at innovative residential services for people with learning disabilities, a raw young researcher who did not know much about anything. Conventional wisdom then turned around a fairly simple set of notions that institutions were damaging and inevitably harmful. There was a considerable optimism, some might say a naive hope, that much could be rectified by reversing institutional conditions. Institutions were crudely characterised by their scale; there were strong rationales for why small would be beautiful.

A more sophisticated account of quality in residential settings and its relationship to key provision variables such as setting size and staffing was given by King, Raynes and Tizard in a book published in 1971. Their scale of quality of care had operationalised what Goffman (1961) had described earlier as the four negative attributes of total institutions: block treatment, rigidity of routine, social distance and depersonalisation. Their analysis was a milestone in the development of applied research in this area, their work has been much cited and their scale much used since. However, the focus of attention was still relatively narrow and the attempt to look at determinants of quality only concentrated on a few service characteristics, such as size, as if a single factor could have an overridingly powerful effect.

The development of PASS was roughly contemporaneous. What is impressive to me looking back is the broad base its authors gave to the factors affecting the lives of service users and other people with disabilities. Wolfensberger and Glenn were already working on the second edition of PASS at the beginning of the 1970s. The third edition we all know and love was published in the middle of the decade. For all of the problems in deciding the scoring system to make it a quantitative evaluation tool, PASS is remarkable for its breadth of conceptualisation. Compared with the almost simple basis of the King, Raynes and Tizard scale, PASS offered a complex framework for considering the relationships between potential causes and effects. Moreover, it provided a positive dimension to quality as well as a negative one. Whereas the understanding of quality in the King, Raynes and Tizard work had been derived from the avoiding of negative conditions, PASS set pointers to good practice in relation to integration, status, autonomy, development and quality of setting. So, as we embark on an appraisal of PASS, I think that it is worth recognising the important contribution that it and the conceptualisation on which it was based has made to thinking over the last 18 years about how defining service quality could be approached.

References

Goffman, E. (1961) *Asylums*. New York: Doubleday.

King, R., Raynes, R., and Tizard, J. (1971) *Patterns of Residential Care*. London: Routledge and Kegan Paul.

Wolfensberger, W. and Glenn, L. (1975) *Program Analysis of Service Systems. Handbook and Manual*, 3rd edition. Toronto: National Institute on Mental Retardation.

Chapter 1

The PASS and PASSING Evaluation Instruments

Paul Williams

Introduction

PASS was originally developed in order to monitor the quality of newly developed community services for people with learning disabilities in Nebraska, USA. It was envisaged that a sample of individual services or programmes could be evaluated in order to identify quality issues for the service system as a whole to address: hence the name 'Programme Analysis of Service Systems', and the acronym PASS.

This first edition of PASS was devised in 1969, and revised and improved editions were produced in 1972 and 1975. The latter third edition is the version still in use; it is sometimes known as PASS3. As will be described in this chapter, PASS is based on a set of principles known formerly as 'normalisation' and now as 'social role valorisation' (SRV). In the early 1980s, a similar but completely revised version was devised, called PASSING – Programme Analysis of Service Systems' Implementation of Normalization Goals. Following an initial pilot edition, the second and current edition of PASSING was published in 1983.

The primary author of both PASS and PASSING is Professor Wolf Wolfensberger of Syracuse University, New York. Both PASS3 and PASSING were co-authored by colleagues of Wolfensberger: Linda Glenn for PASS3 and Susan Thomas for PASSING. Both instruments are published by the National Institute on Mental Retardation in Toronto, Canada, now known as the G. Allan Roeher Institute.

The Instruments and the Process

PASS3 consists of a Handbook giving technical background information and instructions for use, and a Field Manual containing the detailed evaluation criteria. PASSING consists of a single volume of narrative and evaluation criteria. A monograph intended to accompany both instruments, authored by Wolfensberger and also published by the National Institute on Mental Retardation in Toronto, was published in 1983: *Guidelines for Evaluators during a PASS, PASSING or Similar Assessment of Human Service Quality* (Wolfensberger 1983a).

PASS and PASSING each consist of a number of 'ratings' of specific aspects of a programme; there are 50 independent ratings in PASS3 and 42 in PASSING.

The instruments are designed to be applied by teams of raters, not by individuals. This is because the process of making judgements about service quality in PASS and PASSING depends on debate within a team of people.

Members of the team should have had prior training in the principles of normalisation or SRV, and in the use of PASS or PASSING. An ideal team will contain representatives of a wide range of interests in services: for example, a user, a manager, a carer and a specialist professional; teams can vary in size from around three to eight.

The Manuals provide guidance on the issues to be considered in making judgements. After debate, the team reaches agreement on a summary of the performance of the programme in the particular aspect covered by a rating. This summary is compared with statements in the Manual that correspond to levels of quality, from Level 1, extremely poor, to Level 4, 5 or 6 (5 in PASSING), very good. There is a scoring system whereby a weighted score is attached to each level, enabling scores to be calculated for individual ratings, clusters of ratings, or for performance on PASS or PASSING as a whole. The scoring systems will be discussed further in a later chapter.

The Content of PASS3

One of the reasons why PASS3 has not been entirely superseded by PASSING is that it includes consideration of issues of management and administration of a service in addition to criteria derived from normalisation or social role valorisation principles, whereas PASSING is solely based on SRV-related criteria.

The management and administration issues covered in PASS are as follows:

- comprehensiveness (the range of coverage and effectiveness of coordination within the wider service system of which the programme being evaluated is part)
- extent of use of generic resources by the programme
- extent of consumer and public participation at various levels, from receipt of information to involvement in management
- efforts to educate the public about the programme and the needs of its users
- innovativeness of the programme, locally, nationally or internationally
- extent of links between the programme and centres of academic research, and the degree to which research is welcomed and supported
- contribution of the programme to regional priorities in terms of need
- training and development of existing staff, and encouragement of interest by young people who may be potential future staff
- effectiveness of administrative structure and responsibilities of managers
- extent and effectiveness of planning processes
- extent and effectiveness of programme evaluation and efforts to renew the energies and enthusiasm of staff
- effectiveness of documentation of financial expenditure

- cost-effectiveness and avoidance of financial waste.

The normalisation-related issues covered in PASS3 are divided into five sections: Integration; Appropriate interpretations and structures; Model coherency; Developmental growth orientation; and Quality of setting. Model Coherency is a single rating in its own right, but each of the other sections has a number of component aspects to be separately rated.

The Integration section has fourteen ratings, covering aspects of the building used, its siting, the nature and resources of the surrounding neighbourhood, and the people with whom the programme facilitates contact for its users. As will be explained later in this chapter, an important consideration in PASS is the 'message' likely to be conveyed to the public about the service users by aspects of the structure or content of the programme. Thus, one rating in the Integration section is called Image Juxtaposition, which rates the presence of positive or negative 'messages' in the history, name, design, siting, furnishing or decor of the building, or in notices, posters, pictures or decorations displayed.

The section on Appropriate interpretations and structures has twelve separate ratings of aspects of the programme that may help or hinder the achievement of two outcomes: age-appropriateness and culture-appropriateness. Each of these has components of self-esteem and public status.

Age-appropriateness refers to the need of users to feel they are the age they are, and for the public to perceive them as the age they are; in particular, for adults to feel adult and to be seen as adult, with corresponding status, respect, rights and, as far as possible, responsibilities. Culture-appropriateness refers to the need of people to feel they are part of a meaningful culture, and to be perceived as members of that culture.

Aspects of a programme that can affect achievement of these things include the design and appearance of the building used, the support given to the personal appearance of users and their ability to present themselves to others, the activities facilitated and their timing and duration, the rights and autonomy accorded to users, the terminology used to refer to users, the possessions people are supported in having, and the support given to sexual identity and relationship skills and behaviour.

The concept of 'model coherency' again contains the dual elements of efficiency in helping users directly to overcome disabilities or disadvantages, and a clear 'message' to the public that the people served are valued citizens. To achieve these two things, a service needs to combine a wide range of features in a sensible, effective and efficient (in short, coherent) way. The features comprise: Who is doing What, To Whom, Where, When, How and Why?

The section on Developmental growth orientation includes ratings of the conduciveness of the building and the programme to learning and development, and of the relevance and efficiency of the detailed activities to meeting users' needs.

Finally, the Quality of setting section covers comfort, attractiveness, individualisation, and the quality of interpersonal interactions within the programme.

The Content of PASSING

PASSING makes a more explicit division between aspects of the service that have, in Wolfensberger's view, a primary impact on the public status or 'image' of users, and those that have a primary influence on direct help to people to overcome difficulties. The Manual is thus divided into two large sections: Social image enhancement and Personal competency enhancement.

Within each section are subsections covering aspects of the physical setting and siting of the service, the contacts and relationships facilitated by the service, and the activities the service promotes. There is an additional subsection under 'image enhancement' which covers general support by the programme for social status of its users through terminology, funding, possessions and personal appearance and presentation.

The subsection of aspects of setting and siting that relate primarily to image enhancement includes ratings of the degree to which the building fits into its neighbourhood in terms of design and function, its external and internal aesthetics, the extent to which its size, design, furnishings and decor reflect age appropriateness and culture-appropriateness, the history of the building and site, and the nature of the immediate neighbourhood.

Aspects of setting and site that relate primarily to competency enhancement include access, availability of community resources, comfort, individualisation of the physical environment, and balance of safety and learning opportunities in the building.

The section on contacts and relationships relating to image enhancement consists of ratings on the numbers of users in relation to community resources and competition for those resources from other groups, the actual composition of groups within the service and the potential effect of membership of those groups on the status of individuals, the social status of people outside the service with whom the service supports contact, and the social and professional identity of staff. Ratings on competency-related aspects of contacts and relationships include the conduciveness of the size and composition of groupings within the programme, and of contacts outside the service, to learning and development, the quality of interpersonal interactions within the service, the support in the programme for individualisation, and the development of sexual identity and relationship skills and behaviour.

Ratings on image-related aspects of activities comprise the extent to which the separation of different activities in time and place reflects culture-appropriateness, the positive or negative 'messages' conveyed by the actual activities and their timing, and the extent of support for autonomy and rights (it is interesting that Wolfensberger considers this to be primarily an image rather than a competency issue).

Competency-related aspects of activities include the extent to which activities are relevant to people's needs, the efficiency of use of time by the programme, and the support given to the acquisition by users of possessions that encourage learning and development.

PASS and PASSING in Practice

The PASSING Manual is structured in a more logical way, contains more helpful narrative, reflects more up-to-date thinking, and uses more acceptable terminology than the PASS3 Field Manual. PASS3 is still in use, however, because of its coverage of additional management and administrative issues, and because some people feel that it covers some issues, for example model coherency, age-appropriateness or image juxtaposition, more clearly than PASSING does. Both instruments are still used for teaching and evaluation, at least in Britain at the present time.

Although a large number of commissioned evaluations of services using PASS or PASSING have been carried out, the main use of PASS and PASSING since their publication has been as vehicles for teaching the principles of normalisation or SRV. For many years, there have been regular programmes of training, utilising PASS or PASSING to illustrate the detailed application of normalisation or SRV in services (usually through practice evaluations by teams of participants on the training course),[1] in the USA, Canada, Britain and Australia. There have also been similar events in Ireland, France, Belgium, Spain, Norway, Iceland and New Zealand. There is a French translation of the PASSING Manual in use in France and Canada.

In this way, large numbers of people, primarily professional staff or managers of services, have learned about PASS or PASSING and through them about the application of normalisation and SRV. Around 4000 people in Britain have attended such training since 1980. An organisation, the Community and Mental Handicap Educational and Research Association, was set up in Britain in 1979 specifically to bring this training to Britain, and it has been the main force in sustaining this training here since that time.

For historical reasons, some of which are described later in this chapter, normalisation, SRV, PASS and PASSING have been associated particularly with work with people with learning disabilities, but this is not a necessary feature of the instruments or the principles behind them. PASS and PASSING are designed to be applicable to any service for any group, and they have been used, with clear demonstration of their relevance, to evaluate services for elderly people, people with physical disabilities, children, people with mental health problems, homeless people, people with drug or alcohol dependency, people with AIDS, and many other groups.

The Background

Let us now turn in more detail to the background to PASS and PASSING, their history, and the principles of normalisation and SRV that underlie them.

Wolf Wolfensberger trained as a psychologist in the USA in the 1950s and was one of the first psychologists to obtain specialist training in work with people with learning disabilities. In the early 1960s he spent some time in Britain, during

---

1   Information on PASS and PASSING workshops can be obtained from: CMHERA, 2
    Eastbourne Road, Trowbridge, Wiltshire, BA14 7HN. Tel: 01225–753984.

which he worked with Jack Tizard on a study of day services for adults with learning disabilities in what was then the county of Middlesex.

In his influential book *Community Services for the Mentally Handicapped*, published in 1964, Jack Tizard, then a researcher at the Social Psychiatry Research Unit at the Maudsley Hospital in London, and later Professor of Child Development at London University, mentions Wolf Wolfensberger as one of his collaborators, describing him as 'a visiting psychologist on a United States Public Health Fellowship' (p. 2). There is only a brief description of the study of Adult Training Centres (as day services were called then) in Middlesex, but one observation made is that:

> the work that the trainees are able to do if placed in an industrial setting and given proper instruction is remarkable, but the academic accomplishments they bring with them from the junior centres are few indeed and it cannot be claimed that our present methods of education are very successful. (Tizard 1964, 71)

At the time, before the 1971 Education Act, children with learning disabilities were excluded from the school system and received education in 'junior training centres' run by local health authorities. This distanced both the settings and the teaching methods from those of mainstream education, thereby severely disadvantaging the children on top of their existing disabilities.

Adults with learning disabilities were similarly catered for in 'adult training centres', also run by local health authorities. Due partly to the earlier work of Jack Tizard and others in demonstrating the work potential of many adults with learning disabilities (O'Connor and Tizard 1956), many of these adult centres, including those in Middlesex, were oriented towards work and work training. They made extensive use of industrial contract work provided by local companies. Thus, in contrast to the junior centres, they provided teaching and activities that were similar to the activities of ordinary people of the same age, namely industrial work.

This experience was one influence on Wolfensberger, who also during the 1960s came across the Scandinavian concept of 'normalisation', that people with learning disabilities have a right to the same conditions and experiences of life as other citizens. In 1969, Wolfensberger co-edited a publication by the US President's Committee on Mental Retardation, entitled *Changing Patterns in Residential Services for the Mentally Retarded* (Kugel and Wolfensberger 1969). In this he included a chapter commissioned from Bengt Nirje, then Director of the Swedish Association for the Mentally Retarded, on 'The normalization principle and its human management implications'. This was the first written account of significant length of the idea of normalisation, which had already been influential in Scandinavian services and was to prove equally influential in North America, Britain and other parts of the world.

In *Changing Patterns*, Wolfensberger also included a chapter by himself on 'The origin and nature of our institutional models', later published as a separate monograph (Wolfensberger 1975). In this he presented an analysis of the negative perceptions of people with learning disabilities that could be identified historically and in the present day as determinants of attitudes and behaviour towards those people by the public and by service planners and providers. Eight negative perceptions were identified: the person as subhuman, as a menace, as an object of dread, as an object of pity, as a holy innocent, as sick, as an object of ridicule, and as an eternal child. These were contrasted with the positive perception of the person as a developing human being.

At this time, Wolfensberger was employed as a researcher into learning disabilities at the Nebraska Psychiatric Institute in Omaha. Most of the people with learning disabilities from Omaha who required residential care were housed in a large institution about 150 miles from the city. Wolfensberger became a leading member of a group of concerned professionals and family members who worked throughout the 1960s to achieve a local community-based service for these people back in Omaha and the surrounding area. The end of the decade saw the establishment of a pioneer service there, the Eastern Nebraska Community Office of Retardation (ENCOR), one of the first attempts in the world to establish a comprehensive local service, making extensive use of ordinary housing for its residential component (Thomas, Firth and Kendall 1978).

So here we have a number of factors coming together: Wolfensberger's interest in the Scandinavian idea of 'normalisation'; his experience in Britain of the power of enabling adults with learning disabilities to participate in the same sort of daytime activity, namely productive work, as other people; his historical analysis of the impact of public and professional perceptions of the nature of people with learning disabilities on how those people are treated, especially by services; and finally the practical opportunity to establish a service designed to counteract negative perceptions and give people opportunities for community participation. When Wolfensberger came to devise an instrument to evaluate the quality of the new service in Eastern Nebraska, the principles to underlie the criteria of quality were clear: the extent of support for positive and helpful perceptions of service users by the public, and of support for participation in community life.

The Concepts Underlying PASS and PASSING

Wolfensberger was keen that his evaluation instrument should be a force for identifying the unacceptable features of much conventional service provision, as well as for assessing the quality of newly developing community-based services. He therefore included criteria for judging quality that specified a range of practice from extremely damaging to extremely helpful.

The Scandinavian concept of 'normalisation' was a major influence on the development of PASS, but Wolfensberger's historical researches for his chapter on 'The origin and nature of our institutional models' had led him to see that the problem such a set of ideas needed to address was not just the unsatisfactory life experiences of disabled or disadvantaged people, but the public perception of those people. His concept of 'normalisation' thus included an element of normalisation of relationships between disadvantaged people and the public, as well as an element of opening up normative life experiences and opportunities for those people. This rather richer picture was elaborated in the book which Wolfensberger wrote in 1972, with contributions from Nirje, Olshansky, Perske and Roos: *The Principle of Normalization in Human Services*.

The status of the set of principles outlined by Wolfensberger and called 'normalisation' has always been the subject of heated debate: is it primarily an ideology, or does it have a sound basis in scientific fact? Wolfensberger has always claimed the latter. Nevertheless, critiques of normalisation, some based on misinterpretation, have abounded. A response to some of these was published by Wolfensberger in 1980.

One of the sources of misinterpretation of normalisation lies in the word itself. Many people seem to think they know what it means just by seeing the word, and notions have been prevalent that it has something to do with 'making people normal' or coercing people to conform to statistical norms of behaviour. In fact, in ordinary language, the word 'normalisation' is most often used in the context of diplomatic relationships between countries: 'Britain is seeking to normalise its relations with Syria', for example. This idea of normalisation of relationships, rather than primarily of behaviour or lifestyle, is helpful in understanding the true intent of Wolfensberger's concept. The desired outcome is better relationships between disadvantaged people and the public (Williams 1991).

The negative perceptions of people in society, and the consequent poor experiences of those people, can be described as a process of 'social devaluation': they involve thinking of and treating certain people or groups in society as less valuable than others. The intended outcome of normalisation is that those people or groups will become socially valued, and hence more protected from abuse, oppression or negative experiences.

Normalisation, however, recognises that a revaluation of disadvantaged people or groups in society will not happen simply by exhortation. There has to be a practical strategy to attain it. This strategy involves bending over backwards to support positive, valuing images and reputations of individual people and groups of people, and to support actual behaviours, relationships and experiences that are likely to be helpful to good relationships in society.

Social Role, Identity and Needs

Because of the problems with the word 'normalisation', Wolfensberger wrote a paper in 1983 suggesting the new term 'social role valorisation' (Wolfensberger 1983b), and this has slowly become the commonly used term since. Critiques of SRV have continued, and are important in working towards greater validity, refinement and usefulness of the concept. Some of the most interesting commentaries in recent years have come from anti-racist and feminist perspectives (Baxter, Poonia, Ward and Nadirshaw 1990, Brown and Smith 1992, Bano et al. 1993).

The nub of these critiques is that SRV is insensitive to the ethnic, cultural or gender identities of service users. However, there is a central feature in the process of using PASS and PASSING that is not well described in the literature. It is an essential foundation for the discussion that determines the judgements made by the evaluation team. It can easily incorporate recognition of, and respect for, any aspects of identity that may be valued by any section of the community to which the person may belong. Indeed, this will be essential to any process of redressing the alienation of a person from their community that is a consequence of their devaluation.

In his *Guidelines for Evaluators*, Wolfensberger outlines what is known as the 'foundation discussion' to be held by the evaluation team after data collection and before embarking on the ratings of service performance:

> A major step...is to discuss what the characteristics and needs are of the people served, viewed from an 'existential' perspective. This discussion goes far beyond data and descriptors, professional diagnostic and labelling categories, agency language and conceptualizations, etc. In a sense, it involves 'discovering the truth' about the clients, the nature of their social position, identities and needs. (Wolfensberger 1983a, 75)

In Britain, under the initial stimulus of John O'Brien (see Alan Tyne's chapter on 'Framework for Accomplishment', Chapter 15), this foundation discussion has been developed to include a comprehensive review of the experiences of a sample of service users throughout their lives. To the extent that it is possible and acceptable to do so, information is collected for a sample of individual users in answer to the following questions:

- What has been the person's experience of relationships with their natural family?
- What has been the person's experience of relationships within their community?
- What have been the person's economic status and its consequences?
- What have been the practical consequences for the person of their basic disability or disadvantage?
- What have been the person's experiences at key stages of their life, for example at birth, at starting school, at leaving the family home?
- What has been the person's experience of choice in their life?
- What future has the person had to look forward to?

These questions generate pictures of the impact of devaluation in the lives of individual service users. A summary picture is then generated of the sorts of experiences that are typical for the group of people as a whole who are served by the programme being evaluated. This picture is used to create a statement of the needs of the service users. Where experiences in any of the above areas have been, and remain, good, the need is for them to be maintained and safeguarded; where past experience has been good but there are now problems, the need is for reinstatement of the previous position if possible; where experience has been persistently bad, the need is for positive compensation through support for especially valued opportunities and circumstances.

This foundation discussion on experiences and needs is often the most powerful part of a PASS or PASSING evaluation. The major finding of the evaluation, and focus for feedback of the results, may be that the service's definition of needs differs from that generated by the evaluation team from an SRV perspective. At the very least, the account of needs provides the basis for judgements of service quality on specific ratings. PASS and PASSING cannot be applied without a thorough understanding of the foundation discussion process.

The Core Themes

Following the foundation discussion, the evaluation team is ready to embark on the ratings of service performance in specific areas. In the Manual for PASSING, Wolfensberger outlines seven themes that underlie the criteria for judgements. They are derived from SRV principles, but they are all themes that Wolfensberger believes reflect sound scientific knowledge. The areas of scientific research that potentially bear upon these themes are very wide, and comprehensive reviews of the adequacy of scientific evidence for the themes remains a task to be undertaken. Critics (e.g. Chappell 1992, Emerson in Brown and Smith 1992) have argued that the sociological basis to SRV is weak, but nowhere in the literature known to the present writer has there been a convincing refutation of the factual importance of the 'seven themes'.

The themes are:

1. The role of unconsciousness in human services. Service planners, managers and staff can be unaware of the negative effects of the service on its users, and the function of the service in meeting societal intentions or needs other than those of users. Consequently a major force for change in services to the benefit of users is likely to be greater consciousness of these things amongst service providers (and indeed amongst users themselves).

2. Role expectancy and role circularity. We tend to respond to other people's expectations of us, thus reinforcing those expectations in circular fashion. If expectations of disabled or disadvantaged people are negative, those expectations will tend to be reinforced by poor responses of those people, but if expectations are positive, they will be reinforced by positive responses.

3. The 'conservatism corollary'. To redress the devalued status of many disabled or disadvantaged people, it is not sufficient simply to begin treating them as 'ordinary'. We may need to bend over backwards to provide especially valued experiences and circumstances to compensate for past disadvantage.

4. The developmental model. Personal competency enhancement is a major part of the strategy needed to achieve social role valorisation. The more skilled a person is, the more they can negotiate their own positive relationships with others. To help people to achieve skills, a model of service provision is required that assumes developmental growth potential in all its users.

5. The power of imitation. We learn a great deal of our behaviour and skills through observation and imitation of others. To maximise the positive influence of this process, we need to have access to a wide range of positive models of behaviour, skill, identity and social value. Services

should enhance and support our access to this range, rather than severely restricting it as many services in fact do.

6. The dynamics of social imagery. One of the areas in which we are most unconscious of what we are doing in services is in the 'messages' likely to be sent out to the public about the status and social role of users, by the structure, content and processes we adopt. Buildings, activities, groupings, names, notices, staff identity, and many other features of services, can send out highly negative and unhelpful messages, or alternatively very helpful and positive ones.

7. The importance of social integration and participation. The ultimate aim of SRV is to achieve good relationships between disabled or disadvantaged people and others in society, as a protection against abuse and negative experience. Work on the quality of relationships can only begin if people have the opportunity to meet and socialise together. Extensive support for integration of devalued people with valued people is thus a central plank in SRV strategy.

The Wider Context

While reviews of the evidence in support of these underlying themes, and critiques of SRV as a whole, are important, PASS and PASSING remain evaluation instruments with some of the most extensive and carefully thought-out theoretical backgrounds of any yet devised.

This theoretical background can be seen in a wider context of practical and moral philosophy provided by Wolfensberger. Central in this are his beliefs that modern society is expressing some extremely destructive dynamics towards disabled and disadvantaged people (a phenomenon he calls 'the new genocide'), yet at the same time has created a 'post-primary production economy' in which the economic survival of the western world is dependent on the creation of large numbers of people who can be defined as 'needing' paid services (Wolfensberger 1987, 1989, 1990). To contribute to counteracting these forces, Wolfensberger has written and taught extensively about the need for a moral stance to be taken, and for the adoption of personal unpaid commitments to devalued individuals (Wolfensberger and Zauha 1973).

Ultimately, it is these issues about which we need greater consciousness. PASS and PASSING are merely ways in which we can study the role of particular programmes and service systems in colluding with or counteracting such wider societal forces.

References

Bano, A., Crosskill, D., Patel, R., Rashman, L. and Shah, R. (1993) *Improving Practice with People with Learning Disabilities*. London: Central Council for Education and Training in Social Work.

Baxter, C., Poonia, K., Ward. L. and Nadirshaw, Z. (1990) *Double Discrimination*. London: King's Fund Centre.

Brown, H. and Smith, H. (eds) (1992) *Normalisation: A Reader for the Nineties*. London: Tavistock/Routledge.

Chappell, A. (1992) Towards a sociological critique of the normalisation principle. *Disability, Handicap and Society* Vol 7, 35–51.

Kugel, R. and Wolfensberger, W. (eds) (1969) *Changing Patterns in Residential Services for the Mentally Retarded*. Washington, D.C.: President's Committee on Mental Retardation.

O'Connor, N. and Tizard, J. (1956) *The Social Problem of Mental Deficiency*. Oxford: Pergamon Press.

Thomas, D., Firth, H. and Kendall, A. (1978) *ENCOR: A Way Ahead*. London: Campaign for the Mentally Handicapped.

Tizard, J. (1964) *Community Services for the Mentally Handicapped*. London: Oxford University Press.

Williams, P. (1991) Reaction to Zigler, Hodapp and Edison. *American Journal on Mental Retardation* Vol 96, 224–225.

Wolfensberger, W. (1972) *The Principle of Normalization in Human Services*. Toronto: National Institute on Mental Retardation.

Wolfensberger, W. (1975) *The Origin and Nature of Our Institutional Models*. Syracuse, New York: Human Policy Press.

Wolfensberger, W. (1980) The definition of normalization: update, disagreements and misunderstandings. In R. Flynn and K. Nitsch (eds) *Normalization, Social Integration and Community Services*. Baltimore: University Park Press.

Wolfensberger, W. (1983a) *Guidelines for Evaluators during a PASS, PASSING or Similar Assessment of Human Service Quality*. Toronto: National Institute on Mental Retardation.

Wolfensberger, W. (1983b) Social role valorization: a proposed new term for the principle of normalization. *Mental Retardation* Vol 21, 235–239.

Wolfensberger, W. (1987) *The New Genocide of Handicapped and Afflicted People*. Syracuse, New York: Syracuse University Training Institute.

Wolfensberger, W. (1989) Human service policies: the rhetoric versus the reality. In L. Barton (ed) *Disability and Dependency*. London: Falmer Press.

Wolfensberger, W. (1990) A most critical issue: life or death. *Changes* Vol 8, 63–73.

Wolfensberger, W. and Glenn, L. (1975) *Programme Analysis of Service Systems: Handbook and Field Manual*, 3rd edition. Toronto: National Institute on Mental Retardation.

Wolfensberger, W. and Thomas, S. (1983) *Programme Analysis of Service Systems' Implementation of Normalization Goals: Normalization Criteria and Ratings Manual*, 2nd edition. Toronto: National Institute on Mental Retardation.

Wolfensberger, W. and Zauha, H. (eds) (1973) *Citizen Advocacy and Protective Services for the Impaired and Handicapped*. Toronto: National Institute on Mental Retardation.

Chapter 2

What Have We Been Learning from PASS and PASSING in Workshops and Real Evaluations?

Alan Tyne

In the town I come from, for about 2000 years as far as we know people have built wooden boats and sailed them on our estuary and in the North Sea that lies beyond. Some of the most important learning in my life has taken place in a large old shed by the side of that river with a man called variously George or Taffy. I have learned there about workshops – places where there is a good deal of 'work in progress' and a number of unfinished projects. There is a stock of materials for future use and a large number of things that you do not like to throw away because you think they 'may come in handy one day'. There is much to be learned there about important moral rules too. Being inclined to do a job tolerably well and say, 'I think that's about good enough', George's reply is always the same, 'No, that isn't; and you can do the best you can and that still isn't good enough.' George knows the things we make will be around a good deal longer than we ourselves. One day somebody else will be relying on it, perhaps someone we don't even know, and in George's mind that is an important reason to do always your best and that can never be enough. Another great concern is not to waste. When I am about to cut a piece of wood he says, 'Measure twice and cut once' not just because it is frustrating and annoying to cut things to the wrong size but as he says, 'There is only just so much of that wood; that will all be gone one day; you've got to use it with care.' There is much to be learned about tools as well – that the best are those acquired early in life; as your judgement grows you know only to acquire the best. With care and with luck they will last a lifetime, but only if you sharpen them well each time they are used.

About 15 years ago I had just completed a small project where I had spent the better part of two years travelling around the country living and staying in the places where people who have learning difficulties were living and staying. I was puzzled to know what to make of this accumulated experience of many days and nights and many hours just being with people and trying to understand their experience of life in the services that they were being offered. A chance brought me to a workshop in Wisconsin in the United States where I was able to understand a little about PASS (Wolfensberger and Glenn 1975). It was a very exciting time because I realised that what PASS invited people to do was what I had been doing for the last two years, to go and be with people and understand their experience from doing that – to drop the pride of professionalism and to simply stand with people for a time and to let that experience be your guide to what was going on in their life. I decided to introduce PASS to the United Kingdom and many good people came to join in that endeavour. Initially we intended to use it in the way I had. Many people were struggling to make sense of a changing service-scene. PASS seemed to offer some important and helpful ideas that referred back to essential values. Its main importance seemed to be in teaching and learning about what was really happening in services. As time went by we increasingly felt its original purpose for evaluation of services also had a great deal to commend it.

It is worth thinking a little of the context in which this work began, and in which 'evaluation' seemed a helpful idea. In the 1970s, as always, policy reform involved much political interplay between professional groupings, each making their bid to be included. The development of services was largely the preserve of powerful interest-groups. The great subject of the day was 'multi-disciplinary team working' or how you resolve the conflicts between each of the rival professional groups that wanted to have a piece of the action. There was also a great power and ideology vacuum, particularly in services for people who have learning difficulties. The doctors had virtually abandoned the stage. The medical ideology was a weak one. Having ruled the roost for some 20 years or so since the foundation of the National Health Service and the incorporation of mental handicap services into the hospital system, it was now in decline. This provided a moment, an opportunity, an occasion to explore the nature of the ideologies that guided our work. That was a particularly powerful reason why the normal-isation ideas, PASS, and later PASSING (Wolfensberger and Thomas 1983), found a little window, a moment of opportunity that enabled them to gain some ascendancy on the scene.

We met a lot of very 'closed up' organisations. The whole idea of having external and independent evaluation was a very novel, and for many people an extremely threatening, one. It had been assumed as long as people could remember that simple professionalism would be sufficient to ensure quality in the build-up of the welfare state. The debate about values was itself in its infancy, the welfare state only beginning to come under attack. By and large public service bureaucratic professionalism was still heavily dominant.

To suggest to people a debate about values was in itself seen as bizarre. The sheer intensity of opposition to discussion of values as a basis for action had to be seen to be believed. Talk of values was surrounded by deep suspicion. People working in services suspected we were advocating a return to the do-goodery of the pre-war years and that the church and voluntary services would be marching in and taking over from them if they dare let this new move gain a little toe-hold.

So in thinking about evaluation you need to think about whether the context merits it. When we did it, it did. You need to decide for yourself whether the context still merits the evaluation tools that you are trying to use.

It was instructive to take a small group of people from Colchester recently to visit some extremely innovative 'cutting edge' services in parts of the mid-west of the United States. The Chief Executive of our local NHS Trust and the Chair of his Trustees were fascinated to gain these unique insights into where it is likely that our services will be going in the next ten or fifteen years. On each visit they asked people where did they get the ideas for this kind of thing, what was the basis of it all? Each time we heard 'Oh, basically – PASS training'. Even 18 years on people still find it a valuable resource from which to draw.

PASS and PASSING have both a content and a process and they are described in at least four books and a number of shorter documents, mostly authored by Wolf Wolfensberger and colleagues between 1969 and about 1985. The *content* of PASS and of PASSING is contained in two manuals (Wolfensberger and Glenn 1975, Wolfensberger and Thomas 1983). Reviewers sometimes comment that it is 'value based'. This is a little puzzling since it is hard to imagine what kind of an *evaluation* system would not be *value* based. It is probably more significant to say that it is theory based. The theory is fairly straightforward and refers to the situation of the many people who rely on services for important things in their lives, (and by 'important things' is meant things like:

- where you live and who you live with
- what you do in the daytime and whether it has any meaning to anyone else, let alone yourself
- whether you have scope to make a contribution in the lives of others
- where you go for help and whether any help is available for you, if you have a health need or you need support in learning things that you find difficult or if you need support and encouragement to cope with pain of whatever kind that troubles your life, or if you simply need support to ensure that you stay alive.

The theory begins from the notion that people who rely on services suffer the problem of devaluation. Devaluation in brief is a pattern of images and assumptions held by others, that form a basis for them being treated differently in most areas of their life. It is a tendency that is present throughout our culture and is deeply ingrained into our culture. Jean Vanier gives a most eloquent description of the experience of many disabled people when he speaks of people coming to the L'Arche communities with many 'wounds' – cut after cut after cut received from life. That is a very powerful and evocative way of understanding the situation of people who rely on services. The theory also assumes that, being a part of our culture, service organisations also embody those processes and do those same things. Those processes of wounding people are embodied in and even (usually unconsciously) amplified by the services that set out to help people.

The second step in the theory is that this process of wounding and hurting people offends key values in our society. In reality these values are not particularly explicit in PASS and in PASSING, nor are they particularly well spelled out. But you can hunt carefully through the manuals without finding a large amount of support for competitive individualism, crass materialism or blind obedience to authority. Those are not strongly mentioned values in the PASS and the PASSING manuals. They are indeed examples of strongly held values in our society but they are not the ones on which PASS and PASSING are based. They are values which are partial and sectional – important and useful if you happen to be a pretty strong, powerful person with ample resources available to you; but they do not help a lot if you are one of the people who is not particularly strong, who is 'resource-weak'.

PASS and PASSING seem to be based on a fairly familiar and a fairly old story. Many hours and weeks of study, and many occasions to work on these instruments with others who were similarly struggling towards an understanding of this theory, teach me they are based on three very simple straightforward ideas:

- The first is the idea of justice which is as old as the hills and at different times throughout its history has had a number of different agendas. Sometimes the agenda is peace, sometimes the agenda is freedom and sometimes the agenda is equality and there may be others besides.

- The second key value that seems to come out in PASS and PASSING is the value of stewardship. It is George's notion that we are only here for a limited time on this earth and what we do lasts longer than we do so we have a duty to do it right. The notion of stewardship is a very important one – that we should conserve our whole environment – that we should waste neither things nor people – that we should think long term rather than short term – that we should look for connections between ideas, movements and processes. (To make a small diversion here, it teaches us to look for connections between the problems we address and the solutions we arrive at today and the problems that people will be solving tomorrow. When I began my career I was actively campaigning for 24 bed hostels for people with learning difficulties – it seemed a good idea at the time!) We need to see the connections between the solutions that we propose and the problems that we create. We need to see the connections between the problems that the people who concern us have in their lives and the problems that others have – the connections between the case that is being made by the Women's Movement and that of the Disabled Peoples' Movement, the movement of people toward racial equality, the movement to see a fair balance of justice between the first and the third worlds.

- Whereas Justice is a right and Stewardship a duty, the third value, Community, is, always has been and I suspect always will be a hope. It is something which at all points in history has been an aspiration. It is of course a great paradox too. As the sociologist Robert Bellah said, it is a constant dilemma between our desire for self realisation – 'actualisation' – and the knowledge that we only ever achieve that in company with others. It is the human dilemma: unhappy together, unhappy being apart.

Those three ideas are the key values that guide and support PASS and PASSING. They are the measures of quality that people are encouraged actively to use in their work. They are ideas that have always been important, 'glues' in society – sources of social cohesion and coherence.

The theory continues then that services should seek to redress offences against these values through attention to those things that they control. The services have a limited amount of control over the *settings and spaces* that people occupy each day; over some aspects of the *grouping* – who people meet together with in their day-to-day lives, and over time; *over activities and use of time* which services structure on their behalf; and over the *imagery and the language* with which we surround people. The theory does not address all devaluation. Services have a limited scope and pervasiveness, and a very limited control over people, communities and the society as a whole. Nor is it the only possible theory to be based on these values. If you started from a different sense of what the problem is, it would lead to different analysis, different theory. So the Disabled Peoples' Movement begins with a very similar picture to the one that I gained from going around and spending time living with people. It begins from a very similar analysis of what the situation is, what the wounds are, but it arrives at a very different sense of what is the key root cause. For many organisations of disabled people it is disempowerment which is the cause and empowerment the solution, not devaluation and revaluation. There is a growing movement too, a third movement of people who see the problem in much the same way, but who describe it as exclusion. The problem is about being cut out from sets of integrated social relationships and the solution is, of course, inclusion. Here then are three very powerful strands, very tightly linked together. As a sailor I see them as three intertwined strands of the same rope. But they are also distinct and separate and lead in somewhat different directions. They are important in different ways.

PASS and PASSING direct the attention of observers through a series of discrete questions or issues to aspects of services that impact on these key values. The issues are framed by its theory. The discrete character of these issues and the questions in the two manuals enables observers to identify the areas of strength and weakness within a service. Because they are able to separate out the 50 items in the PASS manual or the 42 items in the PASSING manual it is possible to create a unique profile of the quality of a particular service. The development of PASSING marked at least two things. One was a simple process of revision, a more systematic sorting of the issues, up-dating and correcting of language, a more consistent process of scaling judgements. Second, it reflected some of Wolfensberger's changing concerns. The Administration ratings were dropped in PASSING. Partly this marks a despondency about being able to affect major shifts in a bureaucratic service system. It does though enable a clearer focus on the strength and power of imagery in people's lives, and greater attention to the real effects of services, regardless of whether they can be 'fixed'. After publication of PASSING, he reconceptualised the key idea as 'social role valorisation' (Wolfensberger 1983b), the creation and support of valued social roles in people's lives. He sees this as the highest-order goal of services. Wolfensberger continues to explore the idea of a general theory of social devaluation.

We may reasonably ask a number of questions. For instance, is normalisation or social role valorisation really a theory or simply a collection of useful ideas that seem to lead us towards helpful ways of understanding the mass of material which we collect when we spend time with people who rely on services? Is devaluation really the problem or do we need to understand other analyses of disempowerment and exclusion too if we are to gain a strong sense of the whole web and not just a part of it? Students in workshops and participants in evaluations continue to teach us greatly about the answers to these questions as we struggle towards understanding them. Just now I am more concerned to encourage others to join that struggle, than to share what small insights I may have gained in the past fifteen years.

The process in PASS is described in two of the manuals. There is the handbook that came with the PASS3 manual and later on a set of instructive guidelines with Dr Wolfensberger's (1983a) thoughts about the ideal or near-ideal way in which a team might set about attempting an evaluation of a service using the instruments that he designed. The thing you need to know about PASS and PASSING is they are both designed to be used by trained people. There is a training programme in the UK of five-and-a-half-day residential workshops, six of them a year at the moment, that are designed to ensure a number of things (see footnote 1, p.17). First they try to make sure that people are familiar with the content of PASS and PASSING so that they can find their way around the books. Second they ensure people have a personal experience that deepens their understanding of the theory. Most participants know that 'things are not good enough'. The workshop encourages them to go further – to understand the issues of design and fundamental fitness for purpose that lie at the basis of the instruments. The workshops teach people many of the basic skills of distinguishing between ratings or issues, and understanding the relationship between them; of making clear statements in English of the issues; of collecting information and managing the conciliation process for arriving at a judgement of quality. The teams in which participants work are a political context for arriving at judgements. Some evaluation tools put the book between the observer and the people. It is possible to say, 'Well, it's not me saying that, it's this book that says that.' PASS and PASSING set a very different context in which a team is set the task of arriving at a yardstick using the guidelines and the ideas that are contained within the manual. They place the responsibility on observers to create a standard and to make a judgement. A large part of that is done in a process known as the 'foundation discussion', which is not well described anywhere in the manuals. This process is a good example of the way in which as people have used the instruments and shared their learning, some important innovations have evolved. Finally the process directs people to identifying those individual items and elements of the overall pattern which provide a basis for future service development and the basis for recommendations and feedback.

From using PASS and PASSING we have learned a number of things. First, that it belongs to people who will work with it. It has made evaluation not just the preserve of the universities and the professional researchers, it is available to anyone who will do the work it requires. Further, it is based on an ideology which is everybody's. Participants in evaluations have included: service users themselves, their relatives and friends; concerned and interested citizens who wanted to be sure that the services that they were helping to provide were of good quality; and many people who themselves plan, manage and directly deliver services.

Second, we have learned that evaluation is like the two-edged sword – it needs using with care. There are things that the workshops do not teach. In a 'real' evaluation for instance you have more time but are now working with an experienced team instead of a bunch of trainees. In a real evaluation there is a serious risk that people may listen to what you say and try and do what you recommend.

There are less obvious lessons to be learned from all evaluation, not just from using PASS and PASSING. *First* that the contract is everything. There are many deals struck where one person engages another person to evaluate a third – those contracts are best avoided. If misunderstanding and unhappiness are to be kept to a minimum, we have learned to make the contract with the person most concerned. 'Come and look at the service I provide. Be an interested outsider because we value what you have to show us and what you have to tell us' – that seems to be the only basis for a contract that works. *Second* that preparation and follow-up take a great deal longer than evaluation itself. A piece of work that takes a team a week or a couple of days may be a year in the making. A year of preparation and six months in the follow-up, because there is a great deal of work to be done to be sure that each side is clear about what they expect from one another. Follow-up needs time, and is impossible to plan adequately beforehand. *Third*, it is beguilingly easy to learn wonderful insights from participating in evaluation. It is another matter to share these with the people from whom you learned. Part of this is because the whole premise of evaluation is that some change is necessary. In order to undertake that notion you first have to encompass the idea that what you did before probably was not as good as it could have been. In fact it may have been downright bad, in fact it may have been hurting people badly. Those are hard things to hear and hard things to learn. The very people who are the most honest, the most open with you and who will warmly invite you to come and look at what they are doing and use your sharpest tools to measure, are the ones you are most at risk of hurting. Things said in a verbal feedback may be warmly welcomed and received with great joy. The very same verbatim account in a written report may create deepest gloom. Some of that has to do with the passage of time; some of it is to do with the new problem – what is said between us is private, what is written is public sooner or later, and that has consequences. There is something close to a clinical syndrome which I can describe as 'post-evaluative depression' and I suspect it always happens no matter how caring and how good are the people who do the evaluating. *Fourth*, the quality of the information that you get relies extensively on the relationships you are able to build and on the social skills of the team you are able to bring to work with you. Each evaluation is a uniquely creative event – packaged techniques do not work.

Now as tools go PASS is particularly sharp-edged. As my father once said, 'Give the boy a sharp knife – it's safer.' The sharp knife cuts into the work. With a blunt one you have to use a lot more force to make it cut and it will fly off and hurt somebody. So use the sharp-edged tools by all means. But be sure to use the right tools. You don't use the finest tools for everything; sometimes an axe is better and sometimes a spade. You do not use sharp fine tools when other things will do the job. If what you want is to invite some interested outsiders to help you look at your work and to remind a service of its essential social purpose, then PASS or PASSING are valuable tools to use. Like all good tools they require some discipline of their users. It is those disciplines which provide for most of us a basis for any craftsmanship and creativity which lies within us.

Summary of Discussion: The Role of Self-Organised Groups of Disabled People

The discussion was concerned with this one issue, a delegate asking Alan Tyne whether there was validity in disabled people working exclusively together. AT replied that there was an injunction in PASS and PASSING that disabled people should not be grouped together in larger groups than is strictly necessary, because grouping together creates a multiplicative effect in terms of the perception of them as different. When people *choose* to be associated together in order to proclaim their strength to the word around them, to work directly on their situation, that is quite a different matter, and a different set of rules apply.

References

Wolfensberger, W. (1983a) *Guidelines for Evaluators during a PASS, PASSING or Similar Assessment of Human Service Quality.* Toronto: National Institute on Mental Retardation.

Wolfensberger, W. (1983b) Social role valorisation: a proposed new term for the principle of normalisation. *Mental Retardation* Vol 21, 235–239.

Wolfensberger, W. and Glenn, L. (1975) *Programme Analysis of Service Systems: Handbook and Field Manual,* 3rd edition. Toronto: National Institute on Mental Retardation.

Wolfensberger, W. and Thomas, S. (1983) *Programme Analysis of Service Systems' Implementation of Normalization Goals: Normalization Criteria and Ratings Manual,* 2nd edition. Toronto: National Institute on Mental Retardation.

Chapter 3

Evaluation and Change in Service Systems for People with Disabilities

Gerald Midgley

Introduction

Between the years 1990 and 1992, Doria Pilling and I were engaged in a research program assessing the validity and usefulness of PASS (Wolfensberger and Glenn 1975) and PASSING (Wolfensberger and Thomas 1983). These are methods which provide quantitative evaluations of service quality. I will provide more specific details of them later. As part of this research, we conducted a general critique of the two methods and also compared their use in practice with another method called ACE. These studies are summarised in two chapters (4 and 7) in this volume. This chapter represents the third and final aspect of our research program: here I wish to ask how PASS and PASSING (from now on referred to jointly as PASS/ING) might be used in conjunction with a number of other methods, all of which are quite different, to answer a much wider variety of questions about services for people with disabilities than PASS/ING could ever hope to answer on its own.

The central assumption of this chapter is quite simple. Following the insights of a large number of authors (such as Patton 1980, Jackson and Keys 1984) I believe that no single evaluation method, or method of directing organisational change, can cope with every single issue that we are faced with when evaluating, or intervening in, service systems for people with disabilities. All methods inevitably have their limitations.

However, scepticism about methodology need not be destructive. By identifying the strengths as well as the weaknesses of the various different methods, we might actually find that they complement one another. The purpose of this chapter is to explore this complementarity. By doing so, we may begin to move beyond some of the entrenched debates that have characterised much of the literature in the areas of evaluation and organisational change. In short, I intend to challenge the convention that authors have to defend their chosen methodological positions by denigrating the value of all others. By making this challenge I hope to point the way to a more flexible, responsive and critically aware evaluation and change practice.

My intention is to begin the chapter by discussing some of the issues that underlie this vision of complementarity. I will then move on to present a framework of four methods, including PASS/ING, that may be used in conjunction with one another to address a variety of moral and organisational issues in the evaluation and change of service systems for people with disabilities.

Critical Systems Thinking

The theoretical perspective underlying this vision of complementarism is called Critical Systems Thinking. One of the concerns of Critical Systems Thinkers has been the need to base methodological complementarism on a solid philosophical foundation. Many writers (e.g. Burrell and Morgan 1979, Tsoukas 1993) have claimed that the various methodological approaches found in the literature are based on fundamentally different and irreconcilable assumptions, so complementarism is simply not possible. The reply of Critical Systems Thinkers is that a *new* set of assumptions can be developed which embraces the best of the old, and which demonstrates that different methods of evaluation and organisational change answer different kinds of question. Those interested in the philosophical foundations of Critical Systems Thinking may like to consult Flood and Jackson (1991a), which is an edited book of key works. Other books have also been written on the subject (Ulrich 1983, Flood 1990, Jackson 1991). In addition, Midgley (1992a, 1995a) and Gregory (1992) should also be of interest as they present new developments in our understanding of complementarism.

1 The System of Systems Methodologies

Various methodological frameworks have been developed by Critical Systems Thinkers over the years, but one of the most widely used is the *System of Systems Methodologies*. This was first designed by Jackson and Keys (1984) to show how

		System	
		Simple	*Complex*
Relationships between Participants	*Unitary*	Simple–unitary: key issues are easily appreciated, and general agreement is perceived between those defined as involved or affected	Complex–unitary: key issues are difficult to appreciate, but general agreement is perceived between those defined as involved or affected
	Pluralist	Simple–pluralist: key issues are easily appreciated, but disagreement is perceived between those defined as involved or affected	Complex–pluralist: key issues are difficult to appreciate, and disagreement is perceived between those defined as involved or affected

Figure 3.1 The System of Systems Methodologies

various systems methods might most usefully be applied in practice. These authors developed a two-dimensional grid, and this is presented in Figure 3.1. One dimension is labelled 'relationships between participants' (actually defined as the *perception* of the relationships between participants) and the other is labelled 'system' (defined as the perception of the degree of complexity in the system under examination). The first of these dimensions, relationships between participants, is seen as having two states: *unitary* (a perception of general agreement between participants on what the key issues are) and *pluralist* (a perception of disagreement between participants).

On the second dimension of the System of Systems Methodologies, the system dimension, we find that there are also two states: *simple* and *complex*. Simplicity refers to a relatively easy appreciation of key issues. Complexity, on the other hand, refers to situations where interactions are difficult to understand, or the situation is rapidly changing.

By cross-referencing the two dimensions we get four boxes – four different contexts of application – with which different methods can be aligned. The four contexts in the System of Systems Methodologies can be labelled *simple–unitary, complex–unitary, simple–pluralist* and *complex–pluralist*.

As an aside, it is worth noting that there is also an expanded version of the System of Systems Methodologies with a third type of relationship between participants: *coercive* – perception of disagreement that is masked, or potential disagreement that is not being allowed to surface, due to power relationships between participants (Jackson 1987). I have chosen not to use this expanded version here because I do not believe that any of the methods of evaluation and change that have been developed in the organisational sciences are able to deal with coercion. Coercion is characterised by closure of debate, and this can only be dealt with adequately through consciousness raising, campaigning and/or political action (see Midgley 1995 for more details). This is not to say that challenging coercion is unimportant. It is simply an acknowledgement that it is not possible for methods designed for evaluation and change to cope with coercion, and therefore this subject lies beyond the scope of the present research.

Returning to Figure 3.1, we should note that various methods have been aligned with the four different contexts (see Jackson and Keys 1984, Banathy 1987, Oliga 1988, Flood and Jackson 1991b, and Midgley 1992b). In broad terms, quantitative, modelling methods are said to be most appropriate for the unitary contexts, while qualitative, debate-orientated methods are best for pluralist situations.

These are not arbitrary alignments. Quantitative methods are said to be best suited to situations where there is general agreement on the nature of the issues faced (unitary contexts) because formulating a model in response to a set of questions will only be of relevance to those people who agree that this is the *right* set. If there is disagreement over what the basic issues are (i.e. the context is pluralist), then this will not be addressed by provision of a model that is orientated to answer questions that only some people regard as important.

In contrast, qualitative methods are aligned with pluralist contexts because, when there is open disagreement, they can be helpful in providing a basis for the revelation of interests and assumptions, the development of mutual understanding, learning, and ultimately practical decision-making. In contrast, when there is basic agreement on most issues (i.e. the context is unitary), discussion-orientated methods become largely redundant.

We therefore see that each type of method has its uses, but each also has significant limitations. By bringing them together in a framework like the System of Systems Methodologies, they may complement one another.

2 Creative Methodology Design
Of course few real-life situations can be conceptualised using only one category of context, and so the research issue often has to be seen as a series of interdependent research questions, each of which will have its own context. We also need to retain the flexibility to allow new issues to surface and be addressed as we learn more about the organisation. Thus we move away from simple choice between working methods toward creative and systemic methodology design. New approaches can be developed that draw on parts of older, previously distinct methods to create a practice that is genuinely flexible and responsive to perceptions of the situation under investigation. This technique of bringing together a variety of methods according to perceived need has been explored by a number of authors (see, for example, Midgley 1990, Flood and Jackson 1991b).

3 An Ideal of Research Practice
It is very important to be aware that the System of Systems Methodologies is most expressly not a 'rule book' to be followed systematically. It should be regarded as *an ideal of research practice that is useful for critical reflection on methodology design*. Let me explain. Ideals are theoretical constructs, and to be critically reflective is to question assumptions. By saying that we should be critically reflective about methodology design, I am suggesting that there is a need to look carefully at the situations we are going into, trying not to take too much for granted. We also need to consider the possible consequences of the methods we might use, and design our approach accordingly. So, by saying that the System of Systems Methodologies is an ideal that can be used to guide critical reflection, I am saying that the theoretical insights it provides can offer direction to our thinking, but should not determine it absolutely. In using the System of Systems Methodologies, we need to recognise that practical situations may require compromises with what we might like to do with methods in an ideal world, and researchers must be flexible enough to achieve these compromises for the greater good of improving services. See Jackson (1990) for a more detailed consideration of this issue.

4 Being Critical about Methodology
We see that it is absolutely vital to remain critical (questioning) about our use of the System of Systems Methodologies as well as the individual methods contained within it. We also need to be aware that our initial contacts with an organisation are just as 'methodological' as when we follow a given method. Who is asking us to do the evaluation, whether we make decisions on methodology ourselves or consult others, who we consult, and how we question initial assumptions, will all be influential in determining how the context of the

evaluation is perceived and therefore what methods will be followed. Critique is therefore essential at all stages of evaluation and change.

In order to be as critical as possible, Critical Systems Thinking asks the researcher to open him or herself to consultation with all those involved in, and/or affected by, the change process right from the start (Ulrich 1983). Of course, this doesn't mean abdicating responsibility for decision-making to a ready-constituted group of participants, but involves entering into a process of negotiation and discovery, *finding out* who might be affected or involved. Being open to consultation means being prepared to engage in communication with other people, in one-to-one conversations and in groups, so as to be able to exercise appropriate critical judgement about how to proceed. Participants in, and those affected by, organisations can be regarded as 'experts', and need to be able to 'own' the decision-making process. Nevertheless, we still need to be able to identify situations where this 'ownership' is masking disenfranchisement. We therefore retain the right to make ethical judgements about whether or not we challenge particular viewpoints, or indeed whether it is legitimate to conduct an evaluation at all.

Services for People with Disabilities

So far I have discussed Critical Systems Thinking, and I have shown how the System of Systems Methodologies can be used to guide critical reflection upon methodology design. Now it is time to align some specific methods with the four contexts in the framework. I will focus on methods that I believe may prove particularly useful in the evaluation and change of services for people with disabilities.

It would be possible to write a multi-volume series spelling out the pros and cons of a whole host of methods, but this would cause information overload for the reader. Instead, I intend to focus upon four very different methods, including PASS/ING, all of which have been well researched and applied in practice. In making this selection, I am not suggesting that these four represent a set of all possible relevant methods. It is for other authors to identify the limitations of my selection and build upon it using their own particular expertise in different areas. Indeed, in making this selection, I am refining and adding to a previous selection of methods made by Flood and Jackson (1991b). The four methods I have chosen to focus on are:

- PASS/ING
- Viable System Diagnosis
- Strategic Assumption Surfacing and Testing
- Soft Systems Methodology.

These can be aligned with the contexts in the System of Systems Methodologies as shown in Figure 3.2.

System

		Simple	Complex
Relationships	*Unitary*	PASS/ING	Viable System Diagnosis
between			
Participants	*Pluralist*	Strategic Assumption Surfacing and Testing	Soft Systems Methodology

Figure 3.2 The four methods in the System of Systems Methodologies

Over the coming pages I will briefly describe each of these four methods in turn and discuss how they might be used in evaluations of services for people with disabilities. The alignments with the various contexts in the System of Systems Methodologies made in Figure 3.2 will also be explained during this discussion. Of course every method has its critics, and these four are no exception. However, because of space restrictions, I do not intend to address criticisms of the methods here – this will be done in an expanded version of the current chapter being prepared for publication elsewhere. My descriptions of the methods will mostly concentrate on providing an overview of their capabilities, and references will be provided for the interested reader wanting more specific details. Let me begin with the first of the four methods, PASS/ING.

PASS/ING

PASS (Wolfensberger and Glenn 1975) and PASSING (Wolfensberger and Thomas 1983) are both quantitative methods for evaluating service quality. A team of researchers rates a service system on a large number of variables. The process by which this is achieved is summarised by Burton (1983) as follows:

> The setting is visited over several days and information pertaining to the ratings gathered in a variety of ways. Staff and clients are interviewed formally and a formal interview takes place with the head of the service. Observations are made, as unobtrusively as possible, of, for example, staff/staff, staff/client, and client/client interactions, of notices, signs, and equipment, of routines, and other practices of the setting. In addition the neighbourhood and exterior of the setting are inspected... Clients, visitors, ancillary staff and others can be talked to, and the team is present for at least the whole of one client's day... After the site visit, the team meets and the evidence in relation to each rating is pooled, and the team works towards consensus on the relative importance of its various observations for each rating... A score may be computed from the ratings... Finally, the team provides verbal and written feedback to the service, in a form comprehensible to those unfamiliar with the jargon... What the foregoing description omits, however, is that despite its concretisation in the PASS manuals, PASS may be used flexibly (provided that the basic principles are not lost)...

The scores that are generated show how the service system measures up against an ideal of service delivery. This ideal is described explicitly in the PASS and PASSING manuals. It is derived from a particular ideology which is spelt out in detail by Wolfensberger and Thomas (1983), and is most commonly referred to as the ideology of 'normalisation' (a term first coined by Nirje 1960, and later adopted by Wolfensberger 1972). The ideology of normalisation suggests that people with disabilities, and all 'disadvantaged' groups, should be able to live as 'normal' a life as possible. Wolfensberger argues that many groups in society are devalued, and the way services are provided to them often reinforces this devaluation by treating them in inappropriate, degrading or humiliating ways. In addition, services tend to isolate people with disabilities from the rest of the community, and present an image of them to others as either abnormal or deviant. PASS and PASSING both evaluate services by assessing how much they contribute to the devaluation of their clients. The ideal service is one which supports people in becoming valued members of their community, and which does not isolate them or mark them out as different in a negative way. Wolfensberger and Thomas (1983) describe this as 'the use of culturally valued means in order to enable people to live culturally valued lives'.

Now, in some of the literature the ideology behind PASSING is described as 'social role valorisation'. This rather less user-friendly term was introduced by Wolfensberger (1983) to counter a common misunderstanding of normalisation. The word 'normalisation' is often assumed to mean 'making people normal'. This smacks of social engineering, where people with disabilities are forced to conform to a stereotypical norm of the average citizen. As Wolfensberger makes clear, this is a misinterpretation, but its continual recurrence in the literature has made him abandon the term in favour of social role valorisation. However, like many other authors (e.g. Brown and Smith 1992), I have chosen to stick with Nirje's original terminology which is already widely known and, in the UK at least, is showing no sign of being replaced.

Although the ideology of normalisation has been codified into a set of criteria by just a few individuals, it seems to me that these criteria represent an admirably comprehensive attempt to identify key symptoms of the devaluation of the clients of service systems. For this reason, PASS/ING should provide important insights when used by people who are concerned with the diagnosis of devaluation. I would recommend looking at each aspect of the service that is evaluated in PASS/ING individually rather than aggregating the subscores for these aspects into one general score. This is because the more detailed information provided by the subscores can be helpful in identifying aspects of the service system that can actually be changed, while the general score will only be of use to service planners who need to decide whether or not to keep a service open.

In terms of the System of Systems Methodologies, PASS/ING has been aligned with the 'simple–unitary' problem context. Let me explain why. I will start with the word 'simple'. PASS/ING is most responsive to a simple context because it assumes two things: first, that the variables it measures are sufficient to provide all the necessary information for an evaluation; and second, that the researchers' observations can be adequately quantified, and this quantification will remain meaningful over time. If there is a feeling that issues will emerge during the evaluation that cannot be assessed using normalisation criteria, it would be unwise to rely for an evaluation upon PASS/ING alone. Similarly, if the service to be evaluated is in a period of rapid change, any 'snapshot' taken using an instrument like PASS/ING would quickly represent the past, not the present or future, of the organisation. Both the opacity of issues and the phe-nomenon of rapid change (which produces opacity) are indicators of complexity, and this complexity highlights the limitations of PASS/ING.

PASS/ING is also most responsive to unitary problem contexts because if there is strong disagreement over the legitimacy of normalisation criteria – disagreement that cannot be resolved by simply using the method flexibly – this cannot easily be taken into account in conducting an evaluation. PASS/ING takes the ideology of normalisation as given, so any evaluation using it will inevitably support the views of people who agree with its basic assumptions. If some stakeholders in a service system find the normalisation criteria problematic, and tinkering with the method does not satisfy their objections, then their views will be marginalised by its use. Indeed, if it is the managers of a service system who disagree with the ideology of normalisation, the results of a PASS/ING evalu-ation are likely to be dismissed out of hand. It is far better, then, to use PASS/ING when there is broad agreement with the ideology of normalisation. This way, it will produce results that are likely to be perceived as useful, and the reaction to it in terms of the stimulation of change is likely to be constructive.

Let me now move on to discuss the second of the four methods of evaluation and change, Viable System Diagnosis.

Viable System Diagnosis

While PASS/ING is a method which can be used to evaluate a service system against normalisation criteria, Viable System Diagnosis (VSD) is slightly differ-ent. This is a method for evaluating management and communication systems, comparing the reality of an organisation with an ideal model. It looks at the relationships between service delivery units (the facilities which actually provide the service), support functions (such as accounts departments, stationery offices, etc.), management, long-term forecasting (of needs, resource availability, threats to the organisation, etc.) and policy-making. It examines both the organisational structure and the quality of communications between the various different people involved in it. VSD was first developed by Beer (1979, 1981, 1985), but good secondary sources of information about it are also available (see, for example, Clemson 1984, Espejo and Harnden 1989).

Like any other organisation, a service system for people with disabilities needs an efficient management structure and an effective communication network. The consequences of the inadequate development of these can be dire for service users (see Midgley and Floyd 1988 for a study demonstrating this). As VSD is particularly useful for diagnosing failures in this regard, service systems could benefit significantly from evaluations that incorporate it.

In terms of the System of Systems Methodologies, VSD has been aligned with the 'complex–unitary' problem context. Let me explain why. In using methods like PASS/ING, one is making the assumption that the issues are straightforward enough for a tool of measurement orientated toward a pre-specified set of variables to be useful. In other words, the context is relatively simple. One does not need to make such an assumption with VSD. Indeed, VSD is not an issue-based form of evaluation in the same sense as PASS/ING: it assesses the viability of an organisation, making the assumption that those within it know what they are doing in terms of the ethics of service delivery. For this reason, it is particularly useful in complex situations when it is not possible to specify in advance exactly what the service should be doing, or when goalposts are being rapidly moved. In such situations ordinary tools of measurement have severe limitations, and one has to trust the people involved to make the best judgements they are capable of. VSD is useful here because, by encouraging the most efficient and effective structuring of the organisation, and by emphasising the need for good quality communications, the human decision-making resource of the organisation is enhanced.

While PASS/ING and VSD differ in the assumptions they make about the complexity of the issues to be addressed (PASS/ING assumes these can be specified in advance while VSD does not), they are nevertheless similar in that both assume general agreement between key stakeholders on the core values of the service system (i.e. in terms of the System of Systems Methodologies, they assume a unitary context). This has to be the case with VSD because of its emphasis on organisational efficiency and effectiveness: there is no scope for explorations of the values being promoted by the service system.

Let me now move on to discuss the third of the four methods of evaluation and change, Strategic Assumption Surfacing and Testing.

Strategic Assumption Surfacing and Testing

PASS/ING and Viable System Diagnosis (VSD) are both methods which seek to evaluate service systems against some kind of ideal – the former evaluates against an ideal of non-stigmatising service delivery, and the latter against an ideal of efficient and effective organisation. However, Strategic Assumption Surfacing and Testing (SAST) is very different: it is essentially a method for structuring and facilitating debate.

To reduce it to its bare essentials, the method can be described as having four stages:

- Group formation – gathering all those involved and affected by a situation and splitting them into small groups according to their views on key issues.
- Assumption surfacing – identifying the preferred strategy or position that each group is adopting, and revealing the assumptions upon which it is based.
- Dialectical debate – presenting the case for each position and discussing them all in a single, large group.
- Synthesis – achieving an accommodation amongst participants so as to find a practical way forward.

SAST was developed by Mason and Mitroff (1981), and their book, *Challenging Strategic Planning Assumptions,* will be the principal source of reference for the reader who wants the fullest account. However, at the time of writing, it is out of print. If it is impossible to obtain, we would recommend consulting Mason (1969), Mitroff and Emshoff (1979), Mitroff, Emshoff and Kilmann (1979), Jackson (1989) and Flood and Jackson (1991b), although these give less detail. My own sketch of SAST (above) is a précis of Jackson's (1989) description.

In my view, SAST has enormous potential for helping to promote democratic decision-making and addressing openly declared conflicts within service systems for people with disabilities. It is arguably ideal for subjecting the rationale of rehabilitation philosophies to scrutiny, and for examining alternative approaches. Often there is said to be a culture of 'openness' in disability services – especially those with a psychodynamic orientation – that should make SAST very appealing. SAST's promotion of debate fits very comfortably with the generally espoused ethos that people should share ideas and have their views respected.

In terms of the System of Systems Methodologies, SAST has been aligned with the 'simple–pluralist' problem context. Let me explain why. First, it makes the assumption that the issues to be debated can be identified in advance, as can the existence of interest groups who have different views on it. This is why it is most responsive to 'simple' contexts. When the issues are complex and unclear, it will be very difficult to get going with a method like SAST. Second, it assumes that there will actually be different views to be debated. Hence its alignment with a 'pluralist' problem context. In a unitary context, when there is basic agreement over issues, SAST will simply be redundant.

Let me now move on to discuss the last of the four methods of evaluation and change, Soft Systems Methodology.

Soft Systems Methodology

Like SAST, Soft Systems Methodology (SSM) is an approach to structuring debate. However, it differs from SAST in that it does not require strategic issues to be identified in advance. This is because SSM encourages participants to generate issues through on-going explorations of their perceptions. A further idea in SSM is that it is possible to model desirable future human activity. Given the necessary commitment from individuals involved in and affected by possible changes, these models can be used as a basis for guiding actual human activity in the world. However, to ensure that the models of desirable future human activity will indeed be useful, it is necessary for participants to relate them back to their perceptions of their current situation. In this way, possibilities for change are tested for feasibility.

SSM was developed by Peter Checkland and co-workers. Key texts are Checkland (1981) and Checkland and Scholes (1990). It is preferable to use these two books rather than the burgeoning secondary literature on SSM because, as Checkland (1993) points out, much of the work by other authors is of variable quality. However, one useful secondary text which I *can* recommend is Wilson (1984).

For the sake of the accessibility of the argument, I will describe SSM as if it were a straightforward method with various stages. However, in doing so, I should acknowledge an important point raised by Checkland (1981). Presenting SSM in the form of a series of stages encourages the reader to make the erroneous assumption that it is a simple set of techniques to be operationalised in a linear sequence. In fact, although Checkland himself presents SSM in stages, he always stresses its essentially *iterative* nature – that is, one moves backwards and forwards between the various stages as and when necessary. In addition, it is quite acceptable to depart from the specific stages, as long as the central idea of SSM is respected – that one works with participants in debate to generate models of desirable future human activity, and then one compares these models with the participants' perceptions of reality to test the models' feasibility.

SSM is usually conducted in a workshop format involving a general group discussion. The method asks workshop participants to do the following:

- *Produce a 'rich picture'*. A rich picture is a visual representation of the situation people currently perceive. It is usually a mess of numerous drawings and arrows showing interconnections between the various facets of the perceived situation.
- *Identify relevant systems to be designed*. From the rich picture, certain themes emerge. These are used to identify a list of relevant systems that need to be designed.
- *Elaborate the relevant systems*. Each of the relevant systems is then looked at in detail to identify who it should serve, who should do the activities associated with it, what its purpose is, what assumptions it makes, who could prevent it from working, and what environmental constraints it has to take as given. This allows the proposed nature and purpose of each system to be rigorously defined.
- *Produce models of desirable future activities needed to bring the relevant systems into being*. For each relevant system a 'map' is produced of the activities that need to be undertaken to realise it.
- *Allocate tasks*. The process then ends with participants discussing who should undertake the activities, how and when. An agenda for practical action is therefore produced.

In terms of the System of Systems Methodologies, SSM has been aligned with the 'complex–pluralist' problem context. Let me explain why. First, it enables people to deal with a considerable amount of complexity because of the fact that participants in workshops are encouraged to learn as they go along, and are not required to generate concrete issues for debate in advance. People may therefore start an SSM workshop being unclear about what the key issues are. Indeed, they may simply perceive the situation they are in as a mess, having no idea at all about what needs to be done, yet they can gain clarity as they proceed. Second, SSM has been aligned with a 'pluralist' problem context because, like SAST, it assumes that there will actually be different views to be debated. Again like SAST, in a unitary context when there is general agreement over issues, SSM will be largely redundant.

Arguably the real strength of SSM lies in its ability to deal with messy situations when there is no clear focus upon any one problem. My own experience in disability projects suggests that these situations arise more often than one might initially suppose. Sometimes a project will be dealing with its day-to-day concerns in the usual way, coming up against familiar difficulties, but there will be a general feeling that maybe, if things were done differently, these recurrent problems might not arise. Nevertheless, this recognition remains vague and unspecified. In other words, there is no problem focus beyond fragmentary, day-to-day experience. An example might be a mental health vocational rehabilitation project sited in a day centre in which staff experience the frustration of dealing with a number of service users who appear unmotivated and apathetic. Whatever staff do to stimulate interest it seems that people just won't participate, and new people who join the project assume the same attitude. This is, of course, an aspect of 'rehabilitation culture' which many professionals who work with people with mental health problems in day care settings will recognise. Nevertheless, despite awareness of the difficulty, it is often notoriously difficult to concretise the problem so that a solution might be devised. SSM offers creative means by which to formulate understanding, and thereby begin to move toward, not 'solutions' as such, but more effective ways of working.

Using the Methods Together

Having presented the four methods and described some of their strengths and weaknesses, we can now move on to look at what it might mean to use these methods together in a truly complementary fashion. Earlier, I suggested that evaluation and change activities can usefully be seen as a series of interdependent and continually evolving research questions. Let me present a hypothetical scenario of how the practice of defining such questions and using the methods together might work.

A researcher has been called in by a service purchaser to evaluate several day centres for people with disabilities. Her initial interviews with stakeholders (service users, carers, policy makers, managers, staff, members of a local self-advocacy forum, etc.) help her define who should be seen as involved in or affected by the services. These interviews do not reveal any significant coercion. While there are issues to be dealt with, there is no obvious reason why these should not be handled through an evaluation, especially as users' views are well developed and represented through the self-advocacy forum. The professionals show some knowledge of normalisation and want this to be the basis for the evaluation. However, other stakeholders do not share this knowledge, so the researcher feels it would be best to debate issues of philosophy first. She discusses this with the various stakeholders, they agree, and she therefore starts with Strategic Assumption Surfacing and Testing (SAST) to subject the ideology of normalisation to scrutiny. This reveals several important matters requiring attention. First, carers are worried that, if services are closed as a result of a PASS/ING evaluation, no alternatives will be put in their place. Through the debate, the carers' fears are allayed by the policy-makers. Second, while there is general support for the ideology of normalisation, there is some concern on the part of members of the self-advocacy forum that, if PASS/ING is used for the evaluation, their own contribution to the local community of people with disabilities will be devalued. This is because the normalisation criteria set out by Wolfensberger and co-workers suggest that grouping people with disabilities together is a bad thing: services should always seek integration into the wider community. The self-advocacy forum engages in consciousness-raising activities which involve people with disabilities coming together to offer each other support and encourage mutual learning. Through debate using SAST, it is acknowledged that the consciousness-raising activities of the self-advocacy forum are extremely useful. It is agreed that the only form of grouping that should be penalised in an evaluation is the kind that happens in institutions when people become cut off from the rest of the community. PASS/ING is therefore selected as the appropriate evaluation method, but it is decided that, in assessing services, particular attention will be paid to the context in which people with disabilities come together.

Having conducted a PASS/ING evaluation, it becomes quite clear that radical changes need to be considered. Most of the services score very poorly, although one centre with links into local adult education and employment initiatives is considered minimally acceptable. The purchaser decides something needs to be done, and asks for plans to be drawn up. Nobody quite knows where to start, so the researcher recommends that two Soft Systems Methodology (SSM) workshops should be run – one, conducted with a broad range of stakeholders, to look at how the poor services might be replaced by something better, and the other, conducted within the minimally acceptable service, to examine how it might be improved. This recommendation is accepted. The SSM workshops allow participants to design positive alternatives and build action plans for change. However, they also surface several further problems: there is a feeling on the part of user representatives and those from the self-advocacy forum that their views are not routinely considered in the planning process. Managers also feel stressed by the complexity of the changes facing them in the health and social services as a whole, and there are complaints from all quarters that people are not being kept properly informed about what is going on. An outcome of the SSM process is a recommendation to use Viable System Diagnosis (VSD) to address issues of communication and control, taking the need for increased user involvement and improved information flow into account. All stakeholders feel this is important, so a VSD is commenced. The consequent organisational restructuring is carried out alongside implementation of the changes suggested through the use of SSM. Finally, in a debriefing session called by the researcher, it is agreed to re-evaluate the newly developed services after five years, once again using PASS/ING.

Of course this is only one of many possible scenarios, and there is no reason why people should not switch between the methods in a more complex manner. While conducting an SSM, for example, a particular difference between people might be identified that could be resolved by switching temporarily to SAST. As soon as one comes up against an issue that might be handled better though the use of another method, there is no reason why that method should not be brought in. The key is to use the flexibility granted by a framework such as the System of Systems Methodologies to maximise both flexibility and creativity.

Conclusion

In this chapter I have offered a rationale for thinking about methods of evaluation and organisational change as complementary tools. I have presented a practical framework highlighting the strengths and weaknesses of four very different methods – PASS/ING, Viable System Diagnosis (VSD), Strategic Assumption Surfacing and Testing (SAST) and Soft Systems Methodology (SSM) – which I believe make a very useful complementary set.

PASS/ING will be extremely effective when there is general agreement that the ideology of normalisation should be the yardstick for evaluation, and when the situation is relatively stable (so that an evaluative snapshot will continue to have meaning after it is taken). Even if there is minor disagreement over some aspects of normalisation philosophy, the method can be adapted following debate. However, PASS/ING will have limited usefulness when there is unresolvable disagreement over its ideological basis: an evaluation using it will inevitably support the views of those who agree with the philosophy of normalisation, but the views of those who disagree with it (or who think other issues should be looked at instead) could well be marginalised by its use. Similarly, PASS/ING will not be particularly useful in situations of instability where the service may not be the same a month or even a week after the evaluation has taken place. Its use may also be unwise when the issues that are going to have to be dealt with during an evaluation are unclear.

Viable System Diagnosis (VSD), on the other hand, will be extremely helpful in situations of instability. This is because its evaluative focus is on organisational communication and control rather than whether a particular service is appropriate. By optimising effectiveness, the organisation is better able to pursue its objectives and handle rapid change. However, like PASS/ING, the usefulness of VSD is dependent on there being general agreement with the prevailing ideology – this time it is the ideology of the organisation rather than the ideology inherent in the method. VSD helps an organisation make itself more effective, but this will inevitably be effectiveness in pursuing whatever objectives it already has on its agenda. People who disagree with these objectives will generally be marginalised by its use unless debate is entered into before a VSD is undertaken to set the terms of reference of the organisation democratically.

In contrast, Strategic Assumption Surfacing and Testing (SAST) will operate best when there are clearly defined distinctions between the views of different individuals or groups. It makes people justify different perspectives rationally before a consensus or compromise is sought, and will therefore be particularly useful for exploring the issues of principle that underpin service philosophies. SAST will be less useful, however, when there is already agreement between those involved in and affected by the service, as they will see little point in opening up their views to challenge. Similarly, it will not be particularly useful in situations where people are unclear about what the key issues are. It is difficult to mount rational challenges when the positions people are adopting are vague and ill-defined.

It is Soft Systems Methodology (SSM) that will deal best with situations in which there are different, but ill-defined, perspectives to be taken into account. This is because it structures a learning experience for people, allowing them to co-construct both their understandings of the situation and any changes that may usefully be pursued. Of course, SSM will be less useful when there is solid agreement on the course to be pursued, or when the issues of disagreement are very clear, because the learning experience it offers will be perceived as redundant.

The best way of using these methods as complementary tools is to switch between them as and when necessary. One word of caution must still be sounded, however. No method of evaluation or organisational change can deal adequately with coercion, and it is therefore important to begin any research project by talking with people confidentially about the issues they feel are important, and their relationships with one another. If coercion is uncovered, and it appears that key issues cannot be addressed, then an appropriate course of action might be to support activities of consciousness-raising, campaigning, and/or direct action – either instead of an evaluation, as a precursor to it, or even alongside it if possible.

Having sounded this note of caution, I nevertheless hope that I have demonstrated the real benefits that a complementarist approach to evaluation and change can bring. Let me end, then, with a call for other researchers to contribute their own expertise to an on-going research program. By working together and learning from one another we have the chance to build an even more flexible and critically aware evaluation and change practice. This is essential if we are to be truly responsive to the needs of people with disabilities, both now and in the future.

References

Banathy, B.H. (1987) Choosing design methods. *Proceedings of the 31st Annual Meeting of the International Society for General Systems Research*, held in Budapest, Hungary, 54–63. Louisville, KY: International Society for General Systems Research.

Beer, S. (1979) *The Heart of Enterprise*. Chichester: Wiley.

Beer, S. (1981) *Brain of the Firm*, 2nd Edition. Chichester: Wiley.

Beer, S. (1985) *Diagnosing the System for Organisations*. Chichester: Wiley.

Brown, H. and Smith, H. (1992) Introduction. In H. Brown, and H. Smith (eds) *Normalisation: A Reader for the Nineties*. London: Routledge, xiv–xxii.

Burrell, G. and Morgan, G. (1979) *Sociological Paradigms and Organizational Analysis*. London: Heinemann.

Burton, M. (1983). Understanding mental health services: theory and practice. *Critical Social Policy* Vol 3, 54–74.

Checkland, P.B. (1981) *Systems Thinking, Systems Practice*. Chichester: Wiley.

Checkland, P.B. (1993) Review of 'Practical Soft Systems Analysis' by D. Patching. *Systems Practice* Vol 6, 435–438.

Checkland, P.B. and Scholes, J. (1990) *Soft Systems Methodology in Action*. Chichester: Wiley.

Clemson, B. (1984) *Cybernetics: A New Management Tool*. Tunbridge Wells: Abacus Press.

Espejo, R. and Harnden, R. (1989) *The Viable System Model: Interpretations and Applications of Stafford Beer's VSM*. Chichester: Wiley.

Flood, R.L. (1990) *Liberating Systems Theory*. New York: Plenum.

Flood, R.L. and Jackson, M.C. (1991a) *Critical Systems Thinking: Directed Readings*. Chichester: Wiley.

Flood, R.L. and Jackson, M.C. (1991b) *Creative Problem Solving: Total Systems Intervention*. Chichester: Wiley.

Gregory, W.J. (1992) *Critical Systems Thinking and Pluralism: A New Constellation*. Ph.D. thesis. London: City University.

Jackson, M.C. (1987) New directions in management science. In M.C. Jackson and P. Keys (eds) *New Directions in Management Science*. Gower: Aldershot.

Jackson, M.C. (1989) Assumptional analysis: an elucidation and appraisal for Systems practitioners. *Systems Practice* Vol 2, 11–28.

Jackson, M.C. (1990) Beyond a System of Systems Methodologies. *Journal of the Operational Research Society* Vol 41, 657–668.

Jackson, M.C. (1991) *Systems Methodology for the Management Sciences*. Plenum, New York.

Jackson, M.C. and Keys, P. (1984) Towards a System of Systems Methodologies. *Journal of the Operational Research Society* Vol 35, 473–486.

Mason, R.O. (1969) A dialectical approach to strategic planning. *Management Science* Vol 15, B403–414.

Mason, R.O. and Mitroff, I.I. (1981) *Challenging Strategic Planning Assumptions*. New York: Wiley.

Midgley, G. (1990) Creative methodology design. *Systemist* Vol 12, 108–113.

Midgley, G. (1992a) Pluralism and the legitimation of Systems Science. *Systems Practice* Vol 5, 147–172.

Midgley, G. (1992b) *Unity and Pluralism*. PhD thesis. London: City University.

Midgley, G. (1995a) What is this thing called Critical Systems Thinking? In K. Ellis, A. Gregory, B. Mears-Young and G. Ragsdell (eds) *Critical Issues in Systems Theory and Practice*. New York: Plenum.

Midgley, G. (1995b) Dealing with coercion: Critical Systems Heuristics and beyond. *Systems Practice* Vol 8, in press.

Midgley, G. and Floyd, M. (1988) *Microjob: A Computer Training Service for People with Disabilities*. London: Rehabilitation Resource Centre, City University.

Mitroff, I.I. and Emshoff, J.R. (1979) On strategic assumption-making: a dialectical approach to policy and planning. *Academy of Management Review* Vol 6, 649–651.

Mitroff, I.I., Emshoff, J.R. and Kilmann, R.H. (1979) Assumptional analysis: a methodology for strategic problem-solving. *Management Science* Vol 25, 583–593.

Nirje, B. (1960) The normalization principle and its human management implications. In R. Kugel and W. Wolfensberger (eds) *Changing Patterns in Residential Services for the Mentally Retarded*. Washington, DC: President's Committee on Mental Retardation, 179–195.

Oliga, J.C. (1988) Methodological foundations of Systems Methodologies. *Systems Practice* Vol 1, 87–112.

Patton, M.Q. (1980) *Qualitative Evaluation Methods*. London: Sage.

Tsoukas, H. (1993) The road to emancipation is through organizational development: a critical evaluation of Total Systems Intervention. *Systems Practice* Vol 6, 53–70.

Ulrich, W. (1983) *Critical Heuristics of Social Planning: A New Approach to Practical Philosophy*. Berne: Haupt.

Wilson, B. (1984) *Systems: Concepts, Methodologies and Applications*. Chichester: Wiley.

Wolfensberger, W. (1972) *The Principle of Normalization in Human Services*. Toronto: National Institute on Mental Retardation.

Wolfensberger, W. (1983) Social role valorization: a proposed new term for the principle of normalization. *Mental Retardation* Vol 21, 234–239.

Wolfensberger, W. and Glenn, L. (1975) *Program Analysis of Service Systems, Volumes I and II*, 3rd Edition. Toronto: National Institute on Mental Retardation.

Wolfensberger, W. and Thomas, S. (1983) *PASSING: A Method for Evaluating the Quality of Human Services according to the Principle of Normalization*, 2nd Edition. Toronto: National Institute on Mental Retardation.

Chapter 4

Do PASS and PASSING Pass?
A Critique of PASS/ING

Doria Pilling

Introduction

In the summer of 1989, the King's Fund invited the RRC at City University to attend a meeting to discuss the possibility of evaluating PASS (Program Analysis of Service Systems, Wolfensberger and Glenn 1975). Paul Williams, the Director of the Community and Mental Handicap Educational and Research Association (CMHERA), the organisation that has promoted PASS and its updated version PASSING (Program Analysis of Service Systems' Implementation of Normalization Goals, Wolfensberger and Thomas 1983) in this country had applied for a grant to enable quantitative analyses of the data from evaluations using these measures to be carried out. The King's Fund had decided that they wanted some objective evidence from independent researchers on the validity of PASS and its usefulness in promoting change. I went to the meeting, at which Paul Williams was also present, and was asked, with his agreement, to write a proposal for investigating these questions. To start with I knew nothing about PASS and PASSING, but, with Paul Williams' co-operation – and the help of Gerald Midgley, who was interested in methodological issues –I put together a proposal which was accepted by the King's Fund Grants Committee. Paul Williams maintained his co-operation throughout the project, allowing Gerald Midgley to act as a participant observer in a PASSING evaluation of day services for people with learning disabilities, giving us access to various unpublished reports, to information as requested, answering many queries, attending meetings of the small Advisory group that we set up, and encouraging the comparison between PASS/PASSING and ACE that I am going to talk about later today. I stress this because of criticism in a recent book, *Normalisation, a Reader for the Nineties* (Brown and Smith 1992), that the ideas in the version of normalisation on which PASS and PASSING are based, those of their main author Wolf Wolfensberger, are 'owned' by a small group of committed people, with whom it is difficult to debate.

Normalisation as the Basis of PASS and PASSING

PASS and PASSING (on Paul Williams' advice we included both in our investigation) – distinct instruments, but closely related in their theoretical bases and rating procedures – were designed to be objective quantitative measures of the quality of any type of service, particularly those for people with disabilities or disadvantages of some kind.

PASS judges service quality mainly – 73 per cent of the items – in terms of adherence to Wolfensberger's principle of normalisation, and PASSING judges it entirely in terms of a refined elaboration of normalisation concepts. This raises the question of what the King's Fund meant when they said that they wanted evidence on the validity of PASS. Did they want us to determine whether PASS measured Wolfensberger's ideas of normalisation? It seems much more likely that they wanted to find out if it was valid for the use to which it being put – to measure the quality of services (see Pilling and Midgley, Chapter 7, for further discussion of this issue). It seemed essential to examine Wolfensberger's normalisation ideas – and the PASS and PASSING ratings derived from them – as well as the criticisms of them that were appearing in various articles, and eventually the book on normalisation.

The initial meaning of normalisation, an idea that evolved in Scandinavia in the 1960s, was 'making available to the mentally subnormal patterns and conditions of everyday life which are as close as possible to the norms and patterns of the mainstream of society' (Nirje 1970). The meaning was that mentally retarded people should be offered the same conditions as other people, including the treatment, education and training needed for their optimal development. The implication is that mentally retarded people are entitled to the same rights as everyone else (Perrin and Nirje 1989).

Wolfensberger re-worked and reformulated these ideas. They are seen by him as applying to any group of people whose disabilities or differences from others in society puts them at risk of being devalued, and normalisation is seen as a means of reversing the devaluation process itself. Devaluation, according to Wolfensberger, is about an extra layer of disadvantage that is nothing to do with any intrinsic characteristic of people who are devalued, but is all about attitudes to these characteristics. This means that instead of being given experiences and opportunities to help them overcome any impairments or disadvantages, people with disabilities are often denied those that others take for granted. Expectations for them are low and become a self-fulfilling prophecy, not only because of the denial of circumstances that would help them in their development, but because low expectations become internalised by those who are devalued. Normalisation is about removing this extra layer of disadvantage.

In its best known formulation, Wolfensberger and Tullman defined normalisation in 1982 as, 'As much as possible, the use of culturally valued means in order to enable, establish or maintain valued social roles for people.' Wolfensberger came to see the aim of normalisation as being to establish and/or maintain people who are or risk being devalued in as many positive social roles as possible – such as friend, worker, partner, owner. According to him, the more people are seen as fulfilling social roles that most people value, the more likely it is that they will be treated positively by others, and attributes which might be otherwise be viewed negatively will assume much less importance.

The implications of these ideas in practice are that a service has to do everything it can to enhance the social image and competency of its clients. These two aspects are reciprocally reinforcing: if people have a more positive image others will have higher expectations of them and they are likely to be given opportunities and experiences which will improve their competency; the more competent people are the more positive their image is likely to be. The extra layers of disadvantage imposed by society will be diminished and there will be a change in public attitudes, people with disabilities no longer being devalued.

PASSING is explicitly based on this idea that the major goal of normalisation is to help people who may be devalued maintain or attain socially valued roles. (PASSING still talks about normalisation, although Wolfensberger 1983a soon afterwards decided that 'social role valorization' was a preferable term – as normalisation was much misunderstood. I am going to continue to use the term normalisation, for convenience, to cover all Wolfensberger's ideas.) A service is judged on the extent to which it conveys positive expectations about its clients, that will help them achieve valued social roles. The PASSING manual states that in order to do this a service should promote:

> normatively attractive, comfortable and challenging settings; age appropriate and challenging program activities; age appropriate and culturally-valued personal appearance of clients; as much as feasible, image-enhancing matches between the needs of clients, the nature of the program, and staff identities; status-enhancing labels and forms of address for clients; etc. (Wolfensberger and Thomas 1983, 25)

Wolfensberger (1988) said later, that '...the things previously considered to be normalizing really contribute to the enhancement of the social role(s) of a person or group in the eyes of others'. A service should provide then, in the area of its concern, life conditions that most people in society would value and which will convey a positive social image of its clients and develop their competence as much as possible.

Most service providers and users, whether or not they are committed to Wolfensberger's concept of normalisation, would probably agree that the kind of provision described above is indicative of quality. But there are a number of features which make PASS and PASSING controversial as instruments of evaluation. The overriding aim is to change public attitudes, to stop people with disabilities and other characteristics that may be negatively viewed from being devalued. Services are rated on the extent they do this. There is not an inevitable coincidence between circumstances that will improve the image of a client group in the long-run, and short-term benefits to specific clients, though they may coincide. Where there is a difference, it is the long-term impact to the group as a whole that takes precedence in PASS and PASSING.

Expectation Theory

Integral to Wolfensberger's aims is the reversal of negative expectations, so that opportunities and experiences will be opened up and people will achieve more. What evidence then is there that others' expectations have an effect in themselves on what people achieve? The idea that prophecies can be self-fulfilling is an old one, but the main research in this area was carried out in the late 1960s and early

1970s, at the time when Wolfensberger was developing his ideas. The Rosenthal and Jacobsen (1968) study that he mentions in his 1972 work on normalisation, as a spectacular example of the effect of role expectancy on children's development, was the subject of intense controversy, and it does appear very doubtful when scrutinised carefully that it demonstrates the power of teacher's expectations on children's achievement. Central to the study was an attempt to artificially alter teachers' expectations of pupils, by informing them that researchers had predicted that children, in fact randomly selected, would make unusual gains during the school year. Design and testing problems make the evidence that they did so dubious, and, above all, it is uncertain that teachers' expectations were really altered. This was also the case in most of the replication studies which followed, some of which appeared more intent on disproving the Rosenthal and Jacobsen findings than investigating the influence of teachers' expectations. In one or two studies in experimental situations, though, where the researchers could effectively control teachers' expectations, the effect on pupils' performance was dramatic, but it is doubtful how long the control could be maintained in the real world. There are also a number of studies which show that teachers' naturally occurring expectations – based on beliefs about children with certain characteristics, rather than their actual ability, have a small but significant effect on pupils' progress. A number of studies also indicate that expectations affect teaching behaviour, though studies are not consistent on the actual effects. My own review (Pilling and Pringle 1978) and the slightly later one by Mortimore and Blackstone (1982) detail the evidence on the effect of teachers' expectations.

A closely associated idea is that labelling people affects their development. It is probably true that the effect is not as powerful as was once believed. It is interesting, though, that one of the main, and oft-cited, critiques of labelling theory (Gordon 1980) relies heavily on ideas of genetically determined differences between ethnic groups (in particular the controversial work of Arthur Jensen 1969). Another review (MacMillan, Jones and Aloia 1974) finds the evidence on the influence of labelling itself equivocal, but points out the difficulty in separating the labelling from consequences, such as special schooling. This is precisely the point. Initially small differences may be accentuated if they lead to environmental circumstances that limit opportunities.

There is also evidence of the underestimation of the abilities of people with learning disabilities. In the 1960s there was considerable experimentation, and the abilities of people with severe learning disabilities to perform various tasks occasioned surprise. In some research by the Clarkes (Clarke and Clarke 1965), for example, it was found that initial abilities on industrial tasks bore little relationship to the final level of performance achieved. A recent study (Rynders and Horrobin 1990) shows that the educability of children with Downs syndrome was underestimated in the 1970s and details the success in reading of a high proportion of children with Downs syndrome who had been involved in early education programmes.

It seems unlikely, overall, that raising the expectations for people with disabilities would not raise achievements, although the extent needs much more research. Some (e.g. Baldwin and Stowers 1987) have queried the emphasis on the development of competency in PASS and PASSING, on the grounds that this would leave behind those whose abilities cannot be developed as a group to be devalued. But it seems to be a false argument to say that because it might not work for everyone, others' potential should not be helped to develop as far as possible. And a more positive view of some people with disabilities might just as easily transfer to everyone rather than meaning that those who cannot develop very far are even more devalued.

Importance of Integration

The main reason for the stress on integration in PASS and PASSING is because of the emphasis on changing public attitudes. In a letter to the *American Journal on Mental Retardation*, Paul Williams (1991) explains that Wolfensberger's version of normalisation is not just about more favourable 'lifestyles', but is about 'normalising' relationships between society and individuals who may be devalued, in the same sense that the term is used to describe 'repairing a diplomatic rift between countries'. Institutional care which segregates people is unlikely to be helpful for this purpose, he says, however 'caring and benign' it might be.

Integration in society, as far as possible, is thus integral to Wolfensberger's interpretation of normalisation. Not every service manager or user would necessarily equate integration with quality although the acceptance of it as an essential feature of quality will go far beyond those who are in entire agreement with Wolfensberger's diagnosis of, as Paul Williams (1991) puts it, 'the problem'.

Agreement that integration is an essential element of quality can be seen simply as a matter of human rights. People with physical disabilities, such as Colin Barnes (1991), in his book on anti-discrimination, argue strongly against segregation, as producing inferior services and opportunities. It can be argued, as Wolfensberger (1980) himself has, that there would need to be unequivocal scientific 'proof' of the benefits of institutionalisation and segregation to justify them, rather than asking for this of community integration, as some researchers have done (e.g. Zigler 1977, Zigler, Hodapp and Edison 1990).

Criticisms of normalisation in terms of problems involved in 'dispersing' people with disabilities (e.g. Szivos 1992) seem to be starting off the wrong way round, as if people actually started off life in institutions rather than families. Of course this is not to underestimate the value of friendships within institutions for people who have lived in them. But segregated living need not be the only way of obtaining friendships with other disabled people, if this is what is wished. Wolfensberger does not deny the value of such friendships, and encouragement of those within the setting are taken into account in one of the ratings in both PASS and PASSING (Interactions; Life-Enhancing Interactions respectively). However it could be argued that they are underestimated: friendships outside a service with other disabled people do not seem to be acknowledged as positive in PASSING, unless they are with those who are more competent (Competency-Related Other Integrative Client Contacts and Personal Relationships).

Image-Enhancement

The emphasis on ratings concerned primarily (though not entirely) with image-enhancement, with others' perceptions of service and its clients is striking in both PASS and PASSING, in the latter in 27 out of the 42 ratings. In PASS only one of the ratings concerned with social integration is about active promotion of contacts with ordinary community members, the aspect that appears most relevant from a 'common-sense' viewpoint. Most emphasis is about features of the service that others might see as off-putting. These include ratings concerned with labels given to the service and its clients, the appropriateness of the building both for the neighbourhood in which it is located and for its function, and other images and symbols which reinforce others' perception that the service is for 'deviant' people. 'Ghettoising' of services for people with disabilities and disadvantages is also seen as adding to the image of 'deviancy'. Client groupings in the service, the identity and characteristics of staff members are seen as possibly having aspects that might be off-putting. The concentration on others' perceptions flows from Wolfensberger's theory, that perceptions will affect the expectations, treatment and ultimately the behaviour of those with characteristics at risk of being devalued.

Is this emphasis realistic in a measure of service quality? What these ratings seem to do above all is draw attention to many attitudes in our society towards people with disabilities or disadvantages and treatment of them that are taken for granted, that usually remain unexamined. For example, funding that has to be raised by a charity through public appeals rather than being given by statutory authorities as a right, is seen to taint a service and its clients as objects of pity and charity. Such issues may throw considerable light on how some groups of people are viewed by society, but should they contribute towards rating the quality of a particular service?

The ratings concerned with client groupings and staff characteristics are perhaps the most controversial in PASS and PASSING. According to these ratings, clients with different types of disabilities or disadvantages should not be mixed together because negative perceptions are likely to transfer from one group to another. And staff who are disadvantaged themselves, and unlikely to get a job elsewhere, should not be employed by a service for people with disabilities because this will give members of the wider society the view that the clients of the service are of low value. Again these ratings draw attention to important issues, that people should not be lumped together simply because they have some kind of disability. Services for people with disabilities should not be staffed by low-paid people without the necessary skills or qualifications to meet their needs. But the exclusion of such workers can also be seen as discriminatory and contrary to equal opportunities policies (e.g. Brown and Smith 1989), quality being preferably judged by the actions taken to implement equal pay policies and obtain the necessary funding to do so.

A general criticism of these and other ratings in PASS and PASSING that are primarily image-related is that far too much attention is being paid to appearance, and to the values of western society (e.g. Baldwin 1985, Brechin and Swain 1989), the dominant ideology being that of the white, middle-class male (Brown and Smith 1989). One argument against this is that the image issues are not so much concerned with making appearances acceptable, as giving people with disabilities access to conditions of life from which they are usually excluded. Wolfensberger and Thomas (1983) stress that there is an enormous range of valued options and the point is not to exclude people involuntarily from them. The guidelines for PASS and PASSING evaluators (Wolfensberger 1983b) suggest that local norms can be taken providing that this does not mean excluding people from the benefits/amenities of the wider society. This does, of course, need sensitive interpretation, particularly in regard to minority ethnic groups, and there are real dilemmas but Wolfensberger cannot be expected to have all the answers to difficult problems in society. Peter Ferns' (1992) view that minority group values should always be followed, also poses problems. Is it true, as he suggests, that arranged marriages are appropriate for Asian girls, although devalued by the wider society? Should they not also have a choice of whether they want to adhere to these values?

Changing Society's Values

The image-enhancement aspect does pose problems at times – e.g. in only scoring relationships with 'valued' people in one of the PASSING (Image-Related Other Integrative Client Contacts and Personal Relationships) ratings. A number of critics have argued (e.g. Brechin and Swain 1989, Dalley 1992, Robinson 1989) that rather than 'packaging' people to make them less 'different' and more 'acceptable', efforts should be made to increase tolerance of differences. This is one strand of normalisation (Wolfensberger 1972), as the critics generally acknowledge (e.g. Dalley 1992), though it is one on which there could be more emphasis. Wolfensberger says:

> We should work for greater acceptance of differentness of modes of grooming, dressing, speaking; of skin colour, race, religious and national origin; of appearance, age, sex, intelligence and education. Also encouraged should be greater acceptance of the physically and sensory handicapped, the epileptic, the emotionally disordered and perhaps the sexually unorthodox.

> Here, it is important to recall that societal response to deviancy tends to be general, rather than specific to a particular deviance. By furthering societal acceptance for one type of differentness, we are also and indirectly gaining increased acceptance for a group in which we have a particular personal or professional interest. (Wolfensberger 1972, 41)

It does seem true that for real community integration – as people like Mark Burton (1983) have said – you need real changes in society's values, from those of individualistic, competitive capitalist society, where it is difficult to have time for anyone else.

De-Institutionalisation

This does not mean that normalisation has had no effect. It has brought about an enormous change in services – as the Normalisation Reader (Brown and Smith

1992) stresses – particularly for people with learning disabilities. But this was, partly at least, because community care policies (not the same as, but compatible with normalisation) have coincided to some extent with the economic motivations of a Conservative government (Whitehead 1992). There are real dangers now of services being cut, when under-funded local authorities have to implement community care. Wolfensberger is certainly not in favour of de-institutionalisation without proper services, and he makes a scathing attack on this in a recent article:

> Rather, what is needed is well-planned adaptive de-institutionalization in concert with the provision of decent, appropriate, relevant and model-coherent (Wolfensberger and Glenn 1975) community services; but of course, these are the very things that the service super-system either withholds or is incapable of providing. (Wolfensberger 1992)

PASS and PASSING as Evaluation Measures

Overall, PASS and PASSING have been important for drawing attention to issues in services that would probably not have been looked at otherwise. It is a strength of PASS/ING that the ratings continually force comparisons with what is regarded as appropriate and valued for people of a similar age in the wider society. The image issues point to ways in which others' perceptions of service users' surroundings, activities or associations may be negative, and can be regarded as warning signals that ask why they are being treated in a way that others would not value for themselves. If there are aspects of a service affecting users' lives which are beyond the control of staff or even managers – such as location, building design, funding – it is appropriate to take them into account in rating quality in measures concerned with enhancing users' status in society, with their access to valued life conditions. However, it is important that staff and managers of a service being evaluated have some understanding of the measure being used, and of why these aspects are included in the ratings. Where this is not the case, feedbacks to staff which emphasise aspects of the service over which they have no control can be very demoralising, particularly where much effort has been made to make improvements in aspects which are under their control. There has been increasing awareness by those carrying out PASS/ING evaluations of these problems, and of finding ways of overcoming them. Possible solutions are different feedbacks to staff with different roles, and degrees of power, or more involvement of staff/service users/others with an interest in the service in the actual evaluation. What seems to be agreed (as Alan Tyne has said, see Chapter 2) is that the preparation for, and follow-up after, a PASS/ING evaluation require longer time than the evaluation itself.

Summary of Discussion

The discussion covered several issues: the relationship between attitude change and behaviour modification; user groups determining their own agendas; the legitimacy of using the term normalisation to cover Wolfensberger's ideas on social role valorisation, and how to feedback from PASS and PASSING evaluations.

Attitudes and Behaviour Change

Doria Pilling, replying to a delegate, said that in her understanding the whole purpose of Wolfensberger's ideas was not simply to change attitudes to disability but change the behaviour of people in society generally.

Minority Group Viewpoints

A delegate queried what DP had said about taking on user group perspectives, saying he was not clear how client groups could be empowered if somebody else made the decision about which of their needs it was appropriate to take on. In his opinion it was necessary to start from what client groups are saying, irrespective of whether service providers agree with this. DP said that Wolfensberger was often criticised for advocating middle-class white views, and some critics thought that the views of people in the particular group should always be taken. She thought that there could be pitfalls in this position as well, as through lack of opportunities some users might not have had the experiences to know all the options. She thought that the job of service providers was to try to set out the options, but ultimately to let the client choose.

Normalisation and Social Role Valorisation

DP justified her use of the term 'normalisation' to cover the development of the ideas, and said that in a short presentation covering both PASS and PASSING it would have been difficult to keep switching from one term to the other.

Feedback

A delegate said that following an evaluation one would hopefully be providing recommendations about things which were under the control of the service to change, and not about those over which it had no control. DP said that this had not always been the case in evaluations which had occurred. But the strength of PASS and PASSING was that they could point out that radical changes in services are necessary. These might not be in the control of staff and managers to whom the feedback was being presented, and how the changes were pointed out was a sensitive and difficult matter.

References

Baldwin, S. (1985) Sheep in wolf's clothing: impact of normalisation teaching on human services and service providers. *International Journal of Rehabilitation Research* Vol 8, 2, 131–42.

Baldwin, S. and Stowers, C. (1987) Normalisation and elderly persons: in whose best interests? *American Archives of Rehabilitation Therapy*, Spring 34–42.

Barnes, C. (1991) *Disabled People in Britain and Discrimination: A Case for Anti-Discrimination Legislation*. London: Hurst and Company/University of Calgary Press, in association with the British Council of Organizations of Disabled People.

Brechin, A. and Swain, J. (1989) Creating a 'working alliance' with people with learning difficulties. In A. Brechin and J. Walmsley (eds) *Making Connections*. London: Hodder and Stoughton, in association with the Open University.

Brown, H. and Smith H. (1989) Whose ordinary life is it anyway? *Disability, Handicap and Society* Vol 4, 2, 105–118

Brown, H. and Smith, H. (eds) (1992) *Normalisation: A Reader for the Nineties*. London: Tavistock/Routledge.

Burton, M. (1983) Understanding mental health services: theory and practice. *Critical Social Policy* Vol 3, 1, 54–74.

Clarke, A.D.B. and Clarke, A.M. (1965) The abilities and trainability of imbeciles. In A.M. Clarke and A.D.B. Clarke (eds) *Mental Deficiency: The Changing Outlook*, 2nd edition. London: Methuen, 356–84.

Dalley, G. (1992) Social welfare ideologies and normalisation: links and conflicts. In H. Brown and H. Smith (eds) *Normalisation: A Reader for the Nineties*. London: Tavistock/Routledge, 100–111.

Ferns, P. (1992) Promoting race equality through normalisation. In H. Brown and H. Smith (eds) *Normalisation: A Reader for the Nineties*. London: Tavistock/Routledge, 134–148.

Gordon, R.A. (1980) Examining labelling theory: the case of mental retardation. In W.R. Gove (ed) *The Labelling of Deviance: Examining a Perspective*. London: Wiley.

Jensen, A. (1969) How much can we boost IQ and scholastic achievement? *Harvard Educational Review* Vol 39, 1, 1–123.

MacMillan, D.L., Jones, R.L. and Aloia, G.F. (1974) The mentally retarded label: a theoretical analysis and review of research. *American Journal of Mental Deficiency* Vol 79, 3, 241–61.

Mortimore, J. and Blackstone, T. (1982) *Disadvantage and Education*. London: Heinemann.

Nirje, B. (1970) Symposium on 'normalization'. 1 The normalization principle – implications and comments. *Journal of Mental Subnormality* XVI, Vol 2, 31, 62–70.

Perrin, B. and Nirje, B. (1989) Setting the record straight: a critique of some frequent misconceptions of the normalisation principle. In A. Brechin and J. Walmsley (eds) *Making Connections*. London: Hodder and Stoughton, in association with the Open University.

Pilling, D. and Pringle, M.K. (1978) *Controversial Issues in Child Development*. London: Elek. (Part IV – Teachers' expectations and pupil performance).

Robinson, T.(1989) Normalisation: the whole answer? In A. Brechin and J. Walmsley (eds) *Making Connections*. London: Hodder and Stoughton, in association with the Open University.

Rosenthal, R. and Jacobsen, L. (1968) *Pygmalion in the Classroom: Teacher Expectation and Pupils' Intellectual Development*. New York: Holt, Rinehart and Winston.

Rynders, J.E. and Horrobin, J.M. (1990) Always trainable? Never educable? Updating educational expectations concerning children with Downs syndrome. *American Journal on Mental Retardation* Vol 95, 1, 77–83.

Szivos, S.(1992) The limits of integration. In H. Brown and H. Smith (eds) *Normalisation: a Reader for the Nineties*. London: Tavistock/Routledge, 112–133.

Whitehead, S. (1992) The social origins of normalisation. In H. Brown and H. Smith (eds) *Normalisation: A Reader for the Nineties*. London: Tavistock/Routledge, 47–59.

Williams, P (1991) Reaction to Zigler, Hodapp and Edison. *American Journal on Mental Retardation* Vol 96, 224–5.

Wolfensberger, W. (1972) *The Principle of Normalization in Human Services*. Toronto: National Institute on Mental Retardation.

Wolfensberger, W. (1980) Research, empiricism and the principle of normalization. In R.J. Flynn and K. Nitsch (eds) *Normalization, Social Integration and Community Services*. Baltimore, University Park Press, 119–129.

Wolfensberger, W. (1983a) Social role valorization: a proposed new term for the principle of normalization. *Mental Retardation* Vol 21, 6, 234–239.

Wolfensberger, W. (1983b) *Guidelines for Evaluators during a PASS, PASSING or Similar Assessment of Human Service Quality*. Toronto: National Institute on Mental Retardation.

Wolfensberger, W. (1988) *Update on the Teaching and Use of PASS*. New York: Syracuse University, Training Institute for Human Service Planning, Leadership and Change Agentry.

Wolfensberger, W. (1992) De-institutionalization policy: how it is made, by whom and why. *Clinical Psychology Forum* Vol 39, 7–11.

Wolfensberger, W. and Glenn, L. (1975) *PASS 3. Program Analysis of Service Systems. A Method for the Quantitative Evaluation of Human Services, Field Manual*, 3rd edition. Toronto: National Institute on Mental Retardation.

Wolfensberger, W. and Thomas, S. (1983) *PASSING. Program Analysis of Service Systems' Implementation of Normalization Goals: A Method of Evaluating the Quality of Human Services According to the Principle of Normalization*. Toronto: National Institute on Mental Retardation.

Wolfensberger, W. and Tullman, S. (1982) A brief outline of the principle of normalization. *Rehabilitation Psychology* Vol 27, 131–45.

Zigler, E. (1977) Twenty years of mental retardation research. *Mental Retardation* Vol 15, 3, 51–3.

Zigler, E., Hodapp, R.M. and Edison, M.R. (1990) From theory to practice in the care and education of mentally retarded individuals. *American Journal on Mental Retardation* Vol 95, 1, 1–12.

Chapter 5

The Results from PASS
and PASSING Evaluations

Paul Williams

Introduction

This chapter will consider briefly the sort of results that have come from evaluations of services with the PASS and PASSING evaluation instruments (Wolfensberger and Glenn 1975, Wolfensberger and Thomas 1983, Wolfensberger 1983).

First, the quantitative scoring system in PASS and PASSING will be described, including the derivation and use of subscores. Next some analyses using the scores from evaluations will be described, with some British data on the reliability and validity of the scores obtained. The picture of services that emerges from some of the results will be reviewed, with an attempt to explain some of the reasons for the overall level of quality observed. Finally, the qualitative aspect of results from using PASS and PASSING will be illustrated with discussion of the identification of needs of service users and an account of issues in giving feedback.

The Scoring System in PASS and PASSING

As described in the introductory chapter on PASS and PASSING earlier, a team of evaluators reaches a consensus judgement on the 'level' of performance of a service in each of a number of independently considered aspects of the context or practice of the service – 50 aspects in PASS and 42 in PASSING. The 'level' assigned represents, in terms of social role valorisation (see Williams, Chapter 1) – or, in the case of some ratings in PASS, other criteria of good administrative practice – good practice likely to benefit service users, neutral practice likely neither to benefit nor harm users, or bad practice likely to harm users. Weighted scores are assigned to each level of performance. Good practice is given a positive score, neutral practice scores zero, and poor practice is assigned a negative score. A total score over the whole of PASS or PASSING can be calculated, as can various subscores to illustrate themes.

The structure of levels and scores follows a more logical and understandable pattern in PASSING than in PASS, though the basic principles are the same. For each of the 42 aspects of a service considered in PASSING, the Manual gives criteria for judgements and descriptions of five 'levels' of performance. The evaluation team uses the criteria to arrive at an agreed statement of the performance of the service in a particular area of context or practice, according to its likely impact on the social status or competence of service users. This statement is compared with the 'level' descriptions in the Manual; the description that matches most closely represents the level assigned and hence the score achieved.

Broadly, Level 5 represents a world model of good practice, Level 4 represents clear benefit to users, Level 3 represents no clear benefit nor damage to users, Level 2 represents clear damage to users, and Level 1 represents unacceptable reinforcement of highly negative imagery or severe de-skilling of users.

In PASSING, a score of zero is always assigned to Level 3. The positive numerical scores assigned to Levels 4 and 5, and the negative scores assigned to Levels 1 and 2, depend on the weighting given to the particular rating under consideration. Positive scores assigned to Level 5 range from 7 to 50, and negative scores assigned to Level 1 correspondingly range from -7 to -50.

The rationale for the weighting of particular issues in PASS and PASSING is described in the Handbook for PASS3 (Wolfensberger and Glenn 1975). Three main considerations have been used by Wolfensberger in assigning the weights:

- the importance of the item in terms of the achievement of social role valorisation
- the effort, thought and innovation likely to be required to achieve good practice
- the universality of the issue, i.e. its relevance to a wide range of services and client groups.

Highly weighted items are those which, in Wolfensberger's judgement, are very important to the achievement of SRV, are very hard to achieve good practice in, and are applicable to a wide variety of services and groups. Such items in PASS3 are:

- Model Coherency (weighting of 40)
- Socially Integrative Social Activities (39)
- Intensity of Relevant Programming (39)

and in PASSING:

- Programme Address of Clients' Service Needs (50)
- Competency-Related Grouping – Size (46)
- Competency-Related Grouping – Composition (43)
- Competency-Related Integrative Contacts (42)
- Quality of Interactions (42).

Examples of low-weighted ratings are, in PASS3:

- Programme, Facility and Location names (10)
- Research Climate (6)
- Ties to Academia (6)

and in PASSING:

- Image Projection of Service Funding (7)
- Image Projection of Setting History (7).

The overall weighted score, summed over all the ratings, ranges from -947 to +1000 on PASS3, and from -1000 to +1000 on PASSING. In the scoring sheet for PASSING, Wolfensberger assigns value judgements to the achievement of particular bands of score:

+756 to +1000   Excellent

+496 to +755   Good; expected in terms of SRV

-105 to +495   Acceptable; fair

-355 to -106   Below acceptable; poor

-1000 to -356   Totally inadequate; disastrous in SRV terms

There is an alternative way of expressing the scores which we have tended to use in Britain, because it is slightly easier to comprehend and it 'softens' the impact of negative scores for the purpose of constructive feedback to services (Wolfensberger of course does not think we should soften this message). We can express the numerical scores as percentages of total possible score, so that a score of -1000 (on PASSING) becomes 0%, a score of zero becomes 50%, and a score of +1000 becomes 100%. The equivalent value judgements to those above become:

88% to 100%   Excellent

75% to 87%   Good; expected

45% to 74%   Acceptable; fair

33% to 44%   Below acceptable; poor

0% to 32%   Totally inadequate; disastrous

Subscores

There are two approaches to the derivation of subscores. One is the statistical one of trying to identify, through factor analysis, relatively independent subgroups of ratings which correlate together. The other is to group ratings according to themes in order to illustrate service performance in a particular area of practice.

Flynn (1975) carried out a factor analysis of the results of 102 evaluations, using the second edition of PASS. He found four main relatively independent factors which he called 'normalisation programme', 'administration', 'physically integrative facility' and 'human science'. Flynn at the University of Ottawa in Canada, Wolfensberger at Syracuse University in the USA, and CMHERA in Britain, have continued to collect data from PASS and PASSING evaluations, and it is hoped that further factor analyses will be completed on these data.

All evaluation instruments group their individual ratings under headings that imply useful subgroupings. In PASSING there are two main divisions into 'Social image enhancement' and 'Competency enhancement'. Each of these is further subdivided into 'Physical setting', 'Groupings and relationships' and 'Activities and use of time'. There is an additional subdivision of 'Miscellaneous imagery' in the 'Social image enhancement' section. The score sheet gives space for recording subscores (i.e. the summed scores of individual ratings) in each of these subdivisions.

Similarly, PASS3 groups the ratings in clusters for which subscores can be computed. Headings include 'Physical integration', 'Social integration', 'Age-appropriate interpretations and structures', 'Culture-appropriate interpretations and structures', 'Model coherency', 'Developmental growth orientation', 'Quality of setting' and 'Administration'.

Wolfensberger (1983) has also suggested other ways of grouping the ratings to produce potentially useful subscores. In PASSING there are suggested subscores called 'Relevance', 'Intensity', 'Integrativeness', 'Image projection' and 'Felicity'. In PASS3 there are subscores called 'Service location optimality', 'Physical setting appearance' and 'Personal-clinical programme emphasis'.

In Britain, we have experimented with various arrangements of ratings in subgroups to illustrate themes. A number of PASS3 evaluation reports on residential services (e.g. Williams 1992) have used groupings given the following titles:

- Homeliness
- Support for growth and development
- Physical setting support for integration
- Programme support for integration
- Administrative support for meeting needs
- General administration
- Foundations of the service.

Reliability of Scores

The concept of reliability that will be adopted here is that an evaluation instrument should produce the same result when applied by different people to the same situation. Ideal data to examine this for PASS and PASSING would be those from different evaluation teams evaluating the same service on the same occasion. Logistically, this is virtually impossible to achieve; however, there are two alternative approaches. One is to examine the degree of agreement between individual raters making independent judgements within an evaluation team; the other is to examine results from situations as close to the ideal as practically possible.

Wolfensberger (1983) recommends that on training courses in PASS or PASSING, individual raters independently record their personal judgements on each rating before the process of reaching consensus as a team. This is intended to help individuals to learn to make more informed judgements, by comparing their initial judgements with those resulting from the shared insights of the whole team. We have tended not to adopt this procedure on training courses in Britain, because we think the time can be spent more fruitfully on other issues; however, adoption of the procedure on many training courses in North America has produced data from which the inter-rater reliability of individual team members rating independently can be calculated.

Flynn, LaPointe, Wolfensberger and Thomas (1991) have done this using the intraclass correlation method of Shrout and Fleiss (1979) for a sample of 62 evaluations using PASSING. For teams of fewer than nine people, correlations ranged from .54 to .76 (for different sized teams), indicating a satisfactorily high degree of agreement between raters. Reliability was less in larger teams where the diversity of evidence collected by individuals would be expected to be greater; very large teams sometimes occur on training workshops but would be very rare in non-training evaluations.

We have British data from a number of sets of evaluations where, although different teams did not evaluate the same service on exactly the same occasion, we have situations approximating to this. All evaluations reported used PASS3, and all took place as training exercises on courses, though in each case under close experienced and qualified supervision.

Table 5.1

1. A hostel for adults with learning disabilities, run by a health authority. Time between evaluations, two years.

	Time 1	Time 2
Location optimality subscore	36%	39%
Facility appearance subscore	38%	10%
Programme emphasis subscore	11%	8%
Administration subscore	11%	7%
Total score on PASS3	16%	14%

2. A residence within a hospital for adults with learning disabilities. Time between evaluations, one year.

	Time 1	Time 2
Location optimality subscore	17%	11%
Facility appearance subscore	52%	50%
Programme emphasis subscore	19%	11%
Administration subscore	26%	32%
Total score on PASS3	21%	18%

3. A local authority hostel for adults with learning disabilities. Time between evaluations, six months.

	Time 1	Time 2
Location optimality subscore	80%	61%
Facility appearance subscore	75%	39%
Programme emphasis subscore	54%	19%
Administration subscore	32%	38%
Total score on PASS3	51%	31%

4. Another local authority hostel for adults with learning disabilities. Time between evaluations, two years.

	Time 1	Time 2
Location optimality subscore	59%	62%
Facility appearance subscore	59%	64%
Programme emphasis subscore	47%	43%
Administration subscore	29%	33%
Total score on PASS3	44%	41%

5. A residence for adults with physical disabilities, run by a voluntary organisation. Time between evaluations, two years.

	Time 1	Time 2
Location optimality subscore	25%	11%
Facility appearance subscore	36%	0%
Programme emphasis subscore	16%	0%
Administration subscore	17%	0%
Total score on PASS3	18%	2%

6. A local authority day service (adult training centre) for adults with learning disabilities. Time between evaluations, three years.

	Time 1	Time 2
Location optimality subscore	38%	14%
Facility appearance subscore	29%	39%
Programme emphasis subscore	14%	15%
Administration subscore	24%	3%
Total score on PASS3	22%	14%

First (Table 5.1), we have six pairs of evaluations where the same service was evaluated by two different and completely independent teams on two occasions reasonably close in time, where there are no known reasons to suggest the service may have dramatically changed in the intervening period. The period between evaluations varies between six months and three years.

Before supplementing the data in Table 5.1 with those from another source, and giving an overall analysis of reliability, it is interesting to note two possible examples in the data of what is called a 'halo effect'. This occurs when a team develops an overwhelmingly positive or negative view of a service overall that leads them to rate every aspect high or low and removes the capacity of PASS or

PASSING to discriminate between performance on different ratings. We can see in Example 5 in Table 5.1 that the evaluation team at Time 2 rated the service at the lowest level on three of the four subgroups and gave an overall score of only 2%. Of course, it is possible that this was an accurate reflection of service quality, or it may illustrate a negative 'halo effect'. Correspondingly, it may be that the evaluation of Service 3 at Time 1 represents a positive 'halo effect' in the team.

Next we can report (Table 5.2) the evaluation on the same occasion of four residences for elderly people known to be very similar. They were all run by the same social services department with a common senior manager, all had the same architectural design, were geographically quite close and situated in similar neighbourhoods, and had all been opened at the same time.

Table 5.2

	Service			
	1	2	3	4
Location optimality subscore	64%	63%	52%	62%
Facility appearance subscore	30%	27%	34%	29%
Programme emphasis subscore	10%	16%	18%	10%
Administration subscore	9%	8%	18%	10%
Total score on PASS3	21%	24%	24%	20%

We also have an example of three adult training centres, of similar design, size, age and location, run by the same social services department with a common senior manager, evaluated by different teams on the same occasion (Table 5.3).

Table 5.3

	Service		
	1	2	3
Location optimality subscore	65%	39%	14%
Facility appearance subscore	36%	34%	39%
Programme emphasis subscore	9%	21%	15%
Administration subscore	0%	13%	3%
Total score on PASS3	18%	24%	14%

The data in Tables 5.1, 5.2 and 5.3 show that some variation of scores does occur when different teams make judgements of what might be expected to be similar situations. We can summarise the extent of this variation over all the examples described above, in terms of pairs of scores that were within 5, 10 and 20 percentage points (Table 5.4).

Table 5.4

	Within 5%	Within 10%	Within 20%
Location optimality subscore	32%	45%	73%
Facility appearance subscore	55%	82%	86%
Programme emphasis subscore	36%	68%	95%
Administration subscore	45%	77%	95%
Total score on PASS3	64%	86%	100%

Table 5.4 shows that reliability within 5 percentage points is not good, but within 10 percentage points it is reasonable and within 20 percentage points it is good. There is 100% agreement within 20 percentage points for the total score on PASS3. Given the complexity of the judgements involved in evaluating services, this seems certainly an acceptable if not an excellent degree of reliability of an evaluation instrument.

Furthermore, it should be remembered that the data reported here come from non-ideal situations for the testing of reliability. Data from occasions, if they were possible to arrange, where two independent teams evaluate the same service at the same point in time, would almost certainly show higher reliability than reported here.

Validity

Our interpretation here of the question of validity will be: do PASS and PASSING measure something that can meaningfully be called 'quality of services'? This relates of course to the more complex issue of the adequacy of social role valorisation as a framework for identifying criteria of quality. However, our concern here will simply be to examine some evidence of the relationship between scores on PASS or PASSING and other independent evidence of service quality.

The following results (Table 5.5) are from a series of 52 evaluations of residential services for adults with learning disabilities carried out in Britain during the 1980s using PASS3. The services have been divided into nine groups representing different kinds of provision. Data on the scores of these groups on PASS can be used to examine differences in quality between groups as measured by PASS to see if these conform to expectations from other sources. The service groups are listed in Table 5.5 in order of quality as measured by PASS. The size of sample, and median and range of total score on PASS3, are given in each case.

Table 5.5

	Sample size	Median score	Range
1. Wards in hospitals	5	9%	6% to 23%
2. Large residences run by health authorities but not in hospitals	7	16%	5% to 27%
3. Residences in privately-run institutions	2	17%	12% to 21%
4. Bungalows or flats in hospitals	4	19%	12% to 21%
5. 'Village community' residences	2	27%	23% to 30%
6. Social service department large residences (hostels)	17	31%	12% to 51%
7. Ordinary houses managed by health authorities	5	36%	29% to 38%
8. Ordinary houses managed by social services or by voluntary or private agencies	7	44%	38% to 50%
9. 'Life-sharing' houses	3	63%	58% to 64%

Although the sample size is very small for some of the groups in Table 5.5, the overall pattern of differences in quality would seem to accord very well with expectations from independent criteria of quality. There is extensive documentation of the low quality of hospital provision (for example Morris 1969), and a growing awareness of the benefits of ordinary housing provision (Towell 1988). PASS thus seems to place services in a sensible order of relative quality in a meaningful way that accords with independent criteria.

Do the actual PASS scores reflect judgements of quality that are meaningful in a wider context? The answer to this will depend on how the status of SRV is seen.

In the sample in Table 5.5, all groups of services not based in ordinary housing have a median score in the 'totally inadequate, disastrous' range. Ordinary housing options score in the 'below acceptable, poor' range. Only 'life-sharing' options, where disabled and non-disabled people live together and share their social lives together, manage to come up to even the 'acceptable, fair' range.

No services yet evaluated in Britain for which we have data have scored overall in the 'excellent', or even in the 'good' range.

It is almost certainly true that this picture is more negative than would be produced by most other accepted measures of quality (e.g. ACE, see Chapter 6). However, it can be argued that the high standards set by SRV have awakened (made conscious, Wolfensberger would say) large numbers of service planners, providers and managers to the damage done to users by many aspects of large, segregated services, and to the long way we still have to go to provide acceptable services. Thus, although the judgements made by PASS and PASSING are harsher than are likely on other criteria of quality (see Leiper, Lavender, Pilling, and Clifford 1992), the results can be argued to have a wider purpose and usefulness, and hence 'validity'.

Consistency

Two questions related to validity and reliability as defined above are whether PASS and PASSING produce consistent results for particular types of service, wherever the evaluation takes place and whichever evaluation instrument is used. Table 5.6 compares data from Britain and North America, and from PASS3 and PASSING.

The British data are for residential services for adults with learning disabilities; rows 1 and 4 represent the same evaluations as in Table 5.5, supplemented with additional data from evaluations of ordinary housing projects. The North American data are for residential services mostly also serving adults with learning disabilities, but with the inclusion of some residential services for adults with mental health problems; they are taken from Flynn et al. (1991).

Table 5.6

	Sample size	Median/mean	Range
1. Large residences (more than 8 places) in Britain evaluated with PASS3	37	20% (median)	4% to 51%
2. Large residences (more than 8 places) in Britain evaluated with PASSING	31	16% (median)	5% to 39%
3. Institution residences in North America evaluated with PASSING	23	21% (mean)	not reported
4. Small residences (8 or fewer places) in Britain evaluated with PASS3	27	40% (median)	8% to 68%
5. Small residences (8 or fewer places) in Britain evaluated with PASSING	5	38% (median)	18% to 52%
6. Community group residences in North America evaluated with PASSING	79	37% (mean)	not reported

We can confirm from Table 5.6 the general comparability of results between Britain and North America, and between PASS3 and PASSING.

The Results of PASS and PASSING Evaluations

From Table 5.6 we can see that PASS and PASSING, unsurprisingly, rate the general quality of small residences higher than that of large residences. Nevertheless, there is a wide range of scores; some small residences score as poorly as most large ones, and it is possible, though rare, for a large residence to score within the 'acceptable, fair' range. The overall quality of all services on SRV criteria is identified as poor. The median or mean score of large residences is firmly in the 'totally inadequate, disastrous' range, and small residences only manage to achieve a median or mean score in the 'below acceptable, poor' range.

We have data from evaluations of residential services for other client groups, including elderly people, people with physical disabilities, people with mental health problems, people with drug and alcohol problems, and homeless people. The quality of services for these groups, as assessed by PASS or PASSING, is at least as poor as, if not worse than, that of services for people with learning disabilities. Furthermore, moves towards the use of small residences, which would be expected to increase the SRV quality of services, have been less common in services for these other client groups than in learning disability services.

One worrying finding in Britain has been that services for children are no better than services for adults. The data in Table 5.7 can be compared with Sections 1 and 4 in Table 5.6. The data are for residential services for children with disabilities, mostly learning disabilities.

Table 5.7

	Sample size	Median	Range
1. Large residences (more than 8 places) in Britain evaluated with PASS3	11	25%	11% to 48%
2. Small residences (8 places or fewer) in Britain evaluated with PASS3	14	34%	25% to 56%

PASS and PASSING can be used to discriminate between similar service elements within a single agency or project. For example, there have been a number of studies, mainly using PASS3, of ordinary housing projects for people with learning disabilities in Britain. Table 5.8 reports data from two of these studies, showing the range of scores of individual elements within each project in a number of subscore areas. The feedback given to services after such evaluations often includes the recommendation that good practice should be shared more between elements.

The two housing projects are the NIMROD service in South Wales, eight individual housing elements of which were evaluated (Williams 1992), and the North Wiltshire Community Living Project, of which six housing elements were studied (Williams 1988). Each project made use of ordinary houses for small groups, usually just three or four people, dispersed within ordinary community neighbourhoods. Staffing was provided according to the needs of residents; usually staff were non-resident, working complex shift systems to provide 24 hour cover.

Table 5.8

A Total Score on PASS3

NIMROD (8 houses)	Mean score 48%	Range 36% to 68%
NWCLP (6 houses)	Mean score 42%	Range 34% to 57%

B Homeliness

NIMROD	Mean score 52%	Range 33% to 90%
NWCLP	Mean score 51%	Range 30% to 84%

C Support for growth and development

NIMROD	Mean score 45%	Range 31% to 70%
NWCLP	Mean score 29%	Range 13% to 43%

D Physical setting support for integration

NIMROD	Mean score 81%	Range 73% to 100%
NWCLP	Mean score 53%	Range 17% to 75%

E Programme support for integration

NIMROD	Mean score 41%	Range 27% to 65%
NWCLP	Mean score 41%	Range 34% to 52%

F Administrative support for meeting needs

NIMROD	Score for the service as a whole 19%
NWCLP	Score for the service as a whole 48%

G General administration

NIMROD	Score for service as a whole 47%
NWCLP	Score for service as a whole 36%

As well as illustrating differences, sometimes very marked, between elements within an individual service project, such data can be used to compare projects with each other.

The NIMROD service was judged to be better than NWCLP in support for growth and development and in the physical location of the houses; however, NWCLP was judged to have better administrative support for meeting client needs. The latter subscore includes support for staff renewal and staff development, and the finding may be an explanation for the fact that both projects do equally well on programme support for integration, but NWCLP from a poorer base of house location.

A possible picture emerges of well situated houses in NIMROD, but reduced capitalisation on this in terms of actual programme support for integration because of relatively poor support for staff skills and enthusiasm, while NWCLP achieved as much actual integration from a less helpful base because of greater support for staff development and morale. Correspondingly, there was greater support for client growth and development in NIMROD than in NWCLP, probably because much more emphasis had been given to this aspect in NIMROD than in NWCLP when they were first established.

Such pictures of services arising from the quantitative scores need of course to be verified and documented from the qualitative descriptive evidence collected.

A further use of evaluation is to study change in individual services over time. We have data from a number of services that have been evaluated with PASS or PASSING on several occasions. Generally, these data show little change over time, unless the service has undergone a major structural change, such as moving from a single large building to smaller dispersed sites. This reflects the fact that changing practice to achieve greater social role valorisation is very difficult, even where there is a high degree of commitment to do so.

Before leaving this section on the sort of quantitative results that have been obtained with PASS and PASSING, we will give one further illustration. Both in North America and in Britain, a substantial number of day services have been evaluated, especially day centres for adults with learning disabilities. A consistent finding both here and across the Atlantic has been that day services score rather worse than residential services. This was a finding reported by Flynn (1975) and confirmed by Flynn *et al.* (1991).

Table 5.9 gives data from North American evaluations using PASSING (Wolfensberger, personal communication), allowing comparison between residential and day services. They include services for all client groups.

Table 5.9

	Sample size	Mean score
1. Community residences	137	36%
2. Community day services	156	32%
3. Institution residences	43	20%
4. Institution day services	15	17%

A sample of 13 British adult training centres for people with learning disabilities evaluated with PASS3 shows a mean score of 24%, range 13% to 35%, comparable to the scores of North American day services in Table 5.9.

Some of the reasons for poor performance of conventional day services are:

- low model coherency: services are expected to meet a very wide range of needs on a single site with unclear staff identity and a length and timing of daily operation that does not fit with any cultural norms
- unhelpful enforced congregation of large numbers of disabled people together
- low support for autonomy of service users, even where there is some encouragement of self-advocacy

- low use of community facilities and infrequent integration with non-disabled people
- low intensity of activities, with much time spent waiting or doing very little.

The last four of these factors are likely to flow from the first, the lack of model coherency, and this is a likely explanation why the performance of conventional day centres on PASS or PASSING has shown little change over almost twenty years of evaluations, despite numerous official reports, recommendations and reorientations of purpose (see Williams 1995).

As with residential services, PASS and PASSING can discriminate between elements of a project or collection of services. A recent evaluation with PASSING of a day service in Britain consisting of a conventional centre, a supported employment service and innovative use of adult education services, gave the following results:

The centre	36%
Supported employment	55%
Adult education	67%

As with residential services, we can see that a substantial change in PASS or PASSING score is only likely when a service completely changes its structural base. Changes likely to be helpful in day services include greater dispersal and specialisation of elements to meet specific needs, such as employment, education, leisure or therapeutic treatment.

The Needs of Service Users

This chapter has so far concentrated on the quantitative results from PASS or PASSING evaluations. However, often these are the least important or useful results. Of much greater significance, especially for the purpose of feedback to the service, is the analysis of the needs of service users that comes from the 'foundation discussion' prior to the application of the PASS or PASSING ratings.

The picture of needs generated by the PASS or PASSING evaluation team through the 'foundation discussion' may differ substantially from the definition of needs within the service being evaluated, and this can form the focus of feedback and further dialogue. Since the information about the life history of individual service users that forms the basis of the foundation discussion comes from direct care staff, users themselves and those who know them well, there can be immediate engagement of those people with the PASS or PASSING process of determining needs. The service may find this the most useful outcome of the evaluation.

An important point to mention is that the initial description of the needs of users should be independent of the service's current responses. This is difficult to achieve in practice, but ideally the foundation discussion discovers common past experiences and risks in the lives of users that generate needs that set an agenda for services. How services are actually responding to that agenda is discovered independently through the ratings.

There is space here only to give a flavour of what is involved.

Many of the users of a service for people with long-term disabilities are likely to have had very restricted contact with non-disabled people in their community, and what contact they have had may have been very negative. From an SRV perspective, the need is for improved and more frequent relationships within the community, requiring frequent presence in community settings, support for contribution to community life and a good reputation within the community, protection of relationships, and challenging of prejudice and exclusion.

Dialogue with the service about how these needs can be derived from considering the long-term history of devaluing experiences in people's lives, can strengthen the resolve and priority given to meeting those needs. Often, the effort of achieving community participation for severely disabled people results in only rare contact with little planning of how to capitalise on opportunities for relationships. The service may have in effect chosen to prioritise other perceived needs that may be easier to meet, such as privacy, choice, or comfort, resulting in the apparent wellbeing of users but with the sacrifice of true citizenship.

The raising of such qualitative issues with a service is a primary intended function of PASS and PASSING, over and above the service's detailed performance as reflected in the quantitative scores.

Some Issues in Reporting Results

Finally in this chapter, we will mention some considerations in feeding back evaluation results to a service.

The first thing to recognise is that there are many 'stakeholders' in the service: funders, senior managers, middle managers, direct care staff, specialist professionals, users, families. The evaluation may have been commissioned by or arranged through one group of stakeholders, with or without involvement of other groups. There are likely to be implications of giving feedback to one group and not to others.

Feedback to a particular group of stakeholders needs to be tailored to the needs and interests of that group. In practice this often means the preparation of several quite different forms of feedback for different groups (Tyne and Williams 1987, Williams 1987, 1992).

Feedback as a single event, either oral or written, is often unsatisfactory. More fruitful is an interactive dialogue over a period of time. This dialogue might begin before the evaluation, continuing throughout it and afterwards (Tyne 1985, 1987).

The degree of knowledge of, and agreement with, the principles of social role valorisation are likely to vary greatly between and within groups of stakeholders. This will influence the amount of explanation and background argument required to be given.

Decisions have to be made about the purpose of the evaluation and the feedback: is it simply to give a stark account of the facts as seen through SRV and PASS or PASSING, or is it to be constructive with sensitivity to the feelings of service providers? Such decisions will influence, for example, whether to include any mention or analysis of quantitative scores.

Underlying all these factors will be the political undercurrents within any organisation. Information is power: who commissions it, contributes to it, makes judgements about it, disseminates it or keeps it secret, will be decided through a political process. The evaluator's skill in understanding, managing and contributing to this process is likely to be crucial to the usefulness of any evaluation. An evaluator's laudable wish to achieve empowerment of service users, for example, may enormously complicate the evaluation and the feedback process.

Summary of Discussion

Two questions were put to Paul Williams: how PASS/ING would rate a 'normal', rather than a segregated service, the Job Centre and Benefit Office, which is the standard day service for people who are unemployed but who have not got a 'disability' label; whether PASS/ING would allow for it to be said that some services should not exist at all.

PASS/ING Rating of a 'Normal' Service

PW replied that there were two issues. SRV (social role valorisation) is concerned with what is valued, rather than what is normal, and a Job Centre would not be considered 'valued' in our society. Secondly, in saying a service is poor in terms of PASS or PASSING is not to say it is not better than no service at all. There have been PASS/ING evaluations of night shelters for the homeless with scores of minus 998, but this does not mean that people would be better off living on the streets. PASS/ING evaluates against high standards, against what would be required to revalue people in society who are devalued.

Do PASS/ING Evaluations Indicate Some Services Should Be Scrapped?

PW said that this was absolutely so. Before the rating stage was reached in PASS/ING evaluations there was lengthy team discussion. The evaluation and analysis informs the evaluation team of what the issues are and the likely effect of the service on users. This leads to some heavy questions of, first, 'What should be done about it?' and second, 'Do we know how to do it?' The answer to the first question was often, 'There needs to be a social revolution' and to the second, 'No, we haven't got the slightest clue.' This put the team in the mode of preparing a respectful, constructive and sufficiently humble feedback to the service. PW thought some pioneer work had been done in Britain on how to feed back the results sensitively to services.

Acknowledgements

Some of the analyses reported in this chapter were supported by small grants to the Community and Mental Handicap Educational and Research Association from the King Edward's Hospital Fund and the Joseph Rowntree Foundation.

References

Flynn, R. (1975) *Assessing Human Service Quality with PASS2: An Empirical Analysis of 102 Service Programme Evaluations.* Toronto: National Institute on Mental Retardation.

Flynn, R., LaPointe, N., Wolfensberger, W. and Thomas, S. (1991) Quality of institutional and community human service programmes in Canada and the United States. *Journal of Psychiatry and Neuroscience* Vol 16, 146–153.

Leiper, R., Lavender, T., Pilling, S. and Clifford, P. (1992) *Assuring Quality in Mental Health Services: The QUARTZ System.* London: Research and Development for Psychiatry/Sainsbury Centre for Mental Health.

Morris, P. (1969) *Put Away: A Sociological Study of Institutions for the Mentally Retarded.* London: Routledge and Kegan Paul.

Shrout, P. and Fleiss, J. (1979) Intraclass correlations: uses in assessing rater reliability. *Psychological Bulletin* Vol 86, 420–428.

Towell, D. (ed) (1988) *An Ordinary Life in Practice: Developing Comprehensive Community-Based Services for People with Learning Disabilities.* London: King Edward's Hospital Fund.

Tyne, A. (1985) *An Evaluation of an Adult Residential Service using PASS.* Trowbridge: Community and Mental Handicap Educational and Research Association.

Tyne, A. (1987) *Home from Home: Thinking about Improving Family Support Services for People with Mental Handicaps in Clwyd.* Trowbridge: Community and Mental Handicap Educational and Research Association.

Tyne, A. and Williams, P. (1987) *The Relocation of People from Calderstones into Ordinary Housing in Burnley District.* Trowbridge: Community and Mental Handicap Educational and Research Association.

Williams, P. (1987) *The Western Corner Project: Support for Families and Young People.* Trowbridge: Community and Mental Handicap Educational and Research Association.

Williams, P. (1988) *The North Wiltshire Community Living Project: Report of a PASS Evaluation.* Trowbridge: Community and Mental Handicap Educational and Research Association.

Williams, P. (1992) *Evaluation of the NIMROD Project with PASS.* Trowbridge: Community and Mental Handicap Educational and Research Association.

Williams, P. (1995) Residential and day services. In N. Malin (ed) *Services for People with Learning Disabilities.* London: Routledge.

Wolfensberger, W. (1983) *Guidelines for Evaluators during a PASS, PASSING or Similar Assessment of Human Service Quality.* Toronto: National Institute on Mental Retardation.

Wolfensberger, W. and Glenn, L. (1975) *Programme Analysis of Service Systems: Handbook and Field Manual,* 3rd edition. Toronto: National Institute on Mental Retardation.

Wolfensberger, W. and Thomas, S. (1983) *Programme Analysis of Service Systems' Implementation of Normalization Goals.* Toronto: National Institute on Mental Retardation.

Chapter 6

ACE – An Assessment of Care Environments

Paul Wolfson

Introduction: Measuring Care Environments

The environment is a measure of outcome or an intervening variable in many studies involving mental health. Like quality of life it is difficult to define or quantify. It can mean the quality of the food, the number of bathrooms divided by the number of residents, the physical health of the residents, staff practices, staff morale, management structures, the views of the neighbours, ease of access to a public library and almost anything relevant to the context in which people live their lives.

The care environment changes according to the perspective of the person experiencing it. It varies in some important way for each resident of a care setting. The development of PASS (Wolfensberger and Glenn 1975) has clarified our understanding of which perspective is the most important by focusing on the experience of the individual resident. However, there remains the question of how the interests of the individual resident are to be balanced against those of a group of people living together. How this ethical issue is resolved directly impacts on the measured performance of a care setting.

The care environment lacks clear physical boundaries as well as conceptual ones. Decisions have to be made, often in an arbitrary way, about which aspects of the environment are particular properties of the care setting, which relate to the immediate neighbourhood, and which reflect government policy or society. The relative contribution of internal and external factors to the overall evaluation of a care setting poses practical as well as philosophical difficulties for researchers. An environmental measure which does not include external factors poses problems for validity; too much emphasis on wider issues reduces the power of the measure to discriminate between settings and by failing to reward good practice within a setting appears unjust.

The care environment is fluid. It changes every second. Some environmental measures can be used to examine this, others are designed to describe more enduring characteristics of the setting. Ideally a study will use both. Closer examination of what researchers imagine to be enduring features of a setting may reveal abrupt changes in staff practices with a change of shift.

A comprehensive environmental measure tends to yield an unwieldy mass of figures which are difficult to interpret. Measures which focus on a single aspect of the environment (such as interactions) may produce clear results, but these can be dismissed as epiphenomena, the causes of which are unmeasured and unknown.

The Requirements of ACE

The choice of measure for any particular study depends on its focus as well as time and resource constraints. ACE (An Assessment of Care Environments) was developed in response to the evaluation of the closure of Cane Hill Hospital (Pickard *et al.* 1992). Cane Hill is a mental hospital in the south of England with a population of 246 residents (excluding those with a diagnosis of dementia) with a mean length of stay of over 25 years. The study required a single measure which could directly compare the hospital wards with a wide range of new residential settings in the community.

The measure also had to be sensitive enough to find differences between similar types of setting so that the new facilities could be compared with each other. Other requirements were that it should be practical to use for a small research team and that the results should be relatively easy to interpret and feed back to the staff of the settings.

It was the policy of the three District Health Authorities involved in the closure of Cane Hill that the new residential facilities should be tailored to meet the individual needs of the residents. The rationale of ACE (Clifford and Wolfson 1993) was to evaluate each setting by the extent to which this was achieved. There is consequently no ideal standard against which all care settings can be judged. Different settings suit different people because they provide different things.

The hypothesis was that any setting has a range of functions which may be conflicting. The conflict may be expressed in terms of financial resources, e.g. should money be spent on improving the building or on rehabilitation programmes? It may also be expressed psychologically. Providing a home-like environment may conflict with the containment of difficult behaviour; enthusiastic fostering of social relationships within the setting may conflict with the right to privacy. In each setting there is an attempt to balance these conflicts to meet the needs of the residents. The way the conflicts are resolved determines the outcome – the quality of care.

The Components of ACE

ACE has three parts – a measure of the needs of the residents, a measure of what the setting provides both materially and in human terms, and a measure of the quality of care.

The Population Profile

This measures the needs of a group of residents in terms of the type and degree of support they may require.

The Provision Ratings

These are based on six functions of a setting. Each function has five subscales and a global rating:

1. *Home Environment*: the degree of comfort, space, personalisation, accessibility and maintenance.
2. *Mental Health*: the ability of the setting to contain crises, address difficult behaviour, facilities for drug treatment, psychotherapy and review.
3. *Personal Care*: the provision of help with self care, food, domestic activities, physical health care and the closeness with which these are monitored.
4. *Social Care*: the provision of help with benefits and housing, community activities like shopping, structured activities during the day, leisure activities and the way these are reviewed.
5. *Social Relationships*: the provision for work with families, efforts made to improve relationships within and outside the setting, the amount of social support provided for the residents and the way these are reviewed.
6. *Rehabilitation*: the provision for teaching new skills in the areas of domestic and community activities, work and education, money and budgeting and the way this is monitored.

The Quality Ratings

These measure the style of provision and are rated contextually:

1. *Regulation*: the degree of control exerted by staff over residents.
2. *Social Distance*: the presence of social barriers between residents and staff as exemplified by wearing uniforms, separate meals and crockery, ease of access to staff.
3. *Consultation*: resident involvement in decision making.
4. *Flexibility*: the extent to which each resident is treated differently.
5. *Therapeutic Understanding*: the extent to which changes in residents' behaviour are interpreted in terms of life events rather than mental illness and how this informs management.
6. *Expectations*: the extent to which residents are expected to do things for themselves.
7. *Pressure*: pressure exerted on residents to become increasingly self-sufficient.
8. *Integration*: the extent to which the residents use ordinary community facilities.
9. *Sense of Community*: the degree of social cohesiveness amongst the residents.
10. *Laissez-Faire*: the degree of detachment exhibited by staff towards their work with residents.

The Procedure

Initially this involves an informal semi-structured interview with a group of staff. The aim is to produce a relaxed atmosphere where people can speak freely. Two raters are required. One asks the questions, the other keeps a written record. Quality is not asked about directly but is inferred by asking for detailed examples of provision. The researchers then look round the setting and talk informally to the residents. The two researchers then discuss their results and agree on a consensus rating. The whole procedure takes between half a day and a day and a half, depending on the raters' prior knowledge of the setting, and the type of setting.

ACE in Practice

Some examples of the use of ACE are presented in Table 6.1.

Each of the three districts involved in the hospital closure had recruited multi-disciplinary rehabilitation teams. One of the teams felt that rehabilitation work was best done in the new settings rather than the hospital. This provided an opportunity to compare a continuing care ward, not carrying out rehabilitation work, with a ward where active rehabilitation work was being done. These are then compared with a low staff home one and two years after opening.

Columns 1 and 2 illustrate the differences between the continuing care ward and the rehabilitation ward. Apart from the physical environments which were broadly similar, the rehabilitation ward had much greater provision of care. In particular an increased level of monitoring and review of all aspects of care was present on the rehabilitation ward. While disturbed behaviour was tolerated on the continuing care ward, nurses on the rehabilitation ward actively tried to address it. As for quality of care, there were few major differences in the first four indicators – regulation, social distance, consultation and flexibility. This suggests that whatever the philosophy of care operating on a particular ward, being part of a large mental hospital makes it difficult to avoid institutional practices.

On the rehabilitation ward, nurses favoured a social rather than biological approach to behavioural problems, put greater pressure on the residents and were much more involved with their work with the residents. Staff appeared more emotionally detached from their work on the continuing care ward than in any of the 22 settings the measures has so far been used to assess. This raises the question of whether all continuing care wards should have active rehabilitation teams working on them, irrespective of any plans for closure.

Columns 2 and 3 illustrate the marked differences between the rehabilitation ward and the low staff home 1 year after opening. There is a significant reduction in most aspects of the provision of care which is what might be expected in a relatively able group living in a low staffed setting. There was much less regulation and social distance, with more consultation and flexibility. There was a disappointingly low degree of integration with the local community and little involvement by staff with residents. It was the raters' impression from talking to the residents that too little support was offered.

Columns 3 and 4 illustrate the changes occurring over the course of a year in the low staff setting. An analysis of the subscales of the global provision ratings

Table 6.1 Comparison between a continuing care ward, a rehabilitation ward, a low staff home one year after opening and at two years

	1 Continuing care ward Cane Hill	2 Rehab ward Cane Hill	3 Low staff home Year[1]	4 Low staff home Year[2]
Number of residents	19	24	6	6
Provision				
Home Environment	0	1	*	2
Mental Health	1	3	1	2
Personal Care	1	4	1	2
Social Care	1	3	2	3
Social Relationships	0	3	1	2
Rehabilitation	1	3	1	2
Quality				
Regulation	3	3	0	1
Social Distance	4	4	1	0
Consultation	0	1	3	2
Flexibility	0	1	3	3
Therapeutic Understanding	0	3	2	3
Expectations	0	1	2	4
Pressure	1	3	1	3
Integration	0	1	1	2
Sense of Community	0	2	*	1
Laissez-Faire	4	1	3	1

[1] The low staff home Year 1 was evaluated on a pilot version of ACE. The asterisks indicate where ratings were omitted because they were not comparable.

Key: 4 = Very high   1 = Low
        3 = High   0 = Very low
        2 = Moderate

For the sake of simplicity only the global ratings of provision are tabled here.

It is important in interpreting these results to understand that low provision in any particular area does not necessarily mean low standards of care. The provision ratings record the quantity of provision. There can be over-provision. Over-provision of, for example, food – cooked meals for all residents when some are capable of shopping, preparing and serving food – would be reflected in the pattern of the quality ratings. Regulation would be increased, while Flexibility, Expectations, Pressure and Integration would all be reduced. Appropriateness can also be judged by comparing the pattern of ratings in similar settings with residents with similar needs.

revealed that the higher level of provision was achieved by care workers giving more attention to addressing problem behaviour, greater prompting with self care and providing more social support. More time was spent on advice about money and acquiring community skills. This increased level of provision was accompanied by a small increase in regulation, small reductions in social distance and consultation, with a major improvement in staff emotional involvement.

A likely explanation for these changes was that when the residents first left the hospital there was a philosophy of non-intervention amongst care workers. This derived from a feeling that the residents had suffered enough from institutional care and now wanted to live their lives without interference. The improvements in quality and provision of care noted a year later were not achieved by extra staff or resources, but by a change to a more pro-active policy combined with a change in staff deployment. Originally all staff worked in all of the houses on a rota basis to avoid 'burn out'. This was altered so that staff worked intensively in one house at a time and became closely involved with the residents.

Conclusion

The advantages of ACE are that it can be used to directly compare any kind of care environment with results that are relatively easy to interpret. Recommendations can be discussed and fed back to staff so that the effectiveness of their implementation can be reassessed at a later date. A reasonably comprehensive assessment can be made by two researchers in a short time.

However, ACE has only partially resolved many of the methodological problems of measuring care environments outlined at the beginning of this chapter. It is also a new measure, which has had little testing for validity so far. An important development would be a resident's interview with comparable ratings, to examine the relationship between the ACE evaluation and the perception of the individual resident.

References

Clifford P. and Wolfson P. (1993) *ACE – An Assessment of Care Environments.* RDP/Sainsbury Centre for Mental Health.

Pickard, L., Proudfoot, R., Wolfson, P., Clifford, P., Holloway, F. and Lindesay, J. (1992) *Evaluating the Closure of Cane Hill Hospital. Final Report of the Cane Hill Research Team.* London: RDP/Sainsbury Centre for Mental Health.

Wolfensberger, W. and Glenn, L. (1975) *PASS 3. Program Analysis of Service Systems. A Method for the Quantitative Evaluation of Human Services. Field Manual*, 3rd edition. Toronto: National Institute on Mental Retardation.

Chapter 7

PASS/ING and ACE in Action – Similarites and Differences in Evaluating Services

Doria Pilling and Gerald Midgley

How the ACE–PASS/ING Evaluation Came About

A measuring device can be said to be valid if it does what it is intended to do (Carmines and Zeller 1979). PASS (Program Analysis of Service Systems; Wolfensberger and Glenn 1975) and PASSING (Program Analysis of Service Systems' Implementation of Normalization Goals; Wolfensberger and Thomas 1983) could, therefore, be assessed as valid if they accurately measure the extent to which services act in accordance with Wolfensberger's version of the normalisation principle, which is what they are mainly (PASS) or entirely (PASSING) designed to measure (see also Doria Pilling's chapter, Chapter 4, and Paul Williams' chapter, Chapter 1, for discussion of the basis of these measures). However, it seems unlikely that this was the question to which an answer was sought, when the King's Fund initially raised the possibility of the Rehabilitation Resource Centre at City University investigating the validity of PASS[1] as an evaluation measure.

Carmines and Zeller, in fact, go on to argue that the crucial question is not whether a measure is valid but whether it is valid for the use to which it is being put. For example, an intelligence test may be valid for assessing the intellectual potential of students, but not necessarily for forecasting their level of income during adulthood. PASS and PASSING might accurately measure services' adherence to Professor Wolfensberger's normalisation principle, but this does not necessarily mean that they are measuring the quality of the services. Whether they do this, though, is likely to be the question that the King's Fund, and many other people, are interested in, and is the one that we tried to answer in the project that eventually emerged.

Measuring service quality is also the explicit aim of the authors of these instruments. 'PASS and PASSING are tools for the objective quantitative measurement of the quality of a wide range of human service programs, agencies and even entire systems' (Wolfensberger and Thomas 1983).

---

1 See Chapter 4 for a fuller account of how the RRC investigation of PASS/ING originated. PASSING was included as well as PASS, on Paul Williams' advice.

The problem with examining whether they do in fact do this is that there are no generally accepted guidelines of what is a 'good quality' service. There are, though, some 'outcomes' that most people in western society value, and which, it can be argued, a 'good' quality service should facilitate, such as the quality of life of its users or the development of their skills.

The reasons why we did not pursue further the relationship between adherence to normalisation and outcomes such as these for individual clients during the period of the project were mainly practical. However, Wolfensberger and Glenn (1975) have put forward arguments against outcome assessment being an adequate measure of service quality, desirable ends such as skills development possibly being produced by widely differing processes, including some far from desirable means, such as punitive behaviour therapy. Wolfensberger and Glenn also suggest that normalised conditions of life do not necessarily produce feelings of wellbeing or happiness for a service's clients, at least in the short term.

There are also counter-arguments. While a 'good quality' environment might not be the only way of producing desirable outcomes such as skills development, it should surely not be inimical to this? And Wolfensberger and Glenn themselves say in relation to wellbeing and happiness: 'About the only thing that one can say is that PASS measures conditions which are generally optimal when considered in relation to clients in general and over the long run.'

However, in an 18 month study, with only one full-time researcher (and another drawn in on an occasional basis), it was impractical to carry out an investigation of the extent to which PASS and PASSING scores are correlated with some 'outcome' criterion. Evaluations in this country are mainly practice evaluations, that have been carried out during normalisation training workshops over the last decade or so, and it is very unlikely that there is data available which could have been used for this purpose. A possibility might have been to generate such data, using services recently evaluated, but this would have meant finding a suitable outcome measure for diverse types of services, with a variety of user groups, of different ages, and obtaining the co-operation of services to carry this out. This was too formidable a task in the time available.

What we actually decided to do, after much discussion with many people, including experienced users of PASS and PASSING, and researchers with knowledge of evaluation methods, was to investigate whether the rating of service environments by PASS or PASSING was consistent with that produced by other methods, and to determine the reasons for differences where these occurred. This approach also had theoretical appeal, in that Wolfensberger and Glenn (1975) argue that the distinction between outcome and process is not necessarily clearcut, that it depends on one's theoretical orientation, and that from the perspective of normalisation much that others might regard as process, such as social integration, appearance, appropriate surroundings, are outcome measures.

This still left a number of major practical problems. An extensive review of measures to evaluate service quality revealed none that had established reliability and validity, had been successfully used in this country, and was applicable to any client group. The best regarded scales appeared to be the residents' management practice scales (Raynes 1988), based on Goffman's (1961) concept of the total institution, and designed to distinguish institutional from individually oriented practices, but this covered only a relatively small part of the service environment encompassed by PASS and PASSING, and it was designed for use in evaluating services for people with learning disabilities. In the end, if we were to use one overall measure of service quality, rather than a battery of measures, there was little choice. We decided to use ACE (Assessment of Care Environments – formerly known as FACE), recently developed by Paul Clifford and Paul Wolfson (1989) at Research and Development in Psychiatry (now the Sainsbury Centre for Mental Health), which Paul Wolfson has described (Chapter 6). It was designed originally for residential settings, but is easily adaptable to other types of services, such as day or work-centres.

Ideally, both kinds of evaluation would have been carried out by teams experienced in the methods, within a very short period of time. But to set up PASS/ING evaluations with experienced team members especially for this purpose required funding above that available to the PASS/ING evaluation project.

What we did was to evaluate, using ACE, four services that had had relatively recent PASS or PASSING evaluations. For the comparison with PASS/ING to be possible, we not only had to find services that were willing to endure another evaluation, but also a PASS/ING team leader who would both allow us access to the scores and describe how the team had arrived at them.

The ACE evaluations were carried out in three cases of services which had recently been evaluated by teams as part of their training during PASS/ING workshops, and in one case in a service that had had a commissioned PASS evaluation, though this was less recent. Although the teams carrying out the practice evaluations, during workshops, were inexperienced in the method this was, to a considerable extent, counter-balanced by the teams being under the guidance of one of the most experienced PASS/ING team leaders in the country, and we are immensely indebted to him for agreeing to co-operate with us. The commissioned evaluation was carried out by an experienced team, but there was a disadvantage here in that it had been carried out a year earlier. All the ACE evaluations were carried out by the same two researchers, the authors of this chapter, who had received the required day's training in the method.

Using ACE and PASS/ING as Evaluation Methods

ACE was derived from a critique of existing quality measures. Unlike PASS and PASSING it has no explicitly stated values. It views services as having to fulfil a number of conflicting functions – to control the clients' behaviour, to treat each client as an individual, to promote clients' independence from services, to cater for their dependency needs – with limited resources. How these conflicts are resolved determines the character of the setting.

ACE consists of three parts:

I   the Population Profile

II   the Provision Ratings

III the Qualitative Ratings.

The ACE Population Profile

The population profile measures the population characteristics of service users, in terms likely to influence their need for services and support of various kinds.

The provision ratings measure the level of service provision along the following dimensions (see Paul Wolfson's chapter, Chapter 6, p.80, for details):

The ACE Provision Ratings

- *Home environment*
  Comfort
  Space
  Personalisation
  Accessibility
  Maintenance
  Global

- *Mental health*
  Crises
  Problem behaviour
  Drug treatment
  Psychotherapy
  Review
  Global

- *Personal care*
  Self care
  Food
  Physical health
  ADL domestic
  Monitoring
  Global

- *Social care*
  ADL community
  Welfare
  Leisure acts
  Structured acts
  Monitoring
  Global

- *Social relationships*
  Significant others
  Social network (in)
  Social network (out)
  Social support
  Monitoring
  Global

- *Rehabilitation*
  ADL domestic
  ADL community
  Money
  Work
  Monitoring
  Global

The ACE Ratings of Environmental Quality

The ratings of environmental quality measure the style of the provision, and its impact on environmental quality (see Paul Wolfson, Chapter 6, p.80, for details):

1. Regulation
2. Social distance
3. Consultation
4. Flexibility
5. Therapeutic understanding
6. Expectations
7. Pressure for change
8. Integration
9. Sense of community
10. Laissez faire
11. Criticism

Ratings are made in comparison with other services that the raters have had experience of. Data is obtained in ACE primarily through interviews with staff members, supplemented by discussion with users. Direct questions relate to service provision, not to the quality dimensions (with a couple of exceptions), which are inferred from the responses. PASS/ING uses similar methods but puts more emphasis on observation and the use of documentary material.

ACE and PASS/ING are similar in that they are concerned with the appropriateness of the service in relation to the needs of the particular population. The ACE provision ratings, though, are simply concerned with the level of provision in a particular area. It is up to the evaluator, or the service itself, to decide whether these ratings are appropriate in relation to the particular population and in the light of the aims of the service. A high level of provision in a particular area may be inappropriate for the client group. Where provision is inappropriate this should be reflected in the pattern of the ACE environmental quality ratings. As Paul Williams (Chapters 1, 5) and Alan Tyne (Chapter 2) have outlined, a foundation discussion, in which the evaluating team tries to understand the needs of the service users, and how they could be met, is an essential feature of a PASS/ING evaluation. There is no reason why ACE evaluators should not have such a discussion, but the guidelines do not indicate the need for this, and comparisons are essentially in terms of other services.

In PASS/ING all the rating levels are very definitely indicative of service quality, the higher the rating the better being the quality. The decision on appropriateness is part of the process of determining the rating level, and the guidelines are explicit as to the direction of 'goodness', though judgements have to be made in relation to the needs of the particular population and purpose of the service.

In both PASS/ING and ACE each team member makes their own ratings as soon as possible after the fieldwork has been carried out, and conciliation is reached through a discussion process which is an important part of the evaluation.

A distinct advantage of using ACE, given that the services evaluated were doing us a favour in agreeing to this, was that it is relatively quick and easy to administer. We found about a day and a half adequate, giving us time to carry out two separate semi-structured interviews with one or more staff members, have a look round, and talk to the users.

The ACE evaluations were carried out after the PASS or PASSING evaluations, the time period varying from one week to three months in three cases and to over a year in the case of the commissioned evaluation. The question arises of whether the information that the staff informants gave was biased by their earlier experiences of the PASS/ING evaluation. Certainly in one evaluation, where several staff members had taken part in normalisation workshops, there was some defensiveness among interviewees who thought that the service provision was not in accord with normalisation principles. But the issues with which they were concerned were of no importance in making the ACE ratings. As will become apparent when ACE and PASS/ING ratings are compared in some detail, although there is overlap, there is a considerable difference in what is being looked at in the two types of measure. To a large extent PASS/ING ratings are concerned with prerequisites for making the users 'more ordinary' (or less different, more valued), in particular the features in the physical environment and social structure that make this more or less likely. ACE is much more concerned with the activities and attitudes of staff and management.

It is unlikely then that the ACE ratings were influenced by the researchers' knowledge of the values and ideas in PASS/ING. The decisions that have to be made on the ratings are for the most part very different from those in PASS/ING.

The procedure adopted was for the ACE ratings to be made, discussed and finalised jointly by the two researchers immediately after the evaluation. One of the researchers then wrote a report which detailed the evidence on which the ratings were based. This was read by the other researcher and any necessary adjustments were made. A final evaluation report, including the researchers' judgement of the appropriateness of the provision and quality dimensions of the service for the particular population was then written, and agreed between the researchers. Only after this stage was the comparison made with the PASS/ING evaluation results.

PASS/ING scores are weighted according to their relative importance and can then be added up to produce sub-scores of various aspects of the service, and an overall score. ACE scores cannot be added up meaningfully. The comparison between the measures has been made by looking at the picture produced by the PASS/ING scores covering a particular dimension, and at the equivalent, as far as possible, in ACE. An attempt is made to determine reasons for any major differences. The contribution of aspects covered in PASS/ING, but not ACE, is also examined.

ACE evaluations were carried out of the following services, and the results compared with those of PASS or PASSING evaluations, as indicated:

- A privately owned residential home for older people (Residential Home 1) – PASSING practice evaluation.
- A local authority residential home for older people (Residential Home 2) – commissioned PASS evaluation.
- A local authority work opportunities centre for adults with learning disabilities – PASSING practice evaluation.
- Two psychiatric rehabilitation wards – PASS practice evaluation.

This chapter next presents a detailed comparison of the findings from the ACE and PASSING evaluation of Residential Home 1, space restrictions preventing us from detailing all four. It then goes on to make a general comparison of ACE and PASS/ING, using the material from the four comparisons.

Comparison of ACE and PASSING Evaluation Findings for Residential Home 1

There was some difficulty in presenting a picture of how various areas of Residential Home 1 appeared, according to the PASSING evaluation, because although quite extensive discussions were held with the team leader, no written report was available. (The commissioned PASS evaluation, for which an unpublished report is available, is drawn upon in this paper, but is not presented here as the main comparison because of the time-gap between it and the ACE evaluation.) It was decided that a reasonable way to present an overall picture of the PASSING evaluation which could be compared with that obtained from ACE would be to use the PASSING Programatic subscores devised by Wolfensberger (1983). These are titled: Relevance, Intensity, Integrativeness, Image Projection and Felicity. The weighted scores obtained in each of these areas is totalled, and the service's performance categorized according to the percentage of achievable score reached. Wolfensberger's designations of performance are set out as follows:

Percentage of achievable score obtained	Service performance
0 to 32%	Totally inadequate; disastrous
33 to 44%	Below acceptable; poor
45 to 74%	Acceptable; fair
75 to 88%	Good; expected
89 to 100%	Excellent

It should be noted that excellent is near-ideal, and involves the management being consciously aware of the issues involved. It is quite rare for even 'acceptable' levels to be reached.

Overview of Residential Home 1
The ratings for Residential Home 1 were as follows:

Felicity (comfortableness)	–	acceptable (very nearly reaching good)
Image projection	–	acceptable
Integrativeness	–	acceptable (just reaching this level)
Intensity	–	totally inadequate
Relevance	–	totally inadequate

How do the pictures of the service in these areas compare with those presented by the ACE evaluation?

Felicity represents comfortableness of the internal setting, in terms of relationships and attitudes, as well as decor, furnishings and space. The PASSING score very nearly reached good, being 73% of the total achievable score for this area. On both PASSING and ACE, physical comfort and decor were rated excellent, and social relationships were average or better in most aspects on both measures. There was only one substantial difference, in the rating concerned with the extent to which the setting accommodates the needs of the individual client, in which it was rated considerably more favourably in ACE.

ACE ratings are not concerned with the image projected by the service, so no comparison can be made here.

Integrativeness in PASSING is concerned with the participation of service users in the community. The home scored 56% of the attainable score in this area, a score which is in the acceptable range. In PASSING, the service was rated good in a number of aspects in its potential for contact between the residents and others in the community, but poor in actual contacts likely to be beneficial to the service users. ACE ratings on the promotion of social contacts with people outside the home were average, although there were problems for people with mobility problems or the less competent, those on whom the PASSING team seems to have concentrated.

Intensity in PASSING is concerned with the opportunities provided for people to maintain and develop their competencies. The home obtained 27% of the achievable total score in this area, and was rated totally inadequate. On both measures, the overall picture was of very little to do, unless the residents were competent and mobile and could make their own activities.

Relevance in PASSING is about the extent to which the service meets its users' needs. The home received 0% of the total attainable score, and was characterised as totally inadequate. ACE has no specific rating on this question, though the evaluators using the method have to consider this question continually. What was our overall view from the ACE evaluation? It was of a service that was very good in many ways, but one in which considerable improvements could be made in activities and emotional support – about which we made many recommenda-

Table 7.1 PASSING ratings in the Felicity area, and the ACE nearest equivalents

PASSING	ACE
Internal Setting Aesthetics (4)	Comfort (5)= internal aesthetics + comfort + amenities
Physical Comfort of Setting (5)	Personalisation (5) = detailed aesthetic touches
	Maintenance (5) considered as contributing to comfort and aesthetics in PASSING
Individualizing Features of Setting (4)	Space (4) = individualizing features of setting
Life-Enriching Interactions (4) consisting of 5 interactions:	
(i) worker/client	Social Distance (3) = distance between staff an residents
	Laissez-Faire (2) = staff emotional detachment from residents
	Criticism (2) = staff criticism of clients (2)
	Social Support (3)
(ii) worker/worker	No ACE equivalent
(iii) worker/public	Significant Others (4) = staff promotion of residents relationships with others
(iv) client/client	Sense of Community (3)
(v)client/public	Social Network (Out) (3)
Setting Accessibility – Clients and Families (5)	no ACE equivalent
Program Support for Client Individualization (2)	Flexibility (5)
Promotion of Client Socio-Sexual Identity (2)	Partially covered by: Social Network (In) (3) and Sense of Community (3)

The figures in brackets after the PASSING items are the unweighted scores, Level 1 representing a totally inadequate performance, and Level 5 near-ideal. The figures in brackets after the ACE items are the ACE rating levels (also indicated as 1 to 5 here, to make comparison easier, though the figures 0 to 4 are used in the ACE manual), but it is necessary to remember that provision ratings represent the amount available, and not whether this is appropriate for the particular service users (i.e. high is not necessarily good). The higher the environmental quality ratings the more there is of the quality, i.e. 5 means that there is 'a lot' of the quality, which is likely 'good' for items indicative of positive qualities such as Sense of Community or Flexibility, but not for those indicating negative qualities, such as Laissez-Faire (emotional detachment of staff from residents) or Criticism (of residents).

tions. In the case of the most competent people we wondered why they were there at all. But we would not have said that the service was totally inadequate. So where does the difference lie in the two methods? Before trying to answer this, the results of the two evaluations will be compared in greater detail.

PASSING and ACE Compared in the Felicity Area

It will be useful now to consider the comparison between PASSING and ACE ratings in some of these areas in more detail. First, the Felicity area (see Table 7.1).

There was little difference between the teams on the physical comfort of the setting and internal aesthetic items and their ACE equivalents. Both rated the home extremely comfortable, with high quality furnishings that were the result of much thought. The PASSING team rated internal aesthetics 4 and not 5 because people's own rooms varied in quality according to their incomes, and the sitting room was rather formal with chairs around the edge. On Individualizing Features of Setting (Space in ACE) both sets of ratings took into account that all residents had their own room, which they could furnish and decorate as they wished, and some of which were very large. The somewhat formal appearance of the public areas meant that there were no 'nooks or crannies' for a few people to get together and was the reason for the individualizing features of the setting item not being given the highest rating on either measure. (On these provision of homeliness items 'high' in ACE is likely to mean 'good' for most client groups.)

In the social relationships area, most of the ACE ratings –Social Support given to residents, Social Distance, Sense of Community – were average, although the staff were also rated as 'enthusiastic and involved' (low on Laissez-Faire), and the setting was good at welcoming visitors. If anything, the PASSING team rated the service slightly better here, giving it Level 4 on Life-Enriching Interactions (which, as shown above, takes into account interactions: between service workers and service users; among service workers; between workers and the public, including relatives of users; between users; and between users and the visitors to the service). This was probably due to the team's inexperience. They put greater emphasis on the staff's sympathetic attitude and involvement than the team leader did himself, while for him the main point was their appearance of being in service (they were dressed and treated by the owner as domestics), creating social distance.

Accessibility from the setting to the users' home communities – also an important factor in the maintaining of relationships (not included in ACE) – was rated excellent in PASSING, because of the home's central position in the village, and good train services for users and their families coming from other parts of the country. However, the PASSING team rated the home relatively low (Level 2) on Promotion of Socio-Sexual Identity, which is about providing opportunities for sharing, companionship and affection, and, as appropriate, support and guidance on sex roles and sexual behaviour. ACE rated the service as moderate on promoting relationships within the setting, but does not deal with sex roles or relationships unless these are explicitly causing problems.

There was only one item in the Felicity area on which there was a major difference. This was in the rating concerned with client individualization. In PASSING, this rating is concerned with the extent to which all aspects of a service

–including policies and procedures, staff actions and attitudes, programmes and activities – encourage the differentiation of each client from others, and the development of the individual identity and uniqueness of each client. The nearest ACE equivalent is Flexibility – the effort made to accommodate the individual. A high rating describes a setting where there is a considerable variation in provision and policy between individuals. Flexibility was rated high because of the scope for individuality in the residents' rooms, the variation in self-care and other routines, the freedom to go in and out as the residents pleased, and to obtain snacks at any time of day or night. The ACE rating was possibly too generous in that the lack of individual programmes for the residents was not taken into account by the evaluators. Nevertheless, there remains a discrepancy with the Level 2 rating given by the PASSING team to the Program Support for Client Individualization Rating. The reason for this low rating seems to have been that the PASSING team emphasised the lack of actual encouragement for expressing individuality. If residents could establish this for themselves they were not prevented from doing so, but little was done to promote individuality for the rest.

PASSING and ACE Compared in the Intensity Area
A similar comparison was made for the PASSING Integrativeness and Intensity areas, but only the latter will be described in detail (Table 7.2).

**Table 7.2 PASSING ratings in the Intensity area
and their nearest ACE equivalents**

PASSING	ACE
Promotion of Client Autonomy and Rights (1)	Flexibility (5) and Regulation (2)
Challenge/Safety Features of Setting (4)	No equivalent
Competency-related Intra-service Client Grouping – Size (2)	No equivalents
Competency-related Intra-service Client grouping – Composition (2)	
Intensity of Activities and Efficiency of Time-use (1)	Personal Care ratings – particularly Food (5) and Daily Living Activities (5)
	Social Care Ratings, particularly Social Network (In) (3) and Structured Activities (2)
	Rehabilitation provisions (all rated 1 or 2)
	Expectations (3)
	Pressure for Change (1)
Competency-Related Personal Possessions (5)	No equivalent

Several of the ACE ratings are relevant to one of the PASSING ratings, Intensity of Activities and Efficiency of Time Use, which is about the extent to which the service makes the best use of its and its users' time in promoting their competencies. This was rated very low (Level 1) in PASSING. On the ACE Personal Care ratings, provision was rated very high (5) in the areas of Food provision and Daily Living Activities, this meaning that there was no scope for residents to do anything for themselves, even if they were very capable. Only in self-care were residents encouraged to help themselves, with support and supervision being available as necessary. Social Care provision was, in contrast, rated average or lower in some areas. There was little to do unless people were fully mobile and could organise their own activities. Some social events were organised, but they were 'sprung' on the residents, who took no active part in their organisation. Almost the only attempts at rehabilitation were in the self-help area (Rehabilitation provision ratings were all 1 or 2). Expectations – of the residents to be as independent of the service as possible – were rated average as they were mixed – there were no worries about people going out, but in the areas of cooking, cleaning and educational activities expectations seemed to be nil. There was practically no pressure for change, in the sense of increasing independence. Generally the picture provided by the ACE ratings fits in with the PASSING item.

The PASSING team, though, rated the home substantially lower on residents' autonomy and rights than the ACE evaluators. In PASSING a service should extend autonomy and rights to the service users to the maximum degree possible, support them in the exercise of their rights, and intervene if their autonomy and rights are unfairly restricted by others. The ACE Regulation rating is concerned with the extent to which the setting restricts the autonomy of residents. The service was rated as low in imposing regulation (i.e. high in autonomy) because there were no restrictions on residents coming or going, and few rules and regulations. Again, the ACE evaluators may have been over-generous, not taking into account sufficiently the covert restrictions on cooking and housework within the home. Nevertheless the PASSING rating would still have been much less favourable. The home was rated Level 1 on client autonomy and rights in PASSING because the team considered that autonomy was only available for the relatively few residents who were articulate and self-sufficient. There was no encouragement or support for the others in exercising autonomy or rights. This PASSING item takes into account the major losses of choice and control over their lives that are experienced by older people when they enter a residential service – even if the regime is very liberal. Stripping of personal possessions also often occurs, although this particular home was credited in the Competency-Related Personal Possessions item for providing large rooms, often with much storage space, and allowing residents to bring cars and even pets (at the owner's discretion) with them.

The PASSING ratings on client groupings have no direct ACE equivalent, though the appropriateness of the provision for the particular users is fundamental to ACE. In PASSING groups should be composed of the number of people that will best facilitate the development of users' competencies. And group members should have the same, or similar, needs, and where grouped with others, there should be a large majority of more advanced/competent service users. The PASSING team thought that the large number of residents (25) and composition (5 or 6 very competent, the rest less so) was not conducive to the maintenance of skills, and the items on the size and composition of groupings were both rated low (Level 2). The team leader said that the question had come up often in discussion with the more able residents, who felt depressed by the less able.

PASSING on Relevance

The Image Projection area in PASSING has no ACE equivalents. This is also true of the Relevance area, which consists of just one PASSING rating, Program Address of Clients' Service Needs. It is central to a PASS/ING evaluation for team members to try to understand the service-users' needs. Team members try to get to know a few service-users well, to put themselves in their place, to understand their feelings. From this, a list of the major needs of the service users is drawn up, without taking into account whether or not the service is meeting them (in the foundation discussion, mentioned earlier). Rating of the services' practices takes place later, and consideration is then given as to whether these needs are being met.

The list drawn up by the team in this case is unavailable but it was probably not too dissimilar to that in the commissioned PASS evaluation of another home for older people (Residential Home 2), for which an unpublished report is available (Williams 1990). The needs do not apply to every client but they are those that the service should be aware of. Needs included: being able to express feelings of loss, to maintain family relationships, to maintain past status, to retain links with well-known places, for help to maintain control of resources, to retain possessions, to reverse loss of skills and have access to specialist resources/expertise, to have choice, to have advocacy and representation.

The PASSING team considered that there was neglect of the users' needs, that the home could be regarded as a pleasant waiting room for the socially dead or dying, a waiting room for physical death.

How PASSING and ACE Differ Over Residential Home 1

In terms of really fulfilling the residents' needs it is possible to consider the home totally inadequate, although it may well be, as the ACE evaluation findings suggest, at least as appropriate as, if not more appropriate than, similar homes in many respects. It is this that explains how two methods which produce similar pictures of a service in many respects can come to such different conclusions about it. PASSING judges a service in terms of near-ideal meeting of users' needs, while ACE rates in relation to other existing services.

ACE and PASS/ING Findings Compared for Four Evaluations

The last part of this chapter will consider and discuss some of the conclusions that can be reached from all four of the comparisons between ACE and PASS/ING.

Similarities between PASS/ING and ACE

The overall pictures of the services produced by ACE and PASS/ING appeared quite similar.

Where there were very similar items in PASS/ING and ACE, the two sets of evaluators, for the most part, rated similarly. Similar items for the most part related to the physical environment of the service, and the accessibility of community resources, such as shops, restaurants, services. In several instances, PASS/ING ratings were more favourable than those of the ACE evaluators. This was the case, for example, for the Environmental Beauty item in the commissioned PASS evaluation, so that more favourable PASS ratings cannot be solely attributed to the team being inexperienced. At least in these areas, then, PASS/ING cannot be said to have impossibly high standards.

Differences in general were in the same direction in the PASS/ING and ACE evaluations. When rating levels of the two services evaluated by PASSING were compared, the service rated higher was also judged more favourably on ACE, if the ratings dealt with this area. The same was true for the two services evaluated by PASS. To give an example, in the two services rated by PASS, Social Integration was rated worse for Residential Home 2 (Level 1) than for the psychiatric rehabilitation wards (Level 2). Similarly on the two relevant ACE ratings, Social Network (Out) and Integration were rated lower for the residential home (both 2) than for the wards (2.5 on average). This was true although the home was generally rated more favourably on both measures.

Where several ACE ratings covered a similar area to one PASS/ING rating, it was difficult to make judgements, e.g. in the PASSING Life-Enriching Interactions item, but generally differences did appear to be in the same direction.

Differences between PASS/ING and ACE

Certain PASS/ING ratings were low for both services evaluated, while the relevant ACE ratings were higher and differentiated more between the services. The PASSING ratings concerned were the following:

Program Support for Client Individualization

Promotion of Client Autonomy and Rights

Intensity of Activities and Efficiency of Time-Use

Image-Related Other Client Contacts and Personal Relationships

Competency-Related Other Integrative Client Contacts and Personal Relations

PASS ratings concerned were the following:

Individualization

Interactions

Age-Appropriate Autonomy and Rights

Intensity of Relevant Programming

The main reasons for the differences between PASS/ING and ACE appear to be attributable to certain features of the PASS/ING ratings:

- negative experiences of some clients outweigh the more positive experiences of others
- negative aspects of rating areas outweigh more positive aspects
- inclusion in ratings of circumstances over which service has little or no control
- ratings being made in relation to the near-ideal meeting of needs
- the greater specificity of PASS/ING ratings.

Negative experiences outweighing the more positive in PASS/ING. The more negative experiences of a majority of service users are seen as outweighing the more positive experiences of the more competent in PASS/ING. For example, Program Support for Client Individualization was rated Level 2 in the PASSING evaluation of Residential Home 1 and Level 1 for the work opportunities centre, while the respective ACE ratings for Flexibility were 5 and 3. As seen above, Residential Home 1 was rated low in PASSING because the more competent residents could establish their individuality, but little was done to encourage it in the other residents. The work opportunities centre also offered more scope for the more competent, although there was generally little choice of activity.

More generally the more negative aspects of the service are seen as outweighing the positive ones in PASS/ING. For example, in the PASS evaluation of Residential Home 2, Interactions was rated Level 2, although the PASS team concurred with the ACE evaluators' view that relationships at a personal level between staff and clients and the clients themselves were very good. The PASS team placed much emphasis on the two more negative aspects – the lack of time staff had to spend with residents, and the social distance between the staff and residents (signified by uniforms, 'staff-only' places), although the staff distance did not appear to actually impair relationships. The reason for the emphasis on social distance was that it detracted from a close and equal relationship between staff and residents, and made them appear to be separate communities.

Inclusion in PASS/ING ratings of circumstances general in society. The PASS/ING ratings take into account wider aspects than ACE ratings which appear to be similar – this may include circumstances over which services have little or no control, and are virtually inevitable in certain types of service. Promotion of client autonomy and rights was rated Level 1 in both the PASSING evaluations, and Age-appropriate Autonomy and Rights level 2 in both the PASS evaluations. In contrast, ACE rated all four services below average on Regulation (i.e. they were all seen as allowing a relatively high amount of autonomy). PASS/ING sees stripping of possessions, freedom, rights and choice as being almost inevitable, when people enter a large residential home. As with the PASSING evaluation of Residential Home 1 (seen above), the PASS team rated Residential Home 2 low (Level 2) on autonomy and rights, even though the ACE evaluators saw it as having few rules and restrictions. The PASS team took into account the minimal role of the residents in management (there was a users meeting but it was chaired by the CPN), in food preparation (there were facilities, but they were inaccessible to wheel-chair users, who were often the most competent), and restrictions in going out, due to staff availability.

PASS/ING rates in relation to the near-ideal meeting of needs. Intensity of Activities and Efficiency of Time-Use were rated Level 1 in both the PASSING evaluations, as were Intensity of Relevant Programming in both the PASS evaluations. While the ACE evaluators would agree that the programmes were inadequate in all the services they would not consider that they should be rated at the same level: ACE revealed considerable differences between the services. A number of ACE ratings are involved, particularly Rehabilitation – and global ratings varied on these from 1 to 3. Taking the PASS evaluations, those in the psychiatric wards could go out on their own, cook their own food, attend workshops, while the older people in Residential Home 2 had practically nothing to do except attend a structured activity for an hour a day. In both cases needs may have been met inadequately, but the everyday activities were likely to feel quite different to those that experienced them, yet they received the same ratings on PASS.

PASS/ING ratings have a more specific content. Both of the ratings concerned with social relationships with people outside the home in PASSING are for specific purposes – image-enhancement or competency development. Both were rated 1 in both the evaluations, other service-mediated contacts outside the home not being taken into account. In contrast, the ACE evaluators rated Residential Home 1 as placing moderate emphasis (Social Network (Out) – Level 3) on promoting socialisation outside the home, because encouragement was given to residents to attend church, or, in one or two cases, a day centre. Additionally, outside visitors were invited to events like sherry parties. The PASSING team saw service-mediated contacts as being on a charitable basis, to help the 'poor dears'.

Contribution of Image-Related Items in PASS/ING

The comparisons highlighted the contribution of some of the image-related items in PASS/ING, which have no ACE equivalents. To give some examples, the 'dumping' of some very capable older people with others much less capable in Residential Home 1, simply because of age, became very apparent in the rating, Image-Projection of Intra-Service Client grouping, and highlighted attitudes to older people in our society. The same item, in the work opportunities centre, raised questions about the suitableness of the service for some of the more competent service users, who were capable of open employment.

The Building-Neighbourhood Harmony item in the PASS evaluation of Residential Home 2 raised the question of why older people have to live in an institutional-type building, and the Setting-Neighbourhood Harmony and Program-Neighbourhood Harmony items in the work opportunities centre of why people with learning disabilities have to receive 'work training' in a strange-looking building in a residential neighbourhood.

Appropriateness of Service for its Clients

The client grouping ratings in PASS/ING mean that the question of whether the service is appropriate for the different kinds of users has to be explicitly considered (as discussed for Residential Home 1), and the guidelines for doing so are set out. ACE evaluators have to continually consider whether the service is appropriate for the client population, but they do not explicitly rate this, and there are no guidelines.

Emphasis on Prerequisites in PASS/ING

The prerequisites for a service receive more emphasis than the actual activities in some areas in PASS/ING. For example, in the two PASS evaluations, Socially Integrative Social Activities scored higher in the psychiatric rehabilitation wards than in Residential Home 2, but the home had higher scores in support for integration both in locational aspects[1] (65% as opposed to 58%) and social integration aspects[2] (anything about the service that would put people off from making contact – 41% as opposed to 16%).

It is possible to justify the greater emphasis on the prerequisites, on the grounds that these may be the result of planning. Residential Home 2 was deliberately placed in the village so that older people who needed care would not have to leave the area. Favourable prerequisites provide the potential to be built upon. Activities in services which are, say, badly located may arise from a combination of fortunate circumstances, but will be harder to maintain. Nevertheless, this again means that everyday practices could get somewhat obscured in overall PASS/ING scores.

PASS/ING and ACE as 'Snapshot' Measures

Both ACE and PASSING are 'snapshot' methods of evaluation. It is difficult to gauge the frequency of events for particular residents. Both would probably benefit from being supplemented by some systematic record-keeping over a period of time, particularly in relation to social contacts and activities.

Conclusion

PASS/ING and ACE appear to be doing rather different things – although they overlap. PASS/ING is looking at differences in treatment of service users from others in society, at their social status, and whether their real needs are being met. ACE is more concerned with everyday experiences, and how well the service meets their needs in relation to similar kinds of services.

The similarity in rating between PASS/ING and ACE on similar aspects of a service, and the overall similarity in portraits of the services, would suggest that they are valid methods of evaluating the quality of services. The differences are explicable in terms of their different purposes.

---

1 Locational aspects of PASS consist of the following ratings: Local Proximity; Access; Physical Resources; Program-Neighbourhood Harmony; Congregation and Assimilation Potential.
2 The social integration aspects of PASS consist of the following ratings; Program, Facility and Location Names; Function Congruity Image; Building-Neighbourhood Harmony; Deviancy Image Juxtaposition; Deviancy Program Juxtaposition; Deviant Staff Juxtaposition; Deviant Client and Other Juxtaposition; Socially Integrative Activities.

Having said this some caution is necessary. We only made a small number of comparisons, were unable to make rigorous quantitative comparisons between the methods, three of the PASS/ING evaluations were practice ones rather than being carried out by an experienced team, and ACE, although it has been used in several evaluation programmes (Wolfson 1992), is relatively untried. We would like to carry out a more rigorous quantitative comparison with other methods, and investigate the relationship between PASS/ING ratings and some 'outcome' measures, in particular users' views of their quality of life. However, it is encouraging that a recent study (Perry and Felce, in press) has shown broad agreement between PASS and other selected measures in rating several aspects of service quality for people with learning disabilities.

However, one of the strengths of our study was the insight it gave into how ratings are arrived at in actual evaluations. This, and our attempt to assess the contribution of some of the PASS/ING items with no ACE equivalents, helped to clarify the differences between the measures.

PASS/ING seems to us particularly useful in planning and policy-making, in taking a fresh look at services whose form may have come to be taken for granted. ACE could be particularly useful for comparing the everyday experience of people in similar types of service. Both would appear to have a role to play – but it is important that those using either method have some understanding of what the measure is aiming to do, and of what they want to get from it.

Summary of Discussion

(The discussion after this presentation rounded off the day, and Paul Williams and Paul Wolfson, as well as Doria Pilling and Gerald Midgley, were available to answer questions. Brian McGinnis chaired this session.)

Two main issues were covered: whether the values in PASS/ING come entirely from Wolfensberger's own experiences or whether they are more broadly based; and the applicability of measures such as PASS/ING and ACE to people from black minority groups.

Are the Values in PASS/ING in Tune with Those of Others, Particularly Service Users?
A delegate asked whether the norms and values in PASS/ING were built solely on Wolfensberger's own experiences, or if not, how they were built from other people's broader experiences. Paul Williams said that PASS and PASSING did, of course, relate to social valorisation theory (SRV), of which Wolfensberger was the main author. Items were weighted in accordance with his view of the importance of particular aspects of a service's practices in achieving valued social roles for people who have been devalued. He thought that behind the question was a query about whether Wolfensberger and others concerned with the development of SRV were in tune with other possible sources of rating issues, in particular with the views of service users. Some of those concerned with the development of SRV have been supporters of the self-advocacy movement and have been aware of the need to incorporate the views of service users. There were difficulties in how to do this but they were very aware of the need for empow-

erment of users and for them to be involved in decisions about the relative importance of particular issues that PASS and PASSING are looking at.

Gerald Midgley said that he felt a little ambivalence – there was not a consensus round those values but they were the clearest expression yet formulated of what those values could be. Getting involved in a PASSING evaluation – without having been trained first – had enabled him to see some things that people were looking at that he had not thought of before. If it could become part of a dialogue, instead of an absolute 'Bible', so that you could move from the ratings to discussions with disability groups, and ethnic minority groups, to take account of their views of culturally appropriate services, that would be the best option for him.

Doria Pilling thought that the main merit of PASS and PASSING was that they made you look at things that you might not otherwise have looked at. She had recently carried out an evaluation of an employment opportunities service for people with disabilities, and one of the things the service was doing was placing them in residential homes for elderly people. Her own evaluation did not take this into account, but it was an important aspect that PASS and PASSING suggested should be looked at. The measures made you look at symbols and signs which might not be important, but which might indicate that society – not necessarily that particular service – was not treating people appropriately.

A delegate said that she was worried about people saying that maybe there should be a dialogue. Did this get back to people who do the training on PASS/ING or people who have had their service evaluated by it? She thought there was a danger of saying that we want to work this way, but continuing to go ahead with one person's theory.

Another delegate thought that it was not just one person's work, but that a lot of people had looked at the ideologies and theories that have been put into PASS and PASSING. She was concerned about the comparison between PASS/ING and ACE, feeling that they were completely different types of evaluation, coming from different bases. She was also concerned about Gerald Midgley doing the ACE evaluation and also being involved in a PASS or PASSING evaluation.

Doria Pilling replied that the PASSING evaluation in which Gerald Midgley had been involved was of quite a different service from the four involved in the comparisons. She agreed that PASS/ING and ACE were very different, but both were supposedly measuring service quality, and that was what they had wanted to look at. Some people said that PASS/ING is very unrealistic, very idealistic, and this was one of the things they had wanted to compare in practice with another method. They had also wanted to see what PASS/ING would do that possibly another method would not do. It was perfectly true that some of the ratings (of PASS/ING and ACE) were not particularly compatible – but if you are going to make comparisons you have to use the material available – which may not be ideal.

Paul Wolfson said that, as an outsider, he felt that if there was any alternative to PASS or criticisms of it, an undue feeling of emotions was released. His position was that he had read about social role valorisation, liked a lot of what he had read, but that we were talking about a measure of environmental quality, not the Bible.

The Applicability of PASS/ING and ACE to Black Minority Groups

A delegate raised the question of the relevance of the measures under discussion to black minority groups. Paul Williams, in reply, said it was necessary to be specific about what aspects of SRV were being talked about. Carole Baxter (see Chapter 1) had found that some of the issues from Wolfensberger's writings applied to black people. If the basic analysis of the problem is similar then some of the solutions might be too.

Paul Williams also thought it helpful to look at some specific aspects of PASS/ING – for example, judgement of poor quality was made when an unreasonably wide range of activities were taking place in one building, whereas in ordinary society one would expect them to be dispersed in different places. The judgement you were asked to make was the likelihood of reinforcing the image of people as a menace and nuisance to society, because the service was congregating and segregating them in one place, keeping them off the streets. That was a negative image that certain groups in society were at risk of; disabled people were one group and perhaps black people were another. There had also been some checking out as to whether these were actual concerns of disabled or black people – and this had shown some degree of agreement.

A delegate said that Carole Baxter had certainly found that a lot of devaluing issues were the same, but the debate was surely more about whether they should be dealt with by trying to reduce differences between the devalued group and the general population, or follow the lessons learned by, for example, the feminists, and go in for consciousness-raising and positive affirmation of differences.

There was some disagreement among delegates as to whether the measures under discussion could take into account the needs of black people. Gerald Midgley said that any evaluation method using pre-set criteria, whether designed by one person or more, could not deal with disagreement over basic issues. In the planning process there had to be other aspects, such as consciousness-raising groups, as well as evaluation.

A delegate wondered whether PASS/ING should put as much effort into the evaluation of non-specialised mainstream services as it does into specialised – to look at their accessibility for the groups under discussion.

Paul Williams said that PASS/ING had been used to evaluate highly integrated services – it could be most useful here, looking at the areas some of the best services still needed to pay attention to. A delegate from Norway mentioned evaluation of services in Canada where people had been invited to live in people's homes, and used the same services as everyone else.

A delegate said that a common experience for many disabled people who had been offered integration was that it was on other people's terms. Could PASS/ING play a role in redesigning these terms? Paul Williams replied that PASS/ING should have a role in that. The process of using PASS/ING was a complex one, involving the initial preparation, the discussion of people's needs, looking at their history, the evaluation itself, and then the process of working with the people who had commissioned the evaluation as to what they wanted out of it, and the contribution PASS/ING could make. If PASS/ING were commissioned by a group of service users who were about to move from a segregated setting to a more integrated one, that would be a very exciting thing to do. You would want to make strenuous efforts to ensure that the place into which they were integrated was meaningful for them in terms of their past and their identity as people.

Gerald Midgley said that in his view only a minority of people could be revalued by fitting in with the norms. You need a wider process of social change to create revaluation. Normalisation was not enough, as long as it was simply enhancing images, and the main values of society continued to be productivity within a materialist culture. He would like to see a much closer relationship between research and political campaigning.

A delegate from Norway said that there had been a great deal of misunderstanding today of PASS/ING and SRV. These were not about asking us to force people into white man's standards. They were about understanding why people were excluded, why they were at risk in terms of oppression, social devaluation. But the idea that it was a recipe book, asking people to conform, or make people 'normal' or ordinary was a serious misunderstanding of what SRV was about. To her it was one of the more helpful ideologies for getting in touch with oppression and beginning to do something about it. She agreed that normalisation/SRV was not sufficient; it had never claimed to be.

A delegate said that books were being written with theories which were trying to come to grips with what was happening to black people, but he wondered whether these people were quite familiar with what it was to be a black person. He was sure that the writers were white men. To understand being black you had to be black; to understand being a woman, you had to be a woman.

Doria Pilling said that she did not think it was true that only black people could understand black people, and only women could understand women. If that was true there was not a human race. Certainly there were differences: different experiences, and different feelings, and nobody could totally understand anybody else. But what was the point of communication, and people trying to have a dialogue, if they could never gain some understanding; maybe not a complete understanding that comes from experience but something pretty near. Different groups in society were not so different that they did not have common values, problems and experiences, and she would like a dialogue between different groups to a much greater extent, rather than saying that they could not understand each other.

The Chairman ended the session, particularly thanking those who had laboured on PASS and PASSING for many years, and saying that whatever views were held about these measures they had certainly made people think very hard about what they were doing.

References

Carmines, E.G. and Zeller, R.A. (1979) *Reliability and Validity Assessment*. London: Sage Publications.

Clifford, P. and Wolfson, P. (1989) *FACE. A Functional Assessment of Care Environments, the Cane Hill Version*. London: RDP/Sainsbury Centre for Mental Health.

Goffman, E (1961) *Asylums*. New York: Doubleday.

Perry, J and Felce, D. (in press) Objective assessments of quality of life: how much do they agree with each other? *Journal of Community and Applied Social Psychology*.

Raynes, N. (1988) *Annotated Directory of Measures of Environmental Quality*. Manchester: Department of Social Policy and Social Work, University of Manchester.

Williams, P. (1990) Personal communication.

Wolfensberger, W. (1983) *Guidelines for Evaluators During a PASS, PASSING or Similar Assessment of Human Service Quality*. Toronto: National Institute on Mental Retardation.

Wolfensberger, W. and Glenn, L. (1975) *PASS 3. Handbook. Program Analysis of Service Systems. A Method for the Quantitative Evaluation of Human Services*. Toronto: National Institute on Mental Retardation.

Wolfensberger, W. and Thomas, S. (1983) *PASSING. Program Analysis of Service Systems' Implementation of Normalization Goals: A Method of Evaluating the Quality of Human Services According to the Principle of Normalization: Normalization Criteria and Ratings Manual*, 2nd Edition. Toronto: National Institute on Mental Retardation.

Wolfson, P (1992) The environment in the new settings. In L. Pickard *et al. Evaluating the Closure of Cane Hill Hospital. Final Report of the Cane Hill Research Team*. London: RDP/Sainsbury Centre for Mental Health, 159–175.

Part 2

Workshops: Is a Consensus on Quality Standards Possible?

Chapter 8

Evaluating Quality

Peter Allen

My understanding of this workshop session is that it is talking and thinking about evaluating quality. The first thing that we could do is to think about what 'quality' means to us, how we view 'quality'.

Being fairly realistic and feet-on-the-ground in terms of being involved in delivering services, we are learning to operate within a new structure in the UK, of purchasers and providers. At least one person here described himself as having newly become a purchaser. I guess that means he has the responsibility to spend somebody else's money as well as his own. And there is now a new equation around: in terms of purchasers, it is to do with cost, volume and quality. When services are purchased, they are bought at a particular cost to provide the amount of that service to a certain standard. The 'quality' part of the three is as yet the most unsophisticated in the relationship. That is one thing that appears to be happening in the UK at the present time.

I believe the second thing is that there is this political context of user involvement. 'We must involve users in their services.' It feels to me as if some of that has not been particularly well thought through. It appears in many of the documents that are written both nationally and locally by organisations in terms of their unitary community-care plans; but it is in severe danger of spiralling in a nose-dive. However, it is still there, and let us hope that a very firm political statement is being made, to which there is a real commitment.

Underneath all of this, there are users, user groups. My own feeling, concerning the part of East London I work in, is that, in terms of rhetoric, we say the right sort of things. In terms of practice, the involvement of users of services in actually shaping and evaluating and in moving forward the services that they rely on and depend on from day to day, is a bit like attempts to defy gravity. On some days we can jump a bit higher than on others. But, once we achieve weightlessness in services, because it is really pushing against the power of the bureaucracy that is already there, I am pretty sure that we will know about it. It will feel quite different from the experience that we have at the moment.

The local concerns that I have are about how we inform and educate the growing number of purchasers, and learn from each other about quality. In East London, three health authorities have combined to form one. These are the people with whom we perhaps need to be having conversations about quality and about evaluation, because they are the ones who are going to be giving the contracts to providers. If we want a higher quality service, we have to go back to the purchasers.

A Quality Action Group in East London

The area that I want to give a short presentation on now, is around attempts to introduce a 'Quality Action Group' into a day service in East London. A number of us felt that it was appropriate to involve a whole range of people in evaluating the quality of the service that they were receiving. As well as using other monitoring techniques, we wanted something that was much more alive and interactive and really did involve people.

The Quality Action Group that we established was around a day service that, at that time, was organised by the health authority but which was shortly to become a not-for-profit organisation. It is interesting that the reasons which made us embark on looking at quality in this part of the service were twofold. One was that it appeared on a manager's set of objectives – one of the people in the organisation in which I was working was getting performance-related pay depending on some initiatives happening around quality in the service. The other reason was that I had been to a presentation at the Norah Fry Research Unit, at Bristol University, around some materials that they were beginning to develop to address quality and involve service users through a Quality Action approach.

Those two things then met. The manager was looking for something that would address quality. I was looking for permission to use the new ideas that I had picked up on a real-life service.

What is a 'Quality Action Group'? People meet regularly, and the people who meet are those who have a particular stake in the service. What we actually did was to invite a group of people – people who were using the service, people who were working in local colleges, people who were thinking about developing employment schemes: anyone who we felt would have something to contribute. There was a certain degree of selection.

Secondly, managers were supporting the group. It was really important that managers were both supporting and were also actually involved in what was happening.

Thirdly, service users were always involved. The group consisted of about a dozen people; three or four were service users, a relatively small core of people using the facility. There were up to about thirty or forty people who actually used this facility during the week. One of the things we came back to a lot of the time was: how do you get people who perhaps are not used to meetings and who have not got the same level of communication skills actually involved?

Fourthly, we were looking at quality from a service-user's point of view. It was very important to us to be clear that the service users were involved in defining quality, in describing what they thought quality meant. It is quite interesting that, for one of the service users, this came alive to her when we went to Bristol to give a presentation on the work, staying in a hotel. It was one of the first times that she had stayed in a hotel; it was a high quality hotel, and she was very impressed with the range of things that happened to her when she was there. If she asked for things, people tried to help, they would say 'yes'. She felt that the bed was much more comfortable than many she had slept in before. It brought alive to her what quality could mean.

And lastly, we, as a group, attempted to let others know what was happening. It felt like talking to the 'listening bank' at times; you would say things but were not sure that it was going to make much difference to the way some of the people were behaving. But it was important to us to feed back and let others know what was actually happening in the group, so that they did not feel as if a special activity was going on with which they were not connected.

In terms of the process for the quality group, first, we attempted to decide what quality is. This would be an interesting point to stop and think for a bit. We were working with a relatively mixed group of people; thirty per cent of the people used this particular service. How should we go about attempting to decide what quality is?

A Delegate: It is fitness for the purpose. A book I read recently said: 'A Rolls Royce is a high-quality product if you want to buy a very high-quality car. A Skoda is a high-quality product if you want to buy a car to the quality of a Skoda.' There is no absolute so far as quality goes; it is just being right for the job that it is meant to do.

Peter Allen: Being right for the job that it has got to do. Any other thoughts? It is great, is it not? There is a whole industry founded on quality and evaluation, but we find it quite difficult to think of ways of defining what it is.

A Delegate: Is it not about defining the job that it is supposed to be doing as well, because that is surely about comparison of experiences and demands and expectations – which could well vary very much, depending on the client group.

PA: Any other thoughts? I guess it is a difficult one to have a right answer about, but it is quite interesting in terms of being clear about what it is we want to happen, and what would make that happen – bearing in mind it could be different from one situation to another.

One of the ways in which we attempted to define and describe quality was by doing some quality collage. We looked around for images that conveyed quality, looking in books and magazines, doing drawings and pictures. One of the reasons we did that was around issues to do with people's communication and language skills. I wonder if any of you can guess what happened as a result of that: think of the magazines that you or your partner buy. The images that were conveyed were of people that do not really exist, doing things that none of us ever do, wearing things that none of us could ever afford: that was challenging from the point of view of thinking about what this exercise meant. What was interesting for us, though, was that one of the very strong themes that came out of doing this quality-collage activity was something about relationships. For the people who were in the group, one of the things that they said was very important for them in terms of quality of life was having good and strong and meaningful relationships.

One of the first things we did – it sounds very straightforward but it took several gettings together to do this – was to get to know each other as individuals and as a group. That was actually very difficult. One of the things that we very easily do as professionals in groups is to set the agenda that we are going to have for a meeting, to be very clear about the timing, and we become very businesslike. We do not necessarily talk very much about ourselves, and we build certain sort of defences. The Quality Action Group was very different from that, and we did what was called a lifeline exercise, talking about some of the significant things that have happened in our lives. A couple of people in the group were women who had left large mental handicap institutions, and the process of doing this was in itself quite a distressing activity. But I think the benefit of doing this was an enlightening and moving experience.

One of the early successes that we had was making some suggestions about the telephones in this particular building. At the time, it was 50:50 that the phone would get answered, a seventy per cent chance that the person answering would know who you wanted, and about a ten per cent chance that the person would be found. It was important for one of the service users on the Quality Action Group because, for example, if she was doing an activity in the community and for some reason or other it broke down or the transport did not turn up or for some other reason she needed to come back, she would try and get in touch and some of the time she would not get that call answered. One of our early successes was that we got an agreement that people should answer the phone in a consistent way: they should say 'yes' or 'no' as to whether somebody was in; they should go and find them if they were actually there.

A number of other activities were also group-forming. We were involved in a conference in Bristol; people prepared that together. We started preparing a newsletter which was not particularly successful but it was useful for the group itself. We took Polaroid pictures of each other and photocopied these at the end of the first session so that everybody knew the faces of all of the people who had been at the meeting.

Because it was a day facility that was using community resources a lot, transport figured very high as an issue. You did not need to be an expert to know that the buses were often late or the taxis were late. One of the problems we had had earlier on was of some of the taxi drivers being rude to the service users; that was resolved.

I do not think that we ever resolved the issue of how to get more service users involved. We tried lots of different tactics: we held an open morning where we invited as many people as we possibly could to learn more about what we were doing. We had discussions with people who were running the service about work activities – people were saying they wanted more opportunities to work; they wanted to get paid for the work they did. We had discussions with people managing the service about cancelled sessions. As with the taxis, you do not need to be an expert to know when one of the sessions gets cancelled. The statistics were saying that the majority of sessions were taking place but, even if a small minority were not, then that meant an awful lot for the people who were not getting the things that they wanted.

We tried to keep the group in the frame of mind where they were thinking the whole time about solutions. In terms of measuring the quality of bits of the service: I do not know if any of you are old enough to remember Hughie Green's 'Opportunity Knocks', a programme where the audience's reaction and response to a particular artiste was measured on the 'Clapometer', by the loudness of the clap. We developed a similar thing; at the Avenue Resource Centre, we called this thing the ARC-ometer. We would go around measuring what people would do, very snap decisions on what they thought about particular bits of the service, what the service users were doing. It was very subjective, but it often meant an awful lot for the people who were doing it.

We started meeting in January 1990. We met about thirty times. We usually had monthly meetings, but we had summer recesses. The group no longer meets – for reasons that I will come on to.

One of the main issues that came up for us was that people would be late or not be able to come. It seems to be a professional prerogative at times to be late for meetings: 'I'm extremely busy, therefore I can be late.' But service users found this very difficult, and it was very disempowering for them. 'I'm busy, you're not'; 'I can be late, you can't.' There is quite an interesting sort of balance/imbalance there.

Another challenge for us that I have mentioned were the difficulties in trying to get more service users involved, wanting a bigger group. A lot of the earlier work that we did as a group was about getting people to feel comfortable and working together. People might not be used to contributing or might have difficulties in communicating.

People working in a service may leave because they are fed up, or they want promotion. For a group such as this, which had spent time getting to know each other, looking at problems jointly – if a significant person was leaving, then it was quite a challenge bringing a new person in. Both saying goodbye and saying hello could be quite difficult. To keep the group going and to keep new people coming in actually demanded a lot of energy and commitment.

Another point is that some of the issues can seem to be too big. Something needs to be changed; but just addressing it and defying gravity in that way to address it is just too enormous. This came home to us very strongly with a policy decision to move office accommodation for senior managers into the day facility: we felt that whatever we said would have made very little difference.

We have been quite successful in terms of making suggestions about things like the telephone and the transport. Some of those were small things perhaps. I think they were more than cosmetic, but they were not major. Everyone will agree now that the quality of life, the quality of the service that is provided, has changed quite dramatically since those people came in to use that in that way. So there is an issue there for us about what we can do about some of these big points.

Lastly, there were concerns about divided loyalties. There is a need to have people who manage services involved in the Quality Action Group. The problem that we had, though, is that, in that group setting, you could quite easily be seen to be criticising the person who was either second-line managing or managing that service; that person could become a scapegoat, both in the group and in their own management structure.

Summary of Discussion

A major difference of viewpoints emerged during the discussion – between those who thought the small changes that could be made by a Quality Action Group to be valid/worthwhile and empowering, and those who believed that real quality in services and people's lives could not be obtained without a fundamental change in society, through political change.

Who Should Define Quality in Services?

The discussion began with the question of who should define what quality is. Peter Allen said that service users with whom he was working often said to him 'Why are you asking me? You're the one who knows.' One delegate thought that the perception of users was what was important. But another emphasised the importance of having a set of values which were for so-called 'normal' people. Otherwise, there was a danger of saying: 'It's all right for me, but they're different, so they need a different set of values.' This delegate thought that John O'Brien's five accomplishments (see Alan Tyne, Chapter 15, for information about these) did give the basis – relationships, personal development, respect, were things that everybody needs.

PA said that he experiences a dissonance between what people say they are doing, what values they say their services are based on, and what is really happening.

Can Service Quality be Improved Without Major Political Changes in Society?

A delegate who said she came from a socialist country, said that it would be easy for everyone to sit there and say that they believed in justice, equality and various rights, but the practical implications were a total redistribution of wealth and power. Would that be possible in British society?

Another delegate, however, thought that things had to take place in the real world: a world of health authorities and social service departments run by accountants. It was not a question of how we would like things to be, or what users approve of, but whether the managers agree. A different delegate did not think that this situation precluded change. It was a question of using the money available most effectively.

Another delegate thought this was looking at things from the viewpoint of administrators, not of the users. Peter Allen, in his presentation, had shown that a different way of handling the telephone could make a huge difference to the way users feel about a service. That had nothing to do with resources.

PA said that at first he had felt a bit deflated about this. The group might have wanted to change the whole Centre, and somebody thinks that the telephone is the most important thing. Then, when the woman who was talking about it described why, what it had meant to her to stand outside waiting for something to happen, wondering if anyone was going to pick her up, he realised that it did mean a lot. He thought that quality was about these kinds of changes.

The delegate from a 'socialist' country said that it was very dangerous to ask service users what they want and need if they have had very deprived and mismanaged situations. There is evidence from her country that those who have had less will be satisfied with getting something that is just a little bit better – not what they deserve. It was necessary to have a frame of reference to decide what people deserve rather than just relying on what they say. She was worried when quality got down to issues like telephone ringing, when we knew that these people were probably living in below minimally acceptable housing situations, without jobs, without friends.

Two other delegates agreed, saying that there was a danger in involving users in small changes. You might end up thinking these were the only changes that could be made, or leaving the larger issues totally to other people.

Benefits of and Problems with Quality Action Groups
Another delegate saw the main importance of Quality Action Groups being in sharing time with people, beginning to understand what is happening in their minds.

There was further discussion of the difficulties in getting people together in groups, of building up sufficient rapport with service users.

How Can Devalued People have a 'Real' Range of Choices?
The discussion then reverted to the problem of people with little experience being satisfied with what they had. One delegate said that it might be necessary to assist people who had had only the experience of being devalued in making choices; perhaps making choices for them in the short term. But he wanted to get to the base, to prevent people from becoming disempowered in the first place. It was not enough to keep patching things up.

The delegate from a 'socialist' country said that first it was necessary for there to be a decent standard of living. You cannot empower people or give them choices unless there is guaranteed access to a valued range of choices. She thought that the money given to people to evaluate and assure so-called 'quality' could be given to disadvantaged people.

Chapter 9

Exploring Quality of Life and its Relationship to PASS
Looking for Agreement

David Felce

Quality of life is a term which is much easier to use than define. We all know what it means in general terms but we are less likely to analyse how particular aspects of our lives interact to form such a sense of personal wellbeing. We are even less likely to reach a precise assessment of the strength of relative contributions to it.

There is a strong feeling that quality of life is highly subjective – different things are important for different people. However, the notions of a society having a culture, a socialisation process and cultural or societal norms must imply a degree of common ground across individuals about how life is lived. Some attempt to identify such common ground is required if there are not to be as many quality of life definitions as there are people. Researchers on quality of life have attempted a general definition of the concept and to turn this into something measurable. Recently, Cummins, McCabe, Gullone and Romeo (1994) have identified over eighty quality of life scales. The problem remains that not one has achieved a level of acceptance against which other scales can be validated.

Many of these scales, together with other measures of process and outcome, have been developed in order to evaluate the fundamental policy changes affecting the design of services which play a major role in the day-to-day lives of people in need of support, such as those with learning disabilities, chronic psychiatric problems, physical disabilities or infirmity due to old age. In the field of learning disabilities alone, de-institutionalisation has prompted a steady flow of evaluative research which has attempted to capture important aspects of individual development or lifestyle (see, for example, Tizard 1964, King, Raynes and Tizard 1971, Felce, Kushlick and Smith 1980, Felce 1989, Lowe and de Paiva 1991).

In this research, quality was initially equated with developmental gain (e.g. Tizard 1964) but attempts followed almost immediately to broaden the evaluative lens (e.g. King, Raynes and Tizard 1971). The latter's analysis of staff-resident management practices stemmed from the sociological analysis of the characteristics of total institutions (Goffman 1961). At about the same time, other authors were developing alternative ways to assess environments from the perspectives of developmental psychology (McLain, Silverstein, Hubbell and Brownlee 1977), social psychology (Moos 1974), behavioural psychology (Cataldo and Risley 1974), behavioural ecology (Sackett and Landesman-Dwyer 1977) and normalisation (Wolfensberger and Glenn 1975).

A range of methodologies for characterising the quality of service process and outcome thus became available in the 1970s and were represented in some of the more comprehensive research studies of de-institutionalisation. In the USA, the Pennhurst Longitudinal Study (Conroy and Bradley 1985) examined the quality of the living environment using indicators based on some of the above measures in addition to assessing developmental progress, family views and resident satisfaction. Evaluation of ordinary housing services in England (Felce 1989) reported on the extent and quality of staff–resident interaction and its temporal relationship to resident activity, developmental progress, resident activity patterns, family and friendship contact, and community activities. The evaluation of the NIMROD service in Wales (Lowe and de Paiva 1991) also focused on developmental progress, family and friendship contact and community activities but gained family and consumer views as well.

Conceptual Models of Quality of Life

Although broadening the range of measurement indicators makes it more likely that significant aspects of quality of life, such as the use of community, the extent of social networks, the pursuit of constructive activities, and choice and variety in activity, will be reflected, the full implications of the notion of quality of life may still not be addressed. In particular, what is measured may still have a restricted focus and the place of personal satisfaction and individual subjective appraisal in the determination of quality of life may not be dealt with very satisfactorily. Figure 9.1 presents four perspectives on the conceptualisation of quality of life set out in one of our recent papers (Felce and Perry, in press), the first three of which were taken from Borthwick-Duffy (1992): (a) quality of life being defined in terms of the quality of the *life conditions* experienced, (b) quality of life being defined in terms of *satisfaction with life*, (c) quality of life being defined as a combination of an individual's *life conditions* and their *satisfaction with life*, and, (d) quality of life being defined as a combination of *life conditions* and *satisfaction with life* taking account of *personal values and aspirations*.

In the first formulation, life conditions may be described in terms of such factors as physical health, personal circumstances, social relationships, functional activities and pursuits, and wider societal and economic influences impinging on the individual. These may be viewed objectively as constituting one's quality of life. Subjective response to such conditions is the domain of personal satisfaction with life. However, if the latter is viewed as the more important factor, this formulation is at odds with the tradition that quality of life is the ultimate criterion by which to judge personal welfare. From this perspective, the model in Figure 9.1(b) would appear preferable in defining quality of life as synonymous with personal satisfaction. Authors writing on learning disabilities (e.g. Heal and Chadsey-Rusch 1985, Stark and Goldsbury 1990), as well as others

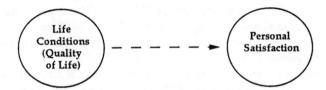

(a) Quality of Life is defined in terms of Life Conditions

(b) Quality of Life is defined in terms of Satisfaction with life

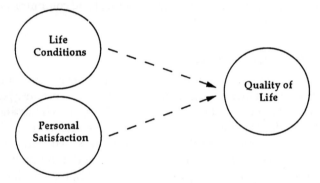

(c) Quality of Life defined as a combination of Life Conditions and Satisfaction

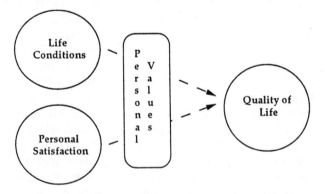

(d) Quality of Life defined as a combination of Life Conditions and Satisfaction weighted by Scale of Importance

Figure 9.1 Conceptualisations of Quality of Life

writing more generally (e.g. Andrews and McKennell 1980, Campbell, Converse and Rodgers 1976, Allen, Bentler and Gutek 1985), equate quality of life with wellbeing or satisfaction with life.

However, whether satisfaction does provide a straightforward touchstone for the evaluation of quality of life is doubtful. Edgerton (1990) has sustained the argument that reports of wellbeing are insensitive to external life conditions and owe more to internal dispositions. Although pleasant or untoward changes in life conditions may induce a temporary change in the reporting of wellbeing, the longitudinal pattern is relatively stable, the best predictor of current wellbeing being that given in the past.

Moreover, the basis of reported wellbeing may essentially be comparative. A person may be satisfied with their wages until he or she discovers that a colleague of equivalent seniority, competence and responsibilities at work earns significantly more. How one reports satisfaction with life's conditions is itself shaped by experience. Expectations and points of reference may be set low or high depending on personal circumstance. Those people whose circumstances and options to date may make them particularly prone to having low expectations may report satisfaction in situations where the majority of other people would not. Evidence that people with learning disabilities expect a relatively poor quality of life is to be found in research which records expressed satisfaction in circumstances which most would find to be unacceptable (Edgerton, Bollinger and Herr 1984, Flynn 1989, Holland 1990). A definition of quality of life which ignores objective assessment of life conditions may, therefore, not provide an adequate safeguard for the interests of vulnerable people.

The accepted importance of subjective assessment coupled with a view that it is also of continuing relevance to assess life conditions and lifestyle objectively produces the third and fourth formulations (Figures 9.1(c) and 9.1(d)). Measures of quality of life in the field of learning disabilities have been constructed to take account of both objective and subjective facets (e.g. Schalock, Keith and Hoffman 1990). A view that an acceptable quality of life has been achieved would require both that the person concerned registers positive satisfaction with the various aspects of their life and that such aspects would be assessed at least non-negatively by a cross-section of other people. How objective and subjective components should be combined for an overall view of quality of life is not addressed by the model in Figure 9.1(c).

Figure 9.1(d) provides one solution. According to the model of Campbell, Converse and Rodgers (1976), individuals judge their objective situation in each of various life domains according to some standard of comparison which is based on aspirations, expectations, feelings of what would be just, reference group comparisons, personal needs and personal values. Their resulting evaluation is their satisfaction with that domain. Domain satisfactions combine to produce a general sense of wellbeing. Cummins (1992) has also suggested combining objective and subjective appraisals via the assessment of personal values as in Figure 9.1(d). Essentially, the significance of either the objective or subjective assessment of a particular life domain is interpretable only in relation to the value or importance the individual places on it.

Agreement on Relevant Life Domains

Although researchers may vary in how they see quality of life in terms of the four models in Figure 9.1, there is considerable agreement that the assessment of quality of life spans a number of different aspects of life or life domains. The paper cited earlier (Felce and Perry, in press) examined fifteen key literature sources, which either described conceptual models or provided operationalisations of quality of life, for evidence as to whether writers categorised life domains similarly. Allowing for a degree of licence in treating a variety of terms which refer essentially to the same thing as synonyms (e.g. standard of living and material wellbeing, interpersonal interaction and social relations), a striking consistency in content emerged.

The majority of aspects mentioned in these sources could be grouped under five domain headings (illustrated later in Figure 9.3). Physical wellbeing subsumes health, fitness and physical safety. Material wellbeing subsumes finance or income, quality of housing or living environment, privacy, possessions, transport, neighbourhood, security and stability or tenure. Social wellbeing includes two major dimensions. Family or household life (i.e. relationships with those one lives with in one's home) and relationships with the natural family, relatives and with more general social friends and acquaintances both reflect a strong concern for the quality and breadth of interpersonal relationships. Community activities and the level of acceptance or support from the community together reflect a similarly strong concern for social involvement. Development and activity is concerned with the possession and use of skills in relation to both self-determination: competence or independence and choice or control; and the pursuit of functional activities: work, leisure, housework, education and a general sense of productivity or contribution. Finally, emotional wellbeing subsumes mood or sense of fulfilment, self-esteem, status or respect, and religious faith.

Combining this analysis of life domains with the earlier conceptual model depicted in Figure 9.1(d) produces an overall model of quality of life (see Figure 9.2). Quality of life is defined as an overall general wellbeing which comprises objective descriptors and subjective evaluations of physical, material, social and emotional wellbeing together with the extent of personal development and purposeful activity all weighted by a personal set of values. The three elements are shown as interdependent, a change in one potentially affecting others (e.g. a loss of religious faith changing one's subjective appraisals). Moreover, each is susceptible to external influence by such variables as genetic, social and material inheritance, age and maturation, developmental history, employment, peer influences and reference points and other factors affecting the social, economic and political context. This makes quality of life a dynamic concept. It may not only be different for different people but also vary for the same person over time. The base against which quality of life is judged may not be a constant.

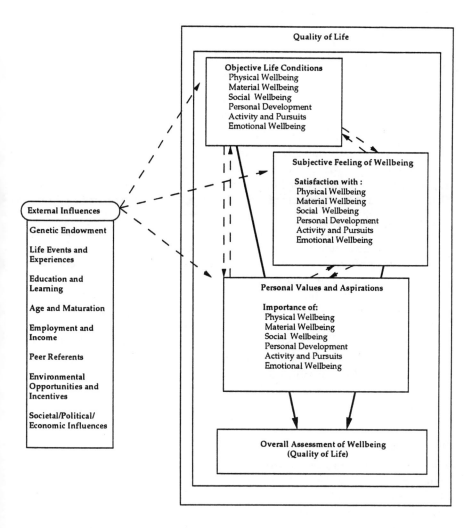

Figure 9.2 A model of Quality of Life

Overlap Between Quality of Life and the Focus of PASS

The basis for reaching an assessment using PASS is also not a constant. PASS assessments are made relative to a cultural set of values which may differ across locations and also change over time. However, variations between cultures may, in some cases, be less great than between individual members of cultures and the values of a particular culture will certainly be less volatile than the personal values of individual members. PASS, however, is not a quality of life measure. It seeks to evaluate in quantifiable terms the extent to which a service uses cultur-ally normative means (familiar or valued techniques, tools or methods) in order to enable the life conditions of people (e.g. income, housing, health) to be as good as those of typical citizens and to enhance and support behaviour, appearances, experiences, status and reputations which are culturally valued. PASS is, therefore, concerned with taking a broad view of the objective life conditions a person experiences across the life domains. It is neither concerned with the subjective assessment of these by the individual nor the precise framework of personal priorities by which he or she may weight such objective or subjective assessments. Rather, consistent with the principle of normalisation, PASS uses cultural norms or values to judge service processes or outcomes.

PASS clearly differs in this way from the quality of life formulation depicted in Figure 9.2. However, Figure 9.3 illustrates that, within its remit, it does embody a breadth of concern which is consistent with the life domains drawn from the various writings on quality of life described earlier. PASS contains 34 ratings which are related to the principle of normalisation, 33 of which relate to a number of distinct issues concerned with six global concerns: physical integration, social integration, age-appropriate interpretations and structures, culture-appropriate interpretations and structures, developmental growth orientation and quality of setting. The thirty-fourth, model coherency, assesses the match between several service characteristics and the specific major needs of the service user.

Figure 9.3 shows how the 33 normalisation-related ratings in PASS other than model coherency map onto the quality of life domains derived earlier.

There is mostly not a one-to-one match; the quality of life domain is usually not the exclusive focus of a PASS rating. Conversely, many quality of life domains cover aspects reflected in several PASS ratings. However, all of the PASS ratings reflect something of one or more quality of life domains and all except one quality of life domain, positive emotional affect or happiness, are reflected in one or more PASS ratings.

Conclusion

Writers on quality of life have gone some way in describing a common set of life domains relevant to the overall assessment of quality of life. PASS, although not being a quality of life measure, is concerned with a similar breadth of issues. This degree of agreement seems to be reassuring to the scope of both endeavours: the attempt to operationalise quality of life on the one hand, and the attempt to assess a service system in terms of the normalisation principle on the other. A fundamental difference in focus, of course, exists between the two. Quality of life looks to interpret objective information and subjective views across the life domains, taking account of personal values and aspirations. PASS interprets largely objective information against general cultural standards. However, such a difference may not set the two approaches so far apart if weight is given to the argument made above that low expectation among those often devalued within society may make recourse to cultural norms a better safeguard of individual welfare than expressed satisfaction.

The use of objective information and normative cultural standards may also be the only approach available if language or communication problems makes the sophisticated elicitation of views and personal values worthy of an assessment of quality of life impossible. This may prove to be the case with respect to

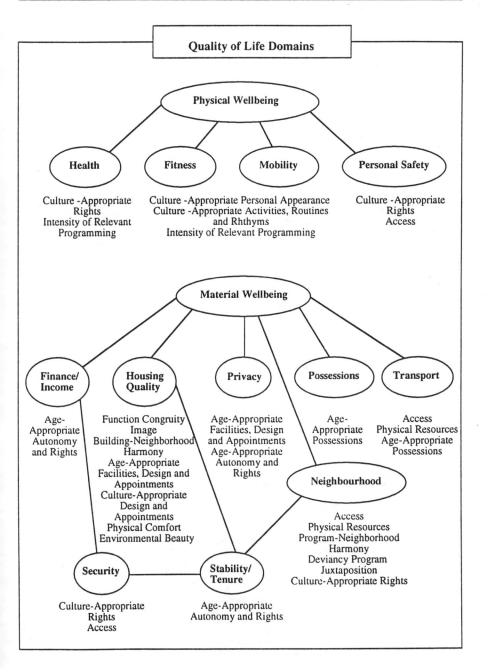

Figure 9.3 Overlap between Quality of Life domains and PASS normalisation ratings

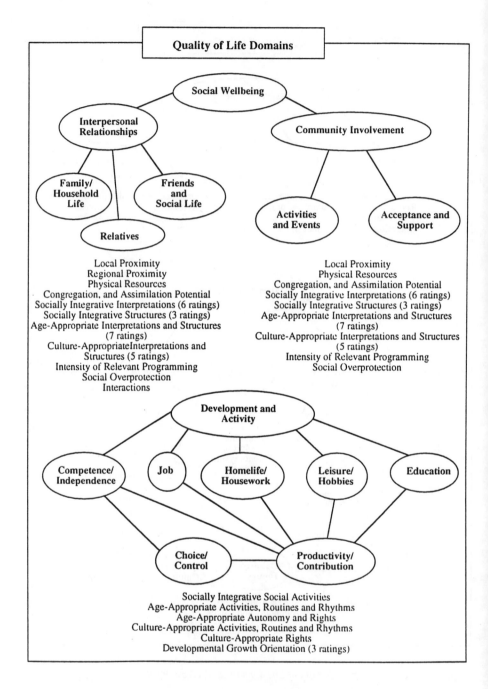

Figure 9.3 Overlap between Quality of Life domains and PASS normalisation ratings (continued)

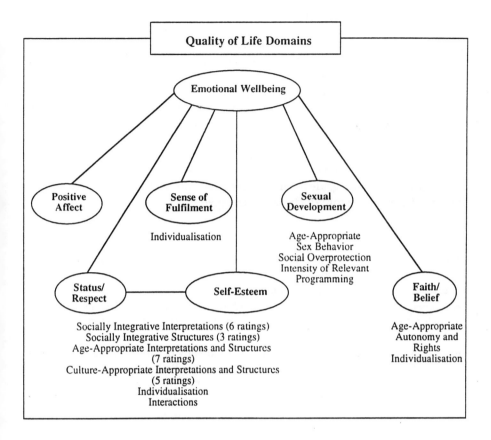

Figure 9.3 Overlap between Quality of Life domains and PASS normalisation ratings (continued)

some people with learning disabilities who lack sufficiently well developed language, some people with chronic mental health problems and some elderly people with mental infirmity. Scales which purport to measure quality of life have been developed for people whose language is poor, such as those with learning disabilities. However, they appear to offer a very simple conceptualisation of that concept. For example, the satisfaction section of the Quality of Life Questionnaire (Schalock, Keith and Hoffman 1990) has ten items which invite respondents to rate each of the following on a three-point scale: an overall view on life, how much enjoyment they derive from it, how well off they are compared to others, whether most events/activities are rewarding or not, their satisfaction with their living arrangements, how well they are treated by neighbours, whether their education prepared them for what they are currently doing, the extent of their problems, whether they feel lonely, and whether they feel out of place in social situations. There is a distinct sense in which the complexities of issues are oversimplified by the level of generality of the items. Moreover, this level of generality makes greater demands on the language abilities of respondents, requiring them both to respond to abstract terms, such as the extent of their problems, and to collate experience and distil a summary position relevant to the issue in question if they are to provide an answer which genuinely represents their position. There is research which shows that gaining a response from people with learning disabilities can be increased by adopting such simplified response formats (Sigelman *et al.* 1981). But to what end? The same research also shows that what is gained may not be valid and reliable information based in real understanding. Where it is not possible to get accurate views from individuals, quality of life assessment may have to be restricted to objectively measurable phenomena, interpreted via societal and cultural norms. PASS may make a contribution here alongside other measurement approaches as well as continuing to serve the purpose for which it was designed.

References

Allen, H.M., Bentler, P.M. and Gutek, B.A. (1985) Probing theories of individual well-being: A comparison of quality-of-life models assessing neighbourhood satisfaction. *Basic and Applied Social Psychology* Vol 6, 181–203.

Andrews, F.M. and McKennell, A.C. (1980) Measures of self-reported well-being: their affective, cognitive and other components. *Social Indicators Research* Vol 8, 127–155.

Borthwick-Duffy, S.A. (1992) Quality of life and quality of care in mental retardation. In L. Rowitz (ed) *Mental Retardation in the Year 2000*. Berlin: Springer-Verlag.

Campbell, A., Converse, P.E. and Rodgers, W.L. (1976) *The Quality of American life: Perceptions, Evaluation and Satisfactions*. New York: Russell Sage Foundation.

Cataldo, M.F. and Risley, T.R. (1974) Evaluation of living environments: the MANIFEST description of ward activities. In P.O. Davidson, F.W. Clark and L.A. Hamerlynck (eds) *Evaluation of Behavioral Programs in Community, Residential and School settings: The Fifth Banff International Conference on Behavior Modification*. Champaign, Illinois: Research Press.

Conroy, J.W. and Bradley, V.J. (1985) *The Pennhurst Longitudinal Study: A report of Five Years Research and Analysis*. Philadelphia: Temple University Developmental Disabilities Center.

Cummins, R.A. (1992) *Comprehensive Quality of Life Scale – Intellectual Disability* (Third edition). Melbourne: Psychology Research Centre.

Cummins, R.A., McCabe, M.P., Gullone, E. and Romeo, Y. (1994) The comprehensive quality of life scale: Instrument development and psychometric evaluation on college staff and students. *Educational and Psychological Measurement, 54*, 372–382.

Edgerton, R.B. (1990) Quality of life from a longitudinal research perspective. In R. L. Schalock (ed) *Quality of Life: Perspectives and Issues*. Washington D. C.: American Association on Mental Retardation.

Edgerton, R.B., Bollinger, M. and Herr, B. (1984) The cloak of competence: after two decades. *American Journal of Mental Deficiency* Vol 88, 345–351.

Felce, D. (1989) *Staffed Housing for Adults with Severe and Profound Mental Handicaps: The Andover Project*. Kidderminster: BIMH Publications.

Felce, D., Kushlick, A. and Smith, J. (1980) An overview of the research on alternative residential facilities for the severely mentally handicapped in Wessex. *Advance in Behaviour Research and Therapy* Vol 3, 1–4.

Felce, D. and Perry, J. (in press) Quality of life: its definition and measurement. *Research in Developmental Disabilities.*

Flynn, M. (1989) *Independent Living for Adults with a Mental Handicap: A Place of My Own.* London: Cassell.

Goffman, E. (1961) *Asylums.* New York: Doubleday.

Heal, L.W. and Chadsey-Rusch, J. (1985) The Lifestyle Satisfaction Scale (LSS): assessing individuals' satisfaction with residence, community setting and associated services. *Applied Research in Mental Retardation* Vol 6, 475–490.

Holland, A. (1990) *People with Learning Disabilities Living in Community Homes: Their Views and the Quality of the Service.* Unpublished doctoral thesis. University of Loughborough.

King, R., Raynes, N. and Tizard, J. (1971) *Patterns of Residential Care.* London: Routledge and Kegan Paul.

Lowe, K. and de Paiva, S. (1991) *NIMROD: An Overview.* London: HMSO.

McLain, R.E. Silverstein, A.B. Hubbell, M. and Brownlee, L. (1977) Comparison of the residential environment of a state hospital for retarded clients with those of various types of community facilities. *Journal of Community Psychology* Vol 5, 282–289.

Moos, R. (1974) *The Social Climate Scales: An Overview.* Palo Alto: Community Psychologists Press.

Sackett, G.P. and Landesman-Dwyer, S. (1977) Toward an ethology of mental retardation. In P. Mittler (ed) *Research to Practice in Mental Retardation Vol II: Education and Training.* Baltimore: University Park Press.

Schalock, R.L., Keith, K.D. and Hoffman, K. (1990) *Quality of Life Questionnaire: Standardization Manual.* Hastings NE: Mid-Nebraska Mental Retardation Services.

Sigelman, C.K., Schoenrock, C.J., Winer, J.L., Spanhel, C.L., Hromas, S.G., Martin, P.W., Budd, C. and Bensberg, G.J. (1981) Issues in interviewing mentally retarded persons: an empirical study. In R.H. Brununinks, C.E. Meyers, B.B. Sigford and K.C. Lakin (eds) *Deinstitutionalization and Community Adjustment of Mentally Retarded Persons.* Washington D.C.: American Association on Mental Deficiency.

Stark, J.A. and Goldsbury, T. (1990) Quality of life from childhood to adulthood. In R.L. Schalock (ed) *Quality of Life: Perspectives and Issue.* Washington D. C.: American Association on Mental Retardation.

Tizard, J. (1964) *Community Services for the Mentally Handicapped.* London: Oxford University Press.

Wolfensberger, W. and Glenn, L. (1975) *Program Analysis of Service Systems. Handbook and Manual,* 3rd edition. Toronto: National Institute on Mental Retardation.

Chapter 10

Quality measurement in the All-Wales Strategy

Judy Renshaw

This workshop describes the aims and progress to date of a joint Welsh Office/Audit Commission project to develop a cost and quality 'tool kit' to assess services developed under the All-Wales Strategy for people with learning difficulties. It is likely that Ministers or others will ask what has been achieved by the All-Wales Strategy over ten years: 'Where has the money gone, and what have we got for our money? Do we know if it has been doing anything useful or not?' Up to now, the answer would have been that various services had been funded but there would have been no way of being able to gauge what actually has been achieved with that money.

The project was undertaken by a small team, comprising a full-time member from the Welsh Office (from the Social Services Inspectorate Wales) and two people from the Audit Commission. To make the project manageable, we decided to focus primarily on social services, which is the lead agency in the All-Wales Strategy, and on services for adults.

What the Welsh Office particularly wanted was to be able to make cost and quality comparisons between services. The counties' needs were rather different: they were for usable and practicable methods of evaluation that would tell them something about the quality of their own services and give them some idea of the directions in which to go – which is not quite the same as having a broad comparison of quality and costs. So the project had slightly dual or diverging requirements.

What Evaluation Methods Were Being Used?

In phase one, we started off by looking round at all eight counties in Wales to see what sort of evaluation methods they were using. The intention was then to go off and to start to develop something of our own, which could be used on a routine basis, drawing on things that were already being used. We spent a little time in each county and looked at the evaluative work going on at different levels.

Evaluation can be at the level of the individual service user: how the quality of services for individuals is assessed. It can be at the level of service units – such as a house or employment service or a family aide service. Or it can be at locality or county level. Mainly because of linking together cost and quality in our project, we decided to examine quality evaluation at the level of service units. So that is quite conventional, the sort of unit that PASS evaluations go for.

We talked to people who were involved in planning evaluations in the counties. We also talked to people who had been doing evaluations and people who had been on the receiving end of them. We felt it was important to talk to people who worked in or were involved in a service that had been evaluated. We asked them what they felt about it, what they valued or disliked about the way they had been evaluated. And as far as possible we talked to service users to get their views of the whole process as well.

First of all: individual plans. These are not only useful at the level of individual service users. The plans also tell you quite a lot about what is going on in terms of the services being monitored. The All-Wales Strategy is quite strong in its emphasis on individual plans, yet we found that, although it varied between the counties, on average only about one in four adults with learning difficulties had an individual plan, despite the ten-year strategy.

There is independent research evidence which indicates the significance of the individual planning process. The Centre for Social Policy Research and Development, based in Bangor, North Wales, found that one of the factors that was related to people's, particularly families', satisfaction with the service was whether there was an individual plan (McGrath, Grant and Ramcharan 1991). Another research project, by the Welsh Office (1991), found something quite similar. Even if all the services were not ideal, families generally felt much more positive about those they were getting if they had individual plans, and a key worker.

That is not to say that there are not sometimes problems with individual plans. Research by the Norah Fry Unit (at Bristol University) indicates some problems: for example, where they focused on the negative rather than on the positive aspects of people, their weaknesses rather than their strengths, or where users' contributions were not fully valued in the individual planning process (Simons 1993). One of the things that some users said to us was that sometimes individual planning meetings would take place in an area that was not private. The user's individual situation was being discussed, and anybody could walk in and out of the meeting and that made them feel very uncomfortable. As a general point, individual plans are important and valued but the way in which the individual planning process takes place is very important.

Annual reports: this is a particularly Welsh dimension in that the Welsh Office required the counties and services to submit annual reports in a fairly structured way until a few years ago. It helped those running services to think about what they were doing because it meant having to state objectives, progress achieved that year, lessons learnt, guidelines for the future, and so on. Although annual reports are no longer a requirement – they are not strictly evaluations – they are an important piece of data, and some counties are still using them. As services have proliferated, the Welsh Office has stopped requiring every service to produce annual reports. This is partly because it was not possible to deal with the volume of information collected, nor to aggregate it in any meaningful way, and so feedback could not be given to the services. That became quite frustrating for the staff who were working away doing quite a good detailed annual report, thinking about their objectives and their achievements – and then it went into a sort of 'black hole'.

Moving on: in a couple of places, there were special groups set up by the county to monitor and evaluate services. By and large, the group was quite a mixture: it would comprise planners from the county joint planning team, people running services, one or two staff from different levels of the service, and nearly always some users and some carers. Typically, there would be a sort of annual programme, and individual services would get picked on to be evaluated by representatives of this group. It was not done in a very systematic way. The group would go out and visit every selected service and spend two or three days there. Sometimes they would draw on existing published evaluation instruments, and at other times they would just go in and say, 'We will have a good look round and see what we think of the service and then write a report.'

There was certainly some value in doing these exercises. We found, for example, members of the county monitoring group were able to comment on things that were going on: such as the use of a staff diary in a house that users felt unhappy about – they did not like the way things were being recorded in this diary for everybody to see. In fact, it was not used in a particularly constructive way, so they are scrapping it.

It was quite difficult for these county evaluation and monitoring groups to gauge the perspective of users because nearly always they would go in and ask people, 'Are you happy here? Do you like it?', and they would usually get quite positive responses. Typically you find this: in that sort of situation, people will tend to say a positive thing; they will acquiesce.

We sometimes found problems also if these monitoring groups were not very clearly linked up with an executive power. Sometimes an evaluation group was quite separate from the planning and management group. The evaluation group would go and visit and make judgements about certain services or make recommendations; but, because it did not automatically have a way in to the management group that had executive power, the recommendations were not taken up. This could be frustrating.

Another thing that people sometimes said to us was that members of the monitoring groups had different perspectives – they were a mix of carers, managers and staff. Although they knew quite a lot about services, they did not have a standard format or a standard way of knowing what they should be going in and looking at. Though they were making quite sensible recommendations, they needed some framework that they could all be working to. As we went around, they often said to us that they valued the opportunity offered by the project. There was a certain hunger for guidance; perhaps for a way of legitimising many things that they were already doing.

Quite a number of the counties had initiated what we have described as internal surveys. For example, a respite care service might have decided that it wanted to do a survey of its users, using a fairly open-ended questionnaire about what they valued or did not value in the service. It asked for any kind of comment – any recommendation. You could describe this as a hotel-type survey where you get a form asking whether there is anything you particularly liked or did not like, any suggestions you would like to make. Sometimes these surveys were found useful but had not been implemented on any very systematic basis and certainly not comprehensively.

There were also structured evaluations going on. These used research tools, which were generated internally within the county. Quite a lot of them would employ an attached researcher, who might belong to the psychology department, say, who would usually go round using their own standard approach with a number of services in the county. In one county, for example, there was an occupational psychologist whose particular interest was in staff, staff satisfaction and staff attitudes and most of the evaluations were about this. In another county, there would be a different orientation, so the type of structured evaluation would be different. All of them are valuable in their own way, but it means you have different things being evaluated depending on the characteristics or professional background of the person who happened to be the evaluator. Sometimes, though, these evaluators were enormously valuable. An example of one: Barnardos came in and did a research project concerned with play schemes (not strictly to do with adults). They were very participative in the way that they set about their evaluation. They got parents and users to contribute to setting the agenda and the main questions at the very early stages. Some practical lessons were learned about how to set up a play scheme, of the development time that is needed, and the kind of work that is needed with parents and families to enable such a scheme to be really effective.

Moving on to other types of activity – in half the counties there were Quality Action Groups. Various different things are going on under the label 'Quality Action Groups'. Nearly all of them seem to have a limited life span, of around 18 months or two years. They seem to reach a peak of activity and then die down. Perhaps Quality Action Groups are most useful carrying out activity over a limited period of time. They were used in quite different ways in different areas. Some of them had turned into more of a support network for the group members. They helped people to establish themselves in groups, to find their identity, rather than achieving a lot in terms of quality assurance. Others of them have gone more for evaluation and have initiated surveys that they sometimes requisitioned others to carry out.

Some of the counties had what we call strategic quality action approaches. An example was one county that had a staff service development plan, a programme that all staff went through. So it was strategic in the sense that it did have an impact on procedures right across the county. In others, we found a kind of ideological value-based framework that underlay everything that happened within the county. There is one county in particular where they have a very strong social role valorisation/normalisation-type approach. It led to a uniquely common understanding across the county, within which there was a higher degree of consensus between staff on what they were about, I think, than anywhere else.

Inspection units: originally they were just looking at residential services that were being accredited by the county, but then their role was extended to in-house services provided by the county. Then, further, it was potentially extended to non-residential services and also beyond inspection and monitoring to development. Although we found to date that their potential has not been realised very much, there is actually a great deal of interest and enthusiasm for working out how they can extend their role into a much more developmental one, and particularly to working on quality.

Finally: external research. This is largely research from the two University-based units, the Mental Handicap in Wales Applied Research Unit in Cardiff (now the Welsh Centre for Learning Disabilities – Applied Research Unit), and the Centre for Social Policy Research and Development in Bangor. National projects from these research units tended to involve all the counties, who were obliged to participate. These were happening just about everywhere, though the counties had possibly less enthusiasm for them than they did for many of the other things.

Lessons Learned about Evaluation

From this trawl around the counties we felt that we had learned some lessons about what was useful and what was not useful locally.

First of all, it is necessary to be clear about what an evaluation is about. In some cases, a county monitoring group would be making a visit, and the people being evaluated felt enormously pressurised – because they did not really know why they were being evaluated. They did not know what the information was going to be used for, nor did they have any idea about what the methods would entail or what they would be expected to do. Just as a very first step, everybody who is involved – those on the receiving end, those participating to any extent – need to be informed about why the evaluation is taking place and what methods are going to be used – just so they know whether to be worried or not.

Rapid feedback: if there is a long time lag between evaluating, going in and asking questions and looking at things and the feedback, it is not going to mean anything. I think that is one of the criticisms of the external research. It would often take them two years to come back with the results and those evaluated would have forgotten what the thing was all about.

Having 'executive teeth': If evaluation information does not have an obvious 'channel' to those with executive power, so that it can make an impact, it is limited and can lead to immense frustration.

Disruptions to people: having a lot of people barging into your small house and asking a lot of questions and looking at things and talking can be disruptive. There is a trade-off really. I think that most of us would believe that, to some extent, going in and monitoring things is valuable; but obviously, if you do it too often, you can disrupt too many people too much, and that is counter-productive. It becomes no longer your home, but a place where evaluators tramp through all the time.

Researcher's style and orientation: depending on the particular bent of the psychologist or the department or whoever is in charge will make a difference to what you are likely to find. If you are hiring somebody to be a regular evaluator, you have to be very clear about the brief that is given to them and to make sure that you are hiring someone who has got the appropriate background and skills to carry out the sort of things that you actually want from them.

Involving people who use services: we have got a long way to go to get good at this in evaluating services. There were some evaluation approaches, where at least users were asked what they thought, but as I mentioned, it can be difficult to get genuine views. On the other hand, some approaches have begun to involve users in undertaking the evaluations, and I think that needs careful thought. Sometimes you will, for example, want to use a standard research format that you have been trained to use and a service user will go in as co-evaluator, along with the rest of the team. In a sense, that it is not terribly satisfactory either – because you are not using the skills and the perceptions of the people who are users in the best possible way. You may actually just be employing them as co-researchers and maybe not quite as good co-researchers as the rest of your team, but you think it is important to have them there. On the other hand, there are very special things that users can do: they have a unique perspective, they are able to talk to other users and often get them to say what they think, in the way that you or I might not be able to. They also might be able to help to set the initial questions, set the agenda for what the evaluation should be about before you even start. So thinking about how users should be involved in evaluation is an evolving process; I think we have not got there yet, but we are beginning to catch on to how to do it.

Process and content: something Alan Tyne said this morning (see Chapter 2) very much echoed our views about process and content. So far we have been dealing largely with the development of our instrument, with the *content* of the checklist. That is probably half – maybe even less than half – of the battle. The rest of it actually is the process of carrying the evaluation out; it is how you involve users, how you do the evaluation, who is involved, what kind of preparation the evaluators get before they go in there, what their understanding is of what it is all about – and then how you use that information when you have got it. Probably more than half of doing this evaluation work is the process; it is not just the content – something that will inevitably be a sort of checklist. People are very rude about checklists; but you have got to have something that lists out a number of items to be looked at. It is not the fact that it is there that is the problem – it is how you use it. It is whether you use it as a tick box without focusing enough on the process.

Devising a New Instrument to Measure Quality

Having been around and learnt about some of the things that were useful and some of the things that were not useful, we had to set out devising our own instrument to look at both content and quality. We said we must devise something that will give meaningful information in a single visit, that does not require repeated measures over a period of six months – that actually going in and doing it once will tell you something that you can use. It might also be useful to repeat it after a period of time to look for change.

There is a big advantage in the All-Wales Strategy having been over a ten-year period. There are lots of policy documents that have been written, that are there, that have a Welsh Office stamp on them, and that set out principles and policies and aims for services – much more explicitly than anything I have ever seen coming from England. So what we first did was to analyse all the documents and strategy for the ten-year period.

This led us to a list of about 40 principles; some of them are quite general and quite broad. For example: 'Everybody is an individual. All individuals are unique, services should be geared to individual needs and should not be offered as a standard pattern of support.' Some are quite specific. There is a circular that came out two years ago on accommodation and that will give you examples: 'People should have a key to their room and should be able to lock it if they wish.' Not surprisingly, as in a lot of policy documents, there is more written about accommodation than there is on any other kind of service. It seems we are better at saying what we want about accommodation than about other services; I think that this is part of the reason why the scores about which Paul Williams was talking earlier (see Chapter 5) tend to be higher on accommodation than on other aspects of services. It is that we have just thought about them more.

The other major source of 'yardsticks' was users' views. Our team member from Wales had a lot of contacts with facilitators from the self-advocacy movement and he contacted them first of all, saying, 'How we are going to do this?' What they said was, 'Why don't you start with what has been already said? We have actually had lots of meetings, lots of day seminars and conferences, and many of those have led to written and published accounts. Very often these quite good documents just go and sit on a shelf and gather dust, so why not pull those together and have a look at what they say before you start doing anything else?' So that is exactly what we did; we took documents that we could get our hands on immediately, particularly those from Welsh users, and, again, we pulled out of them the sets of principles, the things that users had fairly consistently said they wanted. In fact, because we used a number of sources, and there was a huge number of these principles, we took items that had been stated at least twice. The kind of things that came out of this were: 'I should have recognition of the things I do', 'People should give me recognition for things I can do', 'People should see me as a capable person and not always underestimate', 'Labels are for jars, not for people', 'I don't like being called mentally handicapped or mental anything', 'I should not have to travel every day in a vehicle marked "Ambulance" or "Social Services Department"', 'Proper wages for a proper job', 'If I am working, I should get proper wages, the going rate for the job', 'I should have exactly the same rights as other workers', 'Being treated with respect', 'Staff should show some respect and should take my opinions seriously', 'I should have a right to my point of view'.

Again, a list of about forty or so statements like this came out fairly consistently from user groups. So we listed all those out again, and we also put in one or two additional issues that people who knew a lot about evaluating services for people with learning difficulties (The Mental Handicap in Wales Unit, the National Development Team and the Norah Fry Research Unit) thought were particularly important. One example of the extra items was protection against sexual abuse.

Our next step was to examine the extent to which the two lists, from the policy statements and from the service users' publications, were similar. Although there were many similarities, there were also subtle differences between the two perspectives. There were also some areas on the users' list that were not covered in the policy list. These were primarily concerned with process rather than outcome, of how users were treated by other people.

Finally, we compared four instruments, including PASSING (Wolfensberger and Thomas 1983), that we had identified as being widely used, or as exerting considerable influence on the counties' development of their own evaluation tools. The other instruments were: the Service Review Package (Evans and Gray 1990), the Registered Homes Working Group (RHWG) inspection documents (1986), and *Homes are for Living In* (HAFLI)(DH 1989). All of the instruments addressed around half the items on each checklist, but they were slightly more likely to address the items on the list derived from the policy documents.

PASSING addressed rather more items than the other three instruments, about two-thirds. It was strongest in addressing items that were related to promoting ordinary lives. However, there were significant differences between the checklists and PASSING. 'Social image enhancement' was not as strong in either checklist as it is in PASSING. And service users attached much more importance to relationships between the users and staff than is found in PASSING.

We concluded from this analysis that these instruments were only partially adequate for evaluating service quality, or addressing the concerns of service users. The areas that none of the instruments addressed were: financial advice, help in getting a job, consumer involvement, support for carers (on policy checklist); and being allowed to make mistakes, advice on money matters, help with getting a job, voice in policy and planning (on users' checklist).

It is necessary to develop instruments which deal more comprehensively with all the dimensions of service quality. This we are doing in the next stage of the project, building on the foundation provided by the existing instruments.

References

Department of Health (1989) *Homes Are For Living In*. London: HMSO.

Evans, G. and Gray, P. (1990) *Service Review Package*. Developed for Opportunity Housing Trust.

McGrath, M. Grant, G. and Ramcharan, P. (1991) *Service Packages: Factors Influencing Carers' Appraisals of Intermediate Outcomes*. Bangor: Centre for Social Policy Research and Development (CSPRD).

Registered Homes Working Group (1986) *Inspection Documents For Homes For Elderly People*.

Simons, K. (1993) *Sticking Up for Yourself: The Experience of Those Involved in Self-Advocacy for People with Learning Difficulties*. Bristol: Norah Fry Research Centre.

Welsh Office (1991) *The Review of the All-Wales Strategy: A View from the Users*.

Wolfensberger, W. and Thomas, S. (1983) *Programme Analysis of Service Systems' Implementation of Normalization Goals: Normalization Criteria and Ratings Manual*, 2nd edition. Toronto: National Institute on Mental Retardation.

Part 3

Perspectives on Quality

Chapter 11

QUARTZ, PASSING and User Involvement
Meeting Points and Departure Points

Stephen Pilling

Introduction

QUARTZ is a comprehensive quality assurance system developed primarily for use in mental health services providing continuing care services[1] (Clifford, Leiper, Lavender and Pilling 1989, Leiper, Pilling and Lavender 1992a, b, Leiper, Lavender, Pilling and Clifford 1992). It was developed at the Sainsbury Centre for Mental Health (formerly Research and Development for Psychiatry) but has a potential application across a range of continuing care groups beyond mental health. QUARTZ has been subject to an extensive pilot in a wide range of mental health services. This chapter provides an overview of the rationale, development and main components of the system. It also considers the development of user involvement and reviews the similarities with and differences from PASS/ING (concentrating on the updated instrument PASSING; Wolfensberger and Thomas 1983), the two major themes of the conference from which this book emerged.

The QUARTZ system has been subject to an extensive evaluation reported elsewhere (Leiper and Hill 1993). In this regard QUARTZ is one of the few quality assurance systems that has been the subject of a formal evaluation. The central concern of the evaluation was achieving positive change in the quality of the services provided. The evaluation showed positive change in 55% to 69% of

---

1 A copy of the QUARTZ schedules and associated manuals can be obtained from: Pavilion Publishing, 42 Lansdowns Place, Hove BN3 1HH. Tel: 01273–821650.
  Enquiries concerning the development and training in use of the QUARTZ system should be addressed to: Sainsbury Centre for Mental Health, 134–138 Borough High Street, London SE1 1LB. Tel: 0171–403 8790.

services depending on the measures used. QUARTZ focuses explicitly on changing the quality of services, and implementation so far has been limited. PASSING, with much more widespread usage, has broader aims. Training of staff is as prominent a goal as service change. (No doubt this training may of itself exert a positive force for service change.) However, despite this widespread implementation, little formal evaluation of PASSING has occurred (Lindley and Wainwright 1992), an exception being the work described at this conference. This absence of work with a clear focus on quality assurance inevitably limits the comparisons of the two systems. Nevertheless they are links, not least in the content of the QUARTZ schedules, some of which was influenced by PASSING's predecessor, PASS (Wolfensberger and Glenn 1975).

The QUARTZ System

QUARTZ is primarily a process measure and is well described elsewhere (Clifford *et al*. 1989, Leiper, Pilling and Lavender 1992a, b, Leiper *et al*. 1992).

This section briefly describes the development and structure of the system. The development of QUARTZ began with two questions specifically concerned with service quality:

- *What characterises quality services?*
  Quality services can be said to have a clear conception of their task, an appropriate selection and delivery of the care provided. They also pay attention to users' quality of life, demonstrate good team functioning and show clear evidence of integration of the service within the overall care system. It is not difficult to find agreement on these characteristics of good quality services among mental health professionals or service users (Shepherd 1984, Clifford *et al*. 1989). Unfortunately, it is just as easy to identify services where these characteristics are absent in part or whole.

This leads to a second question:

- *If it is a straightforward matter to gain agreement on what constitutes quality services, why does it seem so difficult to provide quality services?*
  There are several factors that contribute to the difficulty in developing and maintaining quality services. They include poor quality staff or training, a lack of management direction, poor care management systems, a lack of awareness or knowledge of appropriate care functions, poor team functioning, and a lack of involvement of clients and carers. Again it is not difficult to add to the list or gain agreement on it. However, it is difficult to identify the precise contribution of each of these factors – there is obviously a complex interaction. In the development of QUARTZ it therefore seemed essential that the system must acknowledge this complexity. The complexity is best addressed through a system that concentrates primarily on process-orientated methodology rather than on outcomes. Failure to address this complexity through excessive concentration on one method (for example external evaluations, user involvement or standard setting),

whilst neither addressing nor acknowledging other aspects of the system, will not achieve positive change.

A review of the existing systems for audit and quality assurance (Clifford *et al.* 1989) identified a number of components that are important in any good audit or quality assurance system. These include:

1. An element of both internal and external review. This means that direct care staff involved in providing the care are also involved in evaluating its quality and its outcome. However, to simply leave this to internal review can, and often does, lead to the avoidance of difficulties, concentration on internal matters and a lack of attention to the wider service system. To require an external element of review is not to promote an inspectorial model, but to insist that the relationship to the wider system, including service-user groups, carers groups and other agencies, is carefully considered.

2. The active involvement of clinicians, carers and management If systems are to be successful they need to engage and promote ownership of the system by direct carers and clinical staff. However, without the support of the management a system is of little value. The interests of both groups (which of course are broadly the same) must be considered if a destructive carer–management split is to be avoided.

3. The system should be an objective setting-based system that acknowledges the multi-faceted nature of the service provided. Objectivity could be provided through appropriate schedules and the promotion of realistic and specific goals. The implication for QUARTZ is that settings (i.e. wards, community teams, group homes) are the proper focus, rather than professional groups. Of course, such settings may be multi-disciplinary, uni-disciplinary or multi-agency. The need to consider comprehensively the service provided means acknowledging and promoting the involvement of users and carers as well as external agencies with a legitimate interest in the care provided.

The Components of the QUARTZ System

In the discussion so far of the QUARTZ system, little mention has been made of values which are, of course, central to PASSING and social role valorisation. Alan Tyne (Chapter 2) in describing normalisation identified three key principles or basic values that he felt underpinned the theory of normalisation; they were justice, stewardship and community. While the QUARTZ system makes no explicit statement of value, its values (Clifford *et al.* 1989) are implicit and are congruent with those expressed by Alan Tyne. Simply stated, QUARTZ is a system that recognises and seeks to promote the rights of individuals to a caring and effective service. It also provides a vehicle for the expression of the duty on all to ensure that the resources and the services they support are monitored and evaluated in a proper manner. It also intends to promote a sense of community through the development of a dialogue between professionals, service users and the wider community. Such an intention may be a forlorn hope but if no talking takes place and no dialogue develops then it is a safe bet that services will not improve. To the extent that these values are made real through QUARTZ, the system will be successful. The system does not, however, promote explicitly a particular theory or ideology nor does it prescribe particular activities. However, it demands that there be 'model coherence' (a notion borrowed from normalisation), which is viewed as the consistent and coherent application of theory and practice in the development and delivery of a service.

The QUARTZ system has two key components:

1. *Quality Review Team (or Person/s)*

QUARTZ can be implemented by a Quality Review Team (QRT) (comprised of a group of individuals drawn together specifically for the purpose), by an individual working alone or by a looser collection of individuals than the QRT described below. (A fuller description of the method of implementation is given in Leiper, Pilling and Lavender 1992a.) As the pilot referred to above operated with QRTs this method will be described; what follows about the QRT and its operation are broadly applicable to an individual or loose collection of individuals working with the QUARTZ system.

QRTs in the pilot services were composed of a group of senior staff drawn from the services under review. (However, it should be noted that in a number of services where QUARTZ currently operates services users have been trained as QRT members.) Whatever the precise composition it is important that the QRT is representative of all stakeholders. The group must not be defined in a narrow professional manner so that it is comprised entirely of service or professional heads. Personal credibility with direct care staff and service users and the skills needed to do the job are the essential requirements. The QRT is neither inspectorial nor managerial; it stands to the side of the management system. To give an example from one pilot site (a health service setting) the QRT consisted of a psychologist, a consultant psychiatrist, two social workers (one from the hospital team, one from a locality team that manages a community care facilities), the co-ordinator of a local voluntary group, a senior housing worker from a group home in the district, the CPN team leader, the manager of a mental health centre and the unit professional advisor for nursing. In other settings there has tended to be a higher representation of more junior staff, more voluntary sector workers and, in a limited number of cases, service users.

In its composition a QRT may or may not differ much from those participating in PASSING workshops or evaluations. However, the constituency from which a QRT is drawn will potentially vary greatly. QRT members will be drawn from the wider service system that they are to evaluate/monitor, although this need not and probably will not be the case for a PASSING evaluation in the majority of cases. This obviously has very different implications for the relation of the groups to the wider service system, for the approach to the work undertaken, the reports provided and the level and potential impact of the work on the service under review. Both methods will be appropriate in different settings, but if used as a routine quality assurance tool it is likely that PASSING will need considerable adaptation as indicated, for example, by Lindley and Wainwright (1992).

2. The Schedules

A QRT member, as a delegate of the QRT, is responsible for facilitating a setting's quality review. The process of the review is guided by a series of schedules and an accompanying manual (Leiper, Pilling and Lavender 1992a, b, Leiper *et al.* 1992). The QRT acts as advisor and supervisor to the team member, and a coordination point for the work of all team members. As such it has obvious advantages over individuals working alone or a less structured group of individuals. The schedules are grouped under four categories and are listed in Table 11.1.

As can be seen from the Table there is a total of 14 schedules. The majority of the schedules relate directly to the services provided to users and rely largely on staff to provide information about services. However, one schedule, 4.4 Users' Views, is specifically concerned with the views of users. This schedule has two parts. Part A is essentially an audit of a setting's methods and motives for user involvement. It attempts to help a setting understand what can be or has been gained from user involvement. For some settings this may reveal serious gaps in their systems of user involvement and consultation or identify areas where further work is needed on staff attitudes. For others it may mean the refinement and enhancement of existing systems. Part B is concerned with direct user consultation and is the least prescriptive of all the schedules. It describes a number of approaches, including questionnaire-based surveys, individual interviews, group meetings, the use of advocacy services and linking with existing user representative groups (e.g. Patients' Councils), all of which may be used to facilitate the collection of user views.

Table 11.1 QUARTZ schedules

Service resources	External links
1.1 *Staffing Resources*	2.1 *Community Links*
A Composition of Staff Team	A Acceptance by Community
B Staffing Levels	B Integration with Community
C Staff Retention	C Participation by Community
1.2 *Financial Resources*	2.2 *Agency Links*
A Budget – Information/Procedures	A Significance of Links
B Budget – Structure/Adequacy	B Communication/Co-ordination
1.3 *Environmental Quality*	2.3 *Relations with Management*
A External Features	A Perceptions of Management
B Client Facilities	B Management Structure
C Therapy/Work Facilities	C Functional Relationship
D Staff Facilities	with Management
E Overall Internal Environment	D Management's Views
F Personal Security and Safety	
	2.4 *Professional Support*
	A Supportive Relationships
	B Training

Working practices	Service provision
3.1 Policy and Procedures	*4.1 Service Utilisation*
A Service Aims	A Information Systems
B Referral/Selection/Admission	B Service Usage
C Programme Planning	C Service Information Profile
D Case Co-ordination	
E Service Review	*4.2 Service Programme*
	A Crisis Stabilisation
3.2 Team Work	B Advocacy
A Team Functioning	C Personal Care Skills
B Meeting Structure	D Domestic Skills
C Meeting Functioning	E Social/Relationship Skills
D Team Working	F Community Functioning Skills
E Leadership/Co-ordination	G Leisure Use Skills
	H Vocational/Work Skills
3.3 Users' Lives	I Educational Skills
A Regulation of Client Activity	J Challenging Behaviours
B Staff/Client Relationships	K Health Care
	L Mental Health – Medication
	M Mental Health – Psychological
	N Mental Health – Substance Abuse
	O External Resources and Supports
	4.3 Individual Care
	A Individual Case Review
	B Case Work
	4.4 Users' Views
	A User Consultation
	B User Feedback

It is not intended that all these schedules be used in any one review. Typically four to seven will be selected arising out of an initial discussion between the QRT member and the staff team. This selection may or may not include user views but in the majority of the schemes so far reviewed Users' Views was chosen. Other services may choose to make the incorporation of user views a requirement.

The purpose of the schedules is to offer the possibility of a comprehensive quality review to a setting. This is achieved through the provision of a structure to examine all aspects of a setting's work. Whatever schedules are used, all information collected is fed back to the staff team highlighting both the strengths and weaknesses of the service. When all the information has been collated and fed back the final stage of the review takes place. This is a goal-setting exercise where all involved in the review meet with the QRT member and generate a list of action goals aimed at improving or maintaining service quality. The feedback from the schedules and the action goals generated form the basis of the setting's quality report. Invariably dates are attached to goals and a cyclical process of review is established.

As can be seen from the above description the QUARTZ system is primarily a staff-based system of quality assurance. The rationale for this has not grown out of tradition, ignorance or contempt for user views. It is based on the belief that in virtually all services the staff of those settings are the primary determinants of the quality of care provided and therefore need to be at the centre of any QA system if there is to be lasting positive change. Nevertheless, a healthy system cannot depend solely on staff if it is to survive: it requires a culture to be established which values and promotes the development of quality. This is primarily the responsibility of management, but users can and should be involved in the promotion and development of that culture.

As can be seen from the above discussion the content of QUARTZ and PASSING varies considerably. PASSING concentrates on two major areas: social image and personal competency. Each of these two areas is then further divided into three areas looking at the physical setting, the ways in which services group individuals and structure their relationships, and the ways in which services structure activities and the use of time. This gives a 42 item questionnaire, the majority of items being concerned with social image. A PASSING evaluation requires all items to be completed. In contrast QUARTZ consists of 14 different schedules, grouped under four major headings: Service Resources, External Links, Working Practices and Service Provision. No schedule specifically addresses the issue of social image but those covering Environmental Quality (1.3) and Community Links (2.1) have been most influenced by the concerns of normalisation theory with social image. Those schedules included under Service Provision are most directly concerned with personal competency. In addition to these areas QUARTZ places considerable emphasis on the operational functioning of a service and team operations. The relationship to the external world, in particular the management system, also receives considerable attention. These differences, which are considerable, reflect the very different origins, aims and outcomes of the two systems. In large part because of its lack of direct emphasis on staff and team functioning, PASSING is unlikely to have structured a review of, or feedback on, a service in a way that will promote effective change.

The use of the QUARTZ system, unlike PASSING, involves considerable choice being exercised by reviewer and the setting staff. No such choice exists with PASSING: all items are used. QUARTZ typically relies on a single reviewer, although group reviews are possible; in contrast, PASSING is a group exercise. Both, however, use group discussion away from the immediate service context to help guide the work of the reviewer/evaluator. The nature of the reviewer's contact with the service is more consistent and clearly prescribed in PASSING. Central to the process is direct experience of the service as received by users. While such an approach is possible with QUARTZ, it is not essential – it is the experience of the staff group that is central to the process. Both stress strongly the qualitative nature of the enterprise (at least in the way in which PASSING is implemented in this country; see Williams, Chapter 5, p.74) and largely avoid a quantitative rating. Although it is possible to produce a global rating of services from PASSING (see Williams, Chapter 5) such a rating must be of limited value in identifying and promoting areas for change.

The systems differ greatly in the way feedback is generated and the form in which it is fed back. QUARTZ places a strong emphasis on the staff role in developing the feedback, in processing and in generating the final report. In contrast, feedback with PASSING is a much more reviewer-led activity. Both systems can of course be valid, according to circumstance, but it is probable that a system which actively involves staff in the generation of reports and feedback is more likely to ensure ownership of the final report and thereby enhance the possibility of positive change.

Finally, QUARTZ is intended to be part of a continuing process of review and evaluation. Such a possibility exists with PASSING but this is not an explicit requirement. The reliance largely on teams of external reviewers and the training requirements raise questions about the feasibility of the repeated use of PASSING as a quality assurance tool. Both systems are, however, concerned with the development of better services and any method that can achieve effectively this should be supported. Both have their limitations in this respect: for PASSING not all the training has successful outcomes (McGill and Emerson 1992); for QUARTZ even where there has been successful piloting associated with positive change there are problems in ensuring continued implementation and uptake (Grover 1993).

User Involvement

There are two primary methods by which users can be involved with the QUARTZ system. The first, already described above, is through the direct feedback of their views of the services by participation in the review. The second is concerned with the developmental and facilitative role that users can develop. This could take a number of forms with regard to QUARTZ. It can include providing advocates for users who need assistance to participate in the feedback process. Alternatively, users may facilitate the establishment of a forum for the obtaining of user views. Users or user groups may be represented on groups charged with steering through the implementation of a QUARTZ system. Finally, users can be involved as reviewers through membership of a QRT, thereby acting as reviewers of services.

The broad structures and possibilities for user involvement have been set out above. Something of the experience of engaging users in the process can be obtained from the four examples given below. They show something of the strengths and weaknesses of QUARTZ as means of promoting user involvement. They are a non-selected sample from a series of reviews in which the author participated. For those readers familiar with PASSING they should enable some further comparison to be made between the two systems.

1 A Psychiatric Day Hospital
This 40 place unit had a well-established staff group and was generally regarded as a good service. The reviewer, who had good contacts with local user groups, had completed a number of schedules with the staff before approaching the

Patients' Council in the Day Hospital. The reviewer felt that a number of important issues had arisen in the course of the review work with the staff that required user comment and involvement. There followed a discussion with the Council of the issues so far identified and to these were added issues raised by the Council. Considerable discussion of the most effective way to obtain the views of a large patient group (fifty plus), many of whom did not attend the Patients' Council, followed. Eventually it was decided to develop a brief (15 item) questionnaire for distribution to all patients. Further discussion then ensued with regard to the responsibility for the distribution of the questionnaire; it was impractical for the reviewer, and both staff and Patients' Council felt their roles might be compromised by getting involved in the distribution of the question- naire. Eventually with the help of a few members of the Council the issue was resolved and the questionnaires were distributed. (A total of 25 responses to the 50 questionnaires sent out was received.)

A number of issues emerged from the survey that were to find their way into the final quality report. The first concerned the lack of privacy in the unit for day patients, the second focused on the need for specific advice on Welfare Rights and the third identified the need for the Patients' Council to develop a better link with the local Users' Forum. Interestingly, the day hospital staff had been convinced that patients received a very poor service from their general practitio- ners, a view they were sure that the patients would share. The survey revealed widespread satisfaction with GPs, a result that, despite the difficulty in interpret- ing the results of such surveys, led to a re-examination of the unit's relationship with GPs. In addition to the clear goals identified, the process of increasing user involvement and consultation had a positive impact on the service.

2 Staffed Group Home I

This was a much smaller setting than the day hospital and so a different method of consultation was chosen. Again the initial stage consisted of the completion of some schedules with the staff group. This proved useful for both staff and reviewer in thinking about the issues that it would be important to discuss with users. The users were informed about progress with the review and then were asked about how they wished to be involved. All wanted to be interviewed about the project, both to discuss with the reviewer the questions that had arisen in the discussion with the staff as well as their own concerns. Three people chose to meet with the reviewer as a group; the remaining four people wanted to be interviewed individually. Some specific concerns emerged from these inter- views. Some, such as locks on bedroom doors and a home visitors policy, had already been identified through the work with staff and the discussion with users centred on clarification of the issues so that clear action plans could be developed which had the support of all involved. One issue not identified in discussion with staff centred on the lack of structured activity in the house. This desire for structured activity ran contrary to the staff view that it was desirable for most activity to take place outside the house. This led to the most useful outcome of the review in that it pushed the staff and the residents into a discussion about policy that was needed but had not so far taken place. Finally, the residents complained about the lack of information on and explanation of their illnesses and the treatment given by professionals outside the home. It was agreed that staff would assist the residents in obtaining this information by whatever means seemed appropriate.

3 Staffed Group Home II

In this six-person group home, consultation with users followed a similar pattern to that of the group home described above with a mix of individual and group interviews. The project had been open for some time and the physical state of the building was deteriorating and considerable dissatisfaction with this was expressed by the users that echoed a theme from the work with the staff. The review provided a useful context in which the views of both users and staff came together and strengthened the setting in its discussions with managers for increased resources. The major issue that emerged from the interviews with users centred on the staff's involvement in the house. The staff and management of the setting were very concerned to preserve and promote the setting as the home of the residents and as a consequence avoided any activity in the house other than was deemed to be absolutely necessary. For example, despite the presence of an office in the group home, all paperwork was done at the agency's head office. However, it emerged from the interviews that the residents liked having staff around and very much wanted the office to be used for paperwork etc. This led to further discussions in the house about the nature of the relationship between staff and residents in a way which had not occurred before despite regular meetings and a sound relationship between staff and residents.

4 A Psychogeriatric Day Hospital

The final example chosen raises a number of interesting issues about user involvement. It was not a successful review as a final report was not produced. This was primarily due to major changes in management structure during the review of the setting. Four out of five of the senior managers responsible for the service changed posts during the course of the review and it was impossible to provide the continuity required for a successful review. Nevertheless the majority of the review was completed although the 'Users' Views' schedule was not. It might be assumed that this was the result of management changes, but the majority of the management changes occurred after the schedules were chosen. Alternatively, the cognitive state of the users of the service could be the explanation; for example, many could have been suffering from dementia and so would have had considerable problems in contributing effectively. However, an examination of the Service Utilisation schedule showed this not to be the case. This, of course, raises an immediate concern about the possible stereotyping of older people, and the lack of consultation is worrying from that point of view alone. However, it also raises an additional question, who are the users of this service? In a setting with the explicit goal of providing a respite service should not carers and families be seen as users of services? This, of course, raises the further question as to how much families and other carers are also users of other mental health services. The challenge for QUARTZ and other QA systems identified in this example is to develop systems that can engage users in some way, however severe the nature of their disability, and also engage carers where appropriate in the reviewing of service quality.

As indicated earlier QUARTZ has been subject to a detailed evaluation reported elsewhere (Leiper and Hill 1993). However, for the purposes of this chapter it may be helpful to report the views expressed by users of services on the QUARTZ system to QRT members and the research worker responsible for the data collection (Hill 1993). In all the settings in the pilot phase there has been positive feedback from users. The general feeling of users was one of validation of their views and pleasure from involvement in the review of services designed to serve them. The staff also reported valuing user involvement and in most cases it appeared to stimulate a fresh dialogue between users and staff.

Conclusion

QUARTZ is a comprehensive quality assurance system that addresses both directly and indirectly the services provided to users. It is primarily a staff-based system but a number of schedules address users' concerns and user involvement. It is a process-orientated measure and demands considerable management and staff commitment. In the pilot phase QUARTZ has been valued by the majority of staff and users who have been involved.

The examples above show that QUARTZ is able to engage the concerns of users in a real and meaningful way. In all the cases described above, where the outcome was positive, it can be argued that the major contribution of the system has been to extend and develop a dialogue between staff and users. In doing so QUARTZ points to the key area in developing user involvement in services; the need for staff and users to talk to each other about the difficulties that they face in delivering and receiving mental health services.

QUARTZ is one of a number of tools available for quality assurance and evaluation. It was developed primarily in the field of mental health but it is already being used with a wide range of other care groups. It is, however, not a panacea and there are limits to its use. It is hoped that the preceding pages have given some indication of the range of its effective use and how its use contrasts with evaluations using PASSING. It is specifically designed as a quality assurance tool for regular and routine use in mental health services. It does not require the use of resources in addition to those available to most services. Nor does it demand training that cannot be provided in-house, although such training will benefit from outside facilitation and advice. As such it has considerable advantages over PASSING as a tool for routine and regular use.

Summary of Discussion

The discussion centred on two related issues: whether the QUARTZ system is value-free, and whether the values of the review team would affect the evaluation report.

Is QUARTZ Value-Relative?

David Felce asked if QUARTZ was value-relative, if values were established in terms of the goals and ambitions of the service providers. Would this mean that a village-community, which provided 'asylum' in the best sense of the word, activities that provide satisfaction and fulfilment, but away from the mainstream, would be assessed in a positive way in QUARTZ?

Stephen Pilling thought this was so. But he thought there were elements of QUARTZ which would also challenge a service like that, make it think about issues. Also implicit in QUARTZ was an incremental position, that you help to clarify and build on what is good, and leave challenge to the next time.

Influence of the Values of the Review Team on the Report

DF said that this led to a related question, the values of individuals in the review team. They did not leave these at the door, so that choice of team might be central to what the report says. Another delegate raised the question of it being more difficult if the team came from the same service. SP thought there were advantages and disadvantages. The relationship with the setting might be indirect, and a person would not look at the setting in which they work. There could be tension, but also a sense of ownership and involvement. Another delegate asked if there were any guidelines in the QUARTZ manuals about representativeness of the review team. SP said that there was emphasis on this, but it could be more explicit.

References

Clifford, P., Leiper, R., Lavender, A. and Pilling, S. (1989) *The Quartz System: Assuring Quality In Mental Health Settings.* London: RDP/Free Associations.

Grover, R. (1993) Personal communication.

Hill, R. (1993) Personal communication.

Leiper, R and Hill, R. (1993) *Evaluating Quality Assurance: an empirical programme evaluation of the pilot implementation of the QUARTZ system.* London: RDP/Sainsbury Centre for Mental Health.

Leiper, R., Pilling, S. and Lavender, T. (1992a) *Implementing a Quality Review System.* Brighton: Pavilion Publishing/RDP.

Leiper, R., Pilling, S. and Lavender, T. (1992b) *Using the QUARTZ Schedules.* Brighton: Pavilion Publishing/RDP.

Leiper, R., Lavender, A., Pilling, S. and Clifford, P. (1992) *The QUARTZ Schedules.* Brighton: Pavilion Publishing/RDP.

Lindley, P. and Wainwright, T. (1992) Normalisation training: conversion or commitment. In H. Brown and H. Smith (eds) *Normalisation: A Reader for the Nineties.* London: Routledge.

McGill, P. and Emerson, E. (1992) Normalisation and applied behaviour analysis: values and technology in human services. In H. Brown and H. Smith (eds) *Normalisation: A Reader for the Nineties.* London: Routledge.

Shepherd, G. (1984) *Institutional Care and Rehabilitation.* London: Longman.

Wolfensberger, W. and Glenn, L. (1975) *PASS 3: Program Analysis of Service System., Field Manual,* 3rd edition. Toronto: National Institute on Mental Retardation.

Wolfensberger, W. and Thomas, S. (1983) *PASSING: Program Analysis of Service Systems' Implementation of Normalization Goals.* Toronto: National Institute of Mental Retardation.

Chapter 12

What Do Users Think About Quality?

Peter Lindley, Jim Band, Bill Gorf, Margaret Guerrero,
Dale Walker and Kath Gillespie Sells

This chapter is in two parts. The first part, by the first five authors looks at what service is, from the perspective of users of mental health services. Kath Gillespie Sells was invited to contribute to the conference to give the perspective of people with physical disabilities, and the second part of the chapter consists of her contribution.

A. MENTAL HEALTH SERVICE USERS' PERSPECTIVE

These notes were compiled by Peter Lindley from contributions by Margaret Guerrero and Bill Gorf of the Lewisham Users Forum and Dale Walker and Jim Band of the Medway Users Forum. They are all members of the South East Training and Consultancy Co-operative. This is a new service development agency set up and run by users and ex-users to provide the users' perspective on all aspects of service development and training in the mental health field. The notes come, not only from the conference presentations made but also from notes of meetings held to discuss and prepare for the conference. Although they are personal views and do not necessarily represent the opinions of the organisations that they belong to, the people concerned have between them many years experience of using mental health services and many years involvement in the user movement where they are continually struggling with the issues they have raised with other users. So, these are not only their views but are opinions that have been shaped by hundreds of other people who are equally critical of mental health services. These opinions, conflicting as they do with the current wisdom of service providers, are *rooted in the experiences of people on the receiving end of services* and as such cannot be dismissed as cranky or inaccurate.

Peter Lindley works at the Tizard Centre, at the University of Kent.

Users and Quality

The original title of our presentation was 'The Insider's view of quality'. Initially we thought that this was a good title but on reflection following the conference decided to change it because in our view service users almost always feel on the outside of the system looking in, not part of it, feeling obliged to accept whatever is offered. Only the staff and service providers who are truly insiders have the real power to make changes. Thankfully this situation is changing. Slowly but surely user forums, Patients' Councils and the three national User networks are making sure that the voices of users are listened to.

No matter what kind of services are at issue or the extent of the disability of the people using them, service users can and should set the agenda for assessing all aspects of quality. This includes not only deciding upon the quality standards that services should aim to achieve but also making a contribution to the methods, processes and assessment schedules used to collect information and assess quality. Even people who are very ill or institutionalised have opinions about the help or lack of help that they receive. It may be hard for them to express these opinions but given time, respect and sympathetic help they can and will have a lot to say. Very few people need to rely on others to speak for them. With a little help and imagination it is possible to help most people, even those without physical speech, to express themselves. Any quality assurance system that does not take account of the users' perspective in its design and use is a *quality assurance system not worth having* and regrettably this is probably so for most of those on the market at present.

What Do Users Mean by Quality Assurance?

When we say much quality assurance is a matter of common sense most professionals we know shake their head and say 'but it's a very complicated business'. Whilst we accept that it is not easy to spell out what a good quality assurance system does in a way that everybody would agree with, we cannot accept that quality assurance has to be as complicated as some of the QA packs on the market suggest. Even the most highly trained professional has to go away on expensive special courses to learn how to use this material that supposedly is central to service provision. Many packs and forms are totally incomprehensible to most users and goodness help those of us who are unable to see, hear, read and write or have trouble learning. This surely cannot be right. The materials, manuals, schedules, forms and questionnaires have to be accessible and understandable by all of us, as do the processes, meetings, workshops, reviews and audit groups that they recommend. We often wonder what service providers did to make sure that things went smoothly before quality assurance!

As far as we are concerned quality assurance can best be defined as: approaches to ensuring that services achieve what they are supposed to achieve or say they are achieving for the people they serve (see Table 12.1).

These approaches should always be collaborative and never exclude users. If users cannot understand them or use them easily and simply or they exclude some users then they are unsatisfactory and need to be changed. Although we are mainly interested in quality assurance in mental health services it is important to point out that we do not know of any approaches that are accessible or even currently under consideration that are presented in languages other than English or in mediums that do not require people to be able to read and write to a very high standard.

Table 12.1 What is quality assurance?

QA ensures

- that services meet the common basic needs that we all share
- that people who rely on services are protected from abuse and exploitation
- service providers collaborate with users to develop and use approaches to setting and monitoring standards that are acceptable to everybody
- regular independent monitoring and evaluation not only by professionals but also by users
- that all aspects of QA including findings are in the public domain, that nothing is hidden or secret or available to staff only
- that staff challenge routine and traditional practices to offer the best service they can
- that services respond to the additional needs of women and people from minority ethnic backgrounds.

A good quality assurance system should enable both service providers and users to be able to see unambiguously to what extent the service is meeting the common basic needs that we all share; that people are protected from abuse and exploitation and that scarce resources are used effectively for patient care and not for administrators' carpets. Quality is also about access to information and users are very often denied or prevented from gaining access to information in subtle ways. Recently one of us wanted to use the hospital library to do research for the local User group. He was advised that the hospital was very happy to allow this to happen and even wanted to encourage it but that unfortunately there would have to be a subscription of fifty pounds a year. This may not seem much to people receiving a wage but to a someone living on benefits this is a fortune. We should add that most User groups would not be able afford this. Most don't have funding to spare and many had none at all when they first started up.

Now we all agree that user involvement is a good thing and we all want to do what we can to encourage it at all levels in services, right up to the very top. A good quality assurance system should also reflect this concern and ask questions and enable discussion about the extent to which services encourage and support user involvement at all levels of the organisation. We are sure that we all also agree that users and user groups can be a pain in the neck. They can slow things down when you want to speed things up and just when you think you have reached agreement with them on a particular policy they change their mind. This can be inconvenient and irritating but what is also clear is that services that support user groups are more likely to be offering the kind of service that users want and need and are amongst the most innovative and exciting for staff to work in. So user involvement in quality assurance is not only good for users but it is also good for staff, particularly staff who want to be challenged to provide the highest possible standards of care.

Collecting Information

As we are sure you are all aware, there are some ways of asking for things that are more likely to lead to a response than others. For example, endless poorly designed questionnaires, with tiny print and little space to write a reply, will obviously produce a poorer response than a more personal relaxed confidential conversation. Most users are convinced that the current crop of 'Quality of Life' measures serve only to remind people how poor services actually are at focusing on needs that really matter. People who rely on services to meet most, and sometimes all, of their needs are unlikely to speak up about abuse and bad practice because victimisation and abuse is a fact in services that is not going to go away overnight. So there are some kinds of feedback that the people using a service find very hard if not impossible to give to staff. This is also so if the information is presented in a way that identifies them.

We have recently been involved in a number of service reviews and were continually being told by the people we interviewed that they found it much easier to confide in another user, particularly when their opinions were critical of the staff and services. We would like to recommend to you that there is an important role for users on quality review teams as well as in providing advice and consultation on the content and design of assessment schedules.

Abuse

Even though there is plenty of evidence that demonstrates that all kinds of abuses of people – sexual, physical and psychological – happen in services, this is very rarely explicitly taken account of or addressed in quality assurance systems. No useful purpose is saved by denying that this is so or hoping that abuse will go away or cannot happen in the services that you work for. One of the major barriers to detecting and dealing with abuse is believing that it cannot happen here or not being prepared to address it publicly. Some people are more prone to abuse, and we have good ideas about who these people might be (see Table 12.2).

Table 12.2 Abuse in services

- Abuse in services happens and will not go away.
- Some people are more prone to abuse than others, e.g. older, more handicapped people, women, people from ethnic minority backgrounds.
- Complaints systems very rarely bring abuse to light.
- QA systems should explicitly address abuse in services.
- QA systems should protect staff and users who speak up about abuse and bad practice.

Services very rarely explicitly recognise or make provision to meet the additional needs of women for protection from abuse, for women-only services, and very few of the QA systems we know of take account of this.

We also know that complaints systems rarely work well. In many major scandals in mental illness and handicap hospitals the abuses were not brought to light by well organised and accessible complaints systems but by courageous junior staff who, having exhausted the complaints systems and achieved little, 'blew the whistle' and went public or took the complaints to very senior people outside of the hospital concerned. Senior people in services very rarely bring abuse to light and often don't believe that it is happening. It seems that the more senior you are the more likely you are to want to deal with abuse in a way that keeps it out of the public eye. This, of course, restricts the opportunities that we have to learn how to deal with it more effectively.

Complaints Systems

Most users we know would agree that effective complaints systems are an important feature of any approach to quality assurance. Unfortunately, most users we know would also agree that complaints systems rarely work and when they do work it is often to the advantage of the service provider. Our experience of making complaints is that we are very rarely believed – our critical opinions of staff, of procedures and practices, of services in general are often dismissed as 'part of our problem' or are thought unreliable because we are after all 'mentally ill' whilst the opinions of staff are almost always referred to as evidence. Even serious complaints are investigated internally by colleagues of the staff concerned. On occasions interviews concerning complaints are conducted in the presence of staff who are the subject of complaints. Some of us have experienced a change for the worse in the services we receive following complaints against staff which were upheld. It is also worth pointing out that the investigations into complaints are rarely published and as far as we know hospital and authorities do not produce annual summaries of numbers of complaints dealt with and their outcomes.

Electro-Convulsive Therapy

Many service users feel very strongly about the use of ECT. Hardly anybody we know supports its use or speaks positively of their experiences of having received ECT. There is a massive and growing user lobby calling for very strict controls and limits on its use and for a complete ban on its use with children. There is no user lobby to make ECT more widely available and increasingly professionals are speaking against it.

Ernest Hemingway wrote about having ECT:

> What's the sense of ruining my head and erasing my memory and putting me out of business. It was a brilliant cure but we lost the patient. (Breggin 1993, 227).

Most people in the user movement feel the same about ECT. It's unpleasant and dangerous to receive and poorly understood by those who advocate its use. Many people report subtle pressure from staff that is very difficult to resist and often find themselves receiving a course of treatment that they really do not want to have and know very little about. They receive very poor information about what to expect or on the mechanism or effects of the treatment. But perhaps most importantly the views of the growing anti-ECT lobby are not listened to and are simply discounted by psychiatrists as being unrepresentative. It is about time that our views were taken seriously and, at the very least, the users' perspective on ECT should be taken account of in its use and in research into its effect. As far as we know none of the published studies offer a consumer perspective on ECT. However, this should be remedied soon. When the Tizard Centre at the University of Kent complete their work on the users' perspective of major tranquillisers they anticipate working on a users' perspective of ECT.

Medication

As you know there is widespread concern about the excessive reliance on medication and the failure to provide sufficient alternatives such as counselling and other talking treatments.

Psychiatrists often prescribe very strong drugs without giving sufficient information on their effects. These drugs can cause an enormous amount of suffering. In the short term they can cause a bewildering array of unwanted or side-effects which can include Parkinsonian symptoms, inner agitation and restlessness and a feeling that all is not well in the head that makes it very difficult to function properly. Some people always feel tired and drained of energy and have great difficulty in rasing the enthusiasm to work or socialise. Their long-term use can cause intense irreversible suffering and the neurological damage called tardive dyskinesia. It is possible to see people in the long-stay and geriatric wards in a pitiful condition trembling, twitching and drooling. You might think that people are this way because of their mental illness, but this is not so. In fact, people are this way because of the medication that they have been given.

Table 12.3 Side-effects of one anti-depressant from the BNF

These side-effects are described as common:
 depression
 reduced blood pressure
 blurred vision
 dry mouth
 excess salivation
 feelings of weakness
 drowsiness
 constipation
 nausea and vomiting
 insomnia
 retention of bodily fluids
Less common side-effects are:
 headaches
 sweating
 neuritis
 liver damage

Most of the medication that we are expected to take, and sometimes forced to take, has dreadful nasty effects that are referred to as side-effects. This is very misleading because these 'side-effects' are often the main effects of the drugs. A list of the side effects of one anti-depressant drug taken from the British National Formulary is given in Table 12.3.

Recently major tranquillisers have been implicated in deaths occurring in mental hospitals. The television programme *Dispatches* recently illustrated this by describing the deaths of two men, one from an overdose many times more that the recommended dosage, and one after taking only 100mg of the drug concerned. A leading professor from the Institute of Psychiatry appeared on the programme to say in his opinion major tranquillisers were implicated in at least one death per week. None of the quality assurance systems we are familiar with tackles this issue of prescribing practices. This and many other issues of medical practice are seen as outside the purview of quality assurance and are dealt with more properly as issues of clinical judgement. If QA systems are not developed to concern themselves directly with monitoring medical treatments they will fail to satisfy users.

Conclusion

We have described for you some of our (and other users!) concerns about quality assurance in mental health services. Although we are not in a position to offer quantitative data in support of our arguments this does not make them any less valid. These and similar views are expressed over and over again by many other service users and increasingly by professionals and they deserve to be taken seriously. At the very least they are relevant to any discussions on the approaches to and the role of quality assurance. But, more importantly, we believe that they offer very important pointers to future collaboration and research. Let us find out together how well they stand up to rigorous study. We would be delighted to be proved wrong. We have touched upon some of the failings of current approaches to QA, particularly their failure to take account of gender, the dangerous, and sometimes fatal, common practice of prescribing doses of major tranquillisers in excess of the recommended BNF dosages and the common failure to provide adequate information to us about the dangerous effects of the drugs we are prescribed.

We do not believe in 'them and us'. We firmly believe that working together is the only way to sort things out and to develop a good working relationship not only in relation to quality assurance but also on all the other issues that concern us. However, from our perspective this situation of them and us really exists. You have all the power and authority and you decide how most things get done. The approaches to quality assurance that you are developing have not been designed to be 'user friendly' and we are rarely asked to offer our views or provide advice. So consequently your quality reviews take ages, sometimes years, and they rarely touch upon the things that concern us. We are still living on the same back wards, going to the same unsatisfactory day centres and the tacky dilapidated drop-ins that do not open in the evenings or at weekends and bank holidays, taking large doses of drugs and suffering unpleasant effects that many of us think are part and parcel of our 'mental health' problems or living isolated lonely lives in community houses that you pretend are our homes but actually do not much feel like it to us. None of the things that we are asking for are new or extraordinary. Is it not about time we put our differences behind us and started working together on these things?

B. THE PERSPECTIVE OF PEOPLE WITH PHYSICAL DISABILITIES

(This was Kath Gillespie Sells' presentation at the conference.)

What is a 'User'?

I have been asked to make a presentation on what a quality service is from the users' perspective.

First it is necessary to consider who the user is. I am supposed to be representing physical disability. I am a wheelchair user, so apparently I fall nicely into that category. However, for some time now the disabled people's movement has been saying that these divisions (based on impairment) are unhelpful and serve to keep us apart and prevent unity and collective action for change.

Secondly, the 'user' or 'client' may represent several impairment groups, i.e. I am talking here about physical impairment but could as easily be sharing a perspective on mental health services. We rarely fall into the neat categories that service providers would wish.

It is important to recognise that the user may also be a service provider or manager. Professionals may also be users. It needs to be remembered too that the carer may be a disabled person and a user of services in their own right. Carers also have needs and these may be different from, and conflict with, those of the user – e.g. respite care is a service for carers, *not* for users/disabled people.

What is Quality?

The simplest answer to the question of what is quality, is that it is what the 'user' wants.

In order to know what the user wants the service provider or professional has to talk to the user to find out. This process of consultation seems to be inordinately difficult for professionals. All too often intermediaries are used so as to prevent a face-to-face confrontation.

In order to discover what quality is, the service provider/professional needs to enter into meaningful consultation with representative disabled people, i.e. those who have a mandate to speak on behalf of their group or organisation of disabled people. Often individual disabled people who are known are 'consulted', to avoid differences of opinion.

Service providers must recognise vested interest: the fear that empowering the user will disempower the professional – that they will lose something by information or skill sharing with the user/disabled person.

The previous situation of the user/disabled person – institutionalisation or abuses along with power imbalances – must be recognised and explored.

Measuring 'Quality'

Some of the tools for measuring quality may have a place, but many have been devised as management tools that permit measurement without input from the user of those services. They serve as more intermediaries.

Disabled people or users have been thinking about quality for some time also. We have devised our own mechanism for measuring a quality service. When examining services to see if they are what the disabled person wants, we need to explore the following five main aspects:

- *Appropriateness – is it what the disabled person wants or needs?* Does Fred really want to do basket-weaving at a day centre? Or should his activities reflect his life experiences – what if Fred was an engineer?
- *Equity – do all disabled people/users get a fair share?* Are the residential units for younger disabled people better staffed than those for the elderly?
- *Effectiveness – does it work for the disabled person?* Does the home-help coming so early in the morning really help the disabled person? Or does the disabled lesbian or gay man have to hide 'sensitive' books etc. for fear of disclosure and loss of a vital service?
- *Acceptability – is the service acceptable to the disabled person?* Does a nineteen year old woman really want to put to bed at 6.30 pm on a Saturday night? Or on any other night? And must she go to bed alone?
- *Efficiency – are resources being wasted?* Is the bath hoist actually used? Was it what the disabled person actually requested? Was the disabled person taught how to use it properly?

Checklist Approach

All too often the checklist is adopted as a short cut and as a means to avoid consultation with disabled people. However, the above checklist is a good guide as to whether a service is in fact a quality service, i.e. whether it is what the disabled person wants and needs.

Talking to Disabled People

Finally, the most important means of testing quality is to ask if the disabled person is satisfied with the service. It is preferable to consult with user-controlled organisations. The absence of jargon and use of simple English is essential in interactions with disabled people.

User Consultants/Trainers

There is a growing number of competent experienced disabled people who are trained trainers and user consultants.[1] They work on many issues, running a variety of tailor-made courses around the country. If real representation and authenticity is to be reflected in service providers'/managers' work, training must be by disabled people.

Finally, it is now popular to talk of user participation, user involvement, even user control and user-controlled service. These may seem lofty ideals but they are practice in some areas of the country. I would suggest that *only* users themselves will have a true understanding of equality. This will be achieved through their participation in planning, provision, monitoring and evaluating services and through training. The extract from *Rules For Radicals* below demonstrates the need for people to be part of the solution to their own problems. This participation is now a demand of 'users/disabled people'!

Dignity

> We learn when we respect the dignity of the people, that they cannot be denied the elementary right to participate fully in the solutions to their own problems. Self respect arises only out of people who play an active role in solving their own crises and who are not helpless, passive puppet-like recipients of private or public services. To give people help, while denying them significant part in the action, contributes nothing to the development of the individual. In the deepest sense, it is not giving but taking – taking their dignity. Denial of the opportunity for participation is the denial of human dignity and democracy. It will not work. (Alinsky 1971)

References

Alinsky, S.D. (1971) *Rules for Radicals*. New York: Random House.

Breggin, P. (1993) *Toxic Psychiatry*. London: Fontana/Harper Collins.

---

1   Consultants and/or trainers can be contacted through: Update Associates, 88 Maidstone Road, London N11 2JR. All associates are disabled people, from a variety of backgrounds, who are trained trainers. Their competence extends along a range of issues, including disability, equality, mental health, HIV/AIDS, community care.

Chapter 13

Quality for People –
Learning From Service Users About Quality

Alison Kerruish

My learning from service users about quality came from working on a project which has just ended. This project lasted two years and was funded by the King's Fund. Firstly I am going to talk about the people who are at the centre of this project and where they live. Then I am going to briefly describe each stage of the project. Finally I am going to mention what I think people have got out of it – the people at the centre of the project, residential services, and me personally.

The Aims of the Project

The first thing to say is that this was an action research project – or service development project. The first aim that we had was to enable residents to establish what constitutes a good quality residential service; the second aim was to develop user-led ways of monitoring the quality of that service. This whole process took two years. The first aim comprised three stages and took about a year; the second aim had two stages and also took about a year.

The People at the Centre of the Project

First of all: the people who are involved in the project. These people all live in supported houses in the London Borough of Bromley. Ten houses are run by Bromley Care Services Ltd which is a limited charity, and one is run by a housing association, Hexagon. We did not cover all of those houses because they were not all open when we started. We covered six houses initially (37 people) and eight in total by the end of the project (49 people). Most of these people had come from two psychiatric hospitals, Cane Hill hospital in Surrey and Maidstone Hospital in Kent, and they had all left hospital between one and three years previously. Most of them had been in hospital for a large part of their lives – for more than ten years. Many had been in hospital between twenty and forty years. Most of the people were over 50, with a large number of people over 60.

Our Philosophy

Before I describe the project, it is important to tell you something about the philosophy of the professional research team. As non-users of mental health services, we wished to be viewed as allies by the residents in the houses. We also wanted to work in partnership with people as far as possible. So we hoped that the process and outcome of the project would be empowering for people – that it would be an empowering process to be involved with and that what they got out of it would also help to empower people. However, we also acknowledge that we had the control over the project. So my view is that empowerment is a matter of degree that is handed out by the researcher, unless of course you can enable people to do research for themselves. We have to acknowledge that there is a power imbalance – and govern our practice by basic human values: the professionals involved have to actually carry out the work in a very open and honest way, and I believe that we did do that.

How the Work was Carried Out

Now something about the process of the project. I am going to skim over this but I do not want to undervalue the initial phase, which was the most important. We spent up to three months in each house getting to know people. Some we never got to know well, with others it took only a matter of days or weeks. But that process was the most important for us in establishing a trust between ourselves and the people who live in the houses – and also for establishing a trust with those who work in the houses and those responsible for providing the services. We then had a series of group discussions in each of the houses, and these were facilitated by a member of the research team. We had about four or five group discussions over a number of weeks in each house. These were very unstructured in nature; we just wanted people to express how they felt about living there –

Table 13.1

Information from Residents	*Themes*	*Component*
Going out with friends or family	People need to maintain contacts with family, and friends from hospital	
Going home to see family/relatives		
Going to places where meet people from hospital	People need to visit family and friends and do things outside of the house with family and friends	Relationships
Having visitors who were with in hospital		
Having family to visit or stay in house		
Having more visits from family or friends		

what was good, what was bad, what was better about living there than being in hospital. The hope was that we would come up with a whole string of issues that are really important in determining a good quality service from the residents' point of view. This was what we got, but it was far more than we expected. The quality as well as the quantity of information was extremely good; people talked about quite personal issues as well as serious issues. So we got a wealth of information. Examples of some things residents said are shown in Table 13.1.

The next task was to summarise all that information and to categorise it as well, because the intention was to provide some sort of framework for quality of the service around what residents had said. We did this by summarising and categorising all the information around the five accomplishments that people are probably familiar with from John O'Brien's work (see Alan Tyne's Chapter 15 for discussion of the five accomplishments), though we amended them slightly. These accomplishments are:

- community integration
- choice and control
- equality and empowerment
- relationships
- developing skills.

An example of how the information from residents was summarised and categorised is shown in Table 13.1.

It was quite a long process; in fact it took us about two months. It would have taken us a lot longer had we actually worked more closely with the residents. Unfortunately, we just did not have the time to do that. There were people from one house who helped us to summarise and categorise all the information, but we could not involve everyone. We took back to the residents our final summary of what they had said – to check whether we had got it right or totally wrong. They made amendments accordingly – adding things in, changing the wording and taking out things that they thought were wrong.

From this quality framework, we then needed to consider the best methods for collecting information and monitoring whether the needs were being met. Issues might be something like:

- 'People need to maintain existing employment skills.'
- 'People need to make friends out in the community.'
- 'People need to know the side effects of their medication.'

All issues were expressed in terms of residents' needs. For each 'need', we tried to work out how best to collect the information and how services could best monitor it. We decided to involve staff in the process, because it was important to gain their acceptance of the content and format of the framework.

I am going to describe the monitoring methods in more detail later, but let me say first that the information obtained was intended to go to service providers – and also back to the residents themselves and to commissioners of the services. I am not going to labour this point but it was very important that the person who commissioned the work in the first place was actually the purchaser of those services. The intention was for us to work very closely with the purchaser and to get some user-led ways of monitoring the services written into contracts. That did not happen for a variety of reasons, most importantly because the commissioning arrangements in Bromley changed radically and the person who commissioned our work was no longer the purchaser. This made it much more difficult to get things done. We found ourselves working very closely with the providers.

In developing the monitoring methods we looked at the issues contained in the quality framework and designed each method accordingly. We did not have set ideas on methods, as do some research projects. We wanted the issues that had been determined by residents to determine the type of monitoring method. Five methods were identified (Table 13.2). The issues were translated into questions that could be addressed by the monitoring method.

Table 13.2

Type of issues	Monitoring method
Image of the house, inside and outside: e.g. Is the garden well maintained? Is it well decorated?	Checklist for a Facility Review – either external or internal
Individual choices and decisions: e.g. Do you need support in using shops and supermarkets?	Via a key worker; a checklist as part of an Individual Service Review or Care Management process
Group decisions within the house: e.g. cooking, having guests to stay	By residents in a House User Group
Citizenship rights: people's rights as citizens in the community, e.g. voting rights	By residents through a Residents' Association for a service, with a representative from each House
Sensitive and personal issues: e.g. opinions on staff working in the house	Confidential and anonymous questionnaire with help from an independent person, if requested

Progress with the Monitoring Methods

By the time the project ended, two or three of these methods were in place in each service and some were being used for monitoring purposes.

The individual service review (ISR) list is a checklist of questions that staff can go through with a resident to help both key worker and resident to prepare more fully for their ISR. It helps them to focus on issues that are important for the resident and not to waste time talking about something that is not important for them. Most of the houses now use this checklist, but only one of the houses uses it in any routine and systematic way, though they do not monitor the information.

Neither of the services have set up a Residents' Association yet. In one service, plans were made a year ago, but it still has not happened.

The Facility Review checklist consists of seven questions that either an internal or external reviewer could use – just by going into the house and looking at it and talking to residents. Questions like, 'Does it look ordinary on the outside and the inside?', 'Do the residents know about the side-effects of medication?' This checklist has not been taken up by either service.

The most progress was made with the House User Groups and confidential questionnaires. For the House User Group, we compiled a list of suggested agenda items for residents, based on the issues in the quality framework. Most groups found this helpful, particularly when they first started. They also added in their own issues. The idea of a House User Group was popular: all the residents in all the houses bar one wanted to set one up. The difficulty was in finding an independent facilitator that residents wanted and felt comfortable with. The service providers vetted and sometimes vetoed suggestions. One of the services is now trying to instigate some sort of system for monitoring how the staff in the houses respond to decisions made by residents in the House User Group. The questionnaire took a long time to devise because of the difficulty in getting the wording right. But it has now been used twice in one service and once with all the residents in the other service. Both services employ somebody independent to offer support to residents in completing the questionnaire if they want it. Virtually all residents have used the independent person, who goes through the questionnaire like an interview. Both services have made use of the information from the questionnaire, but they were unprepared for the amount of information that they got from it. They are still trying to unpack how they will deal with it, even though the people whom they have employed are very skilled at enabling them to look at ways of doing it. Both of these people are co-ordinators of local advocacy schemes.

What Different People Have Got from the Project

The Residents

They have had an input into defining the quality of the service, in setting the agenda for quality through the quality framework, and also in the monitoring of the service through some of the monitoring methods. The whole process of the project may have been empowering for some people, but it is very difficult to stand back and assess whether people have indeed been empowered by it. There are certainly more opportunities for residents to have more control in the service, particularly through the House User Groups. But of course it has to be remembered that the monitoring methods themselves do not guarantee control. A lot depends upon the service provider's willingness to let residents have more control.

The Local Services

It is important to underline that people who have lived in institutions for a long time were more than able and more than willing to work with us in the project, and they were very welcoming towards us as outside professionals. The monitoring methods were implemented to a greater or lesser extent, although not across the entire services. Unfortunately, specifications around user-led monitoring have not yet been written into service contracts.

Services Elsewhere

Other residential services have expressed interest in doing similar work, so we have compiled a training package (Kerruish and Smith 1993). We thought that services might want to develop a framework for quality, although of course that does take some time. Other services might feel that they could just take the framework that we have developed in Bromley and use it or adapt it to their own local needs. Certainly some of the monitoring methods might be taken as they stand by other services. Things like the questionnaires and ISR checklists could also be used as a basis for contract specifications.

The package is in six sections:

- the quality framework itself; how it was developed, how it can be used
- guidelines for developing a quality framework from scratch
- description and documentation of the five monitoring methods
- training and guidelines for the implementation of each method
- recommendations about how to incorporate user-led monitoring into contracts
- a brief résumé of other methods.

Me, Personally

I am a researcher by background, with experience mostly of quantitative research. Working on this project has been an important process for me. I have learnt an enormous amount; too much to say here. I have learnt a lot from the residents and I have grown in my own personal development from working with them. But also as a researcher, it has taught me much more about how to work together with people who are the focus of the research.

Finally, it has enthused me with the idea of training – to provide training and support for people to commission and carry out their own work themselves, instead of employing professional researchers.

References

Kerruish, A. and Smith, H. (1993) *Developing Quality Residential Care.* London: Longman.

Chapter 14

IQA: Inside Quality Assurance – Its Rationale and Use in Residential and Non-Residential Settings

Leonie Kellaher

Introduction

Inside Quality Assurance (IQA) is an Action Pack, published by CESSA (The Centre for Environmental and Social Studies in Ageing, University of North London) in 1992.[1] It has the stated aim of establishing a system of review in individual residential homes – for all client groups and all sectors – which will help create a climate in which individuals have 'good chances to be themselves' whilst living in a setting which has to work collectively.

The IQA Rationale

The two central foci of any evaluation of a service, particularly when an attempt is being made to say something about the quality of that service, must be *what* is being evaluated and *who* is doing the evaluation. Neither of these is a straightforward matter. In starting to develop Inside Quality Assurance in 1989 this complexity was acknowledged and an explicitly partisan line was adopted, with the object of facilitating better understanding of the user's world through the exploration of his or her experiences as a recipient of residential services.

In 1989 a team of researchers at the University of North London (then the Polytechnic of North London) took on a commission within the Department of Health's Caring in Homes Initiative. The title of the particular part of the initiative for which CESSA was responsible was Self Assessment & Performance Review. This commission arose out of one of the recommendations of the Wagner (1988) Group which had reported on residential care in 1988. Although these terms – along with quality control/assurance – were only just starting to be used in the social care field, Self Assessment & Performance Review clearly concerned quality and its evaluation in care settings.

The work was to be carried out in a developmental way, through action research in demonstration projects. Inevitably, the team proceeded from an

---

1 IQA is available from IDU. Tel: 01908–21006.

understanding of residential settings which had emerged in the course of work carried out over several years (Peace, Kellaher and Willcocks 1982, Willcocks, Peace and Kellaher 1987, Kellaher, Peace, Weaver and Willcocks 1988, Peace and Kellaher 1990). For at least a decade, CESSA had been involved in researching the complexities of residential settings – notably those for older people – and especially the ways in which standards in these were regulated. One of the issues that the team had come to acknowledge was that it is not easy for anyone who does not spend considerable and continuous time in residential establishments to have a picture of what goes on, day in and day out. Hence, the original title of the Caring in Homes Initiative commission was adapted to become Inside Quality Assurance.

The idea that insiders are the best people to report on the minutiae of day-to-day living in the relatively closed settings that are many residential homes – for all groups of people, not just older people – requires some expansion, if not a defence. As a general rule, the research and the thinking on residential care (e.g. Davies and Knapp 1981, Booth 1985) has assumed that the permanent, and therefore fundamental, structures which underpin residential care are: first, those of physical structure – the building; and second, the organisation – the staff, the regime. The point that the resident group, in terms of its particular requirements rather than as individuals, is the most consistent element of residential life, tends to have been overlooked by researchers and practitioners. Observing as they necessarily do, from the outside, they fail to note that neither physical fabric nor organisation remains constant even for the duration of an individual resident's stay in care. There are often changes to buildings and constantly to staffing arrangements – called turnover – which may represent threats to the continuity or predictability which individuals naturally seek in their home circumstances.

So in developing IQA the basic rationale for placing the resident centrally was this: that it was not only fair, but it was logical, to regard the resident – or the resident collectivity – as the most fixed point in the complex entity that is residential care. What followed was the proposition that the accounts given by this group of their residential experiences had to be given great weight, something which was beginning to be voiced as an ideal but did not yet seem to be taken seriously in terms of actions.

Inside Quality Assurance came to be based, therefore, upon information given by those who know best – those who live and work in residential settings – along with those who encounter life in homes habitually. The information which this system of quality assurance would process would be around the detail of daily life as experienced by those who were, by definition, most present in the setting. There is, as argued above, a logic to this rationale. In another sense, however, it is a reactive approach. In considering how the objectives of the Caring in Homes Initiative might best be achieved, it was not possible to ignore the existence of a considerable body of research and other literature and the Wagner Report's recommendation for the enhancement of day-to-day life for people living in residential settings of all kinds:

all residential establishments without exception need to have their own internal procedures for self-evaluation and performance review (Wagner 1988, 12)

Much of the research had been generated over the two or three decades preceding the Wagner Report. Sometimes, there had been explicit recommendations as to how residential care might be reshaped and improved; sometimes explanation was offered for the way things were in such settings and suggestions for change were implicitly offered. It was clear, however, in 1989, when the Self-assessment and Performance review initiative was taken on, that residential settings had generally been unaffected by this work. In many respects residential care continued to be institutional in character and the individuality of those who lived in homes – and to a lesser extent that of those who worked there – would frequently be compromised.

The element which appeared to be absent from the research analyses was the voice of residential experience. This is not to say that research and evaluations did not include the 'consumer' voice; they often did, but these were subordinate voices and ones shaped by methodologies which made assumptions as to the form and content which the voice of experience should take. Reactively, a decision was taken to reverse these approaches and to start and finish with the voice of experience in developing a system for assuring quality in homes for all groups, across all sectors of provision.

The Conceptual Basis of IQA

The conceptual basis upon which IQA is founded springs from the rationale which directed early thinking as to how best to match, with a practical tool, the aims expressed within *A Positive Choice*. The first of the conceptual props derived from earlier work within CESSA, particularly work in relation to the regulatory processes entailed in Registration and Inspection functions. Regulation clearly indicates that there are two or more discrete entities which have to be balanced in some way (see Figure 14.1). Despite rhetoric to the contrary: 'This is just like home. We don't have rules here; you don't have rules in your own home' (Kellaher 1982) the domestic analogy does not stand up to scrutiny.

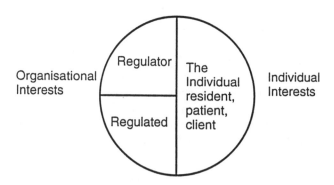

Figure 14.1 Differents sets of interests

It is clear that at least two – and possibly three – sets of interests are represented in residential settings, and need to be kept in balance if one or the other party is not to be disadvantaged. It can be argued that legislation, in this instance the Registered Homes Act 1984, has its moral and judicial foundation in giving weight to parties – groups and individuals – who might otherwise be overwhelmed by stronger organisational influences. In residential homes it is invariably the individual resident whose interests have to be weighted against the stronger influences of the organisation. So in the same way that Inspection has the interests of the resident group in view, a review system working from within should seek to give weight to the resident voice so that this can serve as a constant check upon stronger influences.

Beyond the concept that these different, and perhaps divergent, sets of interests need to be regulated, not only by mechanisms like inspection, which emanate from outside the home, but also by mechanisms which seek to open up common ground for discussion between those who represent internal sets of interests, IQA is operationalised through two premises:

- Any information from these (internal) sources is better than no information.
- Even if just one person makes a point, it is worth taking into account when considering how the home as a whole is.

What this means is that IQA aims to uncover the internal meanings which actors ascribe to events; in this sense it is evaluatively formative rather than summative.

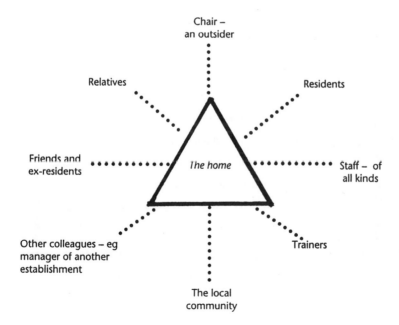

Figure 14.2 A quality group and its possible composition

9 Fourth Quality Group meeting: finishing off and moving on

8 Producing the report

7 Third Quality Group meeting: consolidating everyone's ideas

6 Feedback: checking out with everyone else

5 Second Quality Group meeting: making sense of the information

4 Preparing information for the second quality group meeting

3 Collecting information about the home

2 First Quality Group meeting: introducing IQA

1 Preparing for the IQA review

Values: Respect •Dignity •Rights •Autonomy
Choice • Fulfilment • Equality of opportunity

Figure 14.3 The IQAs process: an overview of the steps that make up an IQA review

IQA: A Description

IQA is a step-by-step process which leads to an account of the home, its work and its aspirations, as expressed by those within. The account is a written record which can be monitored and can lead to things becoming different at the day-to-day level. The IQA process appears to have intrinsic value in that it gives residents and staff a new perspective on what they accomplish and the directions they wish to move in. It also has the capacity to inform those who cannot have an insider's understanding.

IQA is steered by a group made up of both insiders and outsiders. The kind of people who may be involved are shown in Figure 14.2.

The composition of the group will vary from home to home and over the exercises which make up the IQA cycle. An IQA exercise is based upon the two complementary processes which underpin all research, those of collecting and then organising and analysing information. It is structured by the nine progressive steps shown in Figure 14.3, the IQA process, which culminate in the written account of the home's achievements and intentions for the future.

A small number of general topics are the starting point for collecting information through a guided conversation (see Figure 14.4).

People – residents, staff and others, such as friends and relatives as well as professionals, are all approached – are free to interpret these topics in their own terms and in response to two simple but crucial questions and prompts.

The first of these simply asks the informant:

- Can you describe…(the topic)?

and then asks the person to be a little more precise, or even diagnostic, by saying:

- How much do you think it (what they have just talked about) needs to be different?

People can say what they think might be done, and they can use a scale which goes from 1 to 9 to show whether they think a lot or not very much needs to be different, in other words to indicate the intensity with which they hold a view. All of this is optional and people have the right not to be involved.

This summary of IQA, as a system which has been developed through a series of trial demonstrations involving up to 200 homes for all groups of people across the sectors, illustrates just one way of refocusing concerns about quality assurance through the comments of those who receive and experience services day-to-day, rather than through those who organise provision. The point is that those experiencing care directly – principally residents but also front-line staff, relatives, friends and others who have inside experience of a home – view care from a unique perspective.

IQA: What Is It For?

IQA is about *self-evaluation*; that means the people who have most experience of residential life describing, in an open and organised way, how things are in their home, and what ideas they may have for future plans and different approaches.

There are 7 topics to explore

1 Physical care

2 Choice

3 Expression of feeling

4 The home as somewhere to live

5 Knowing how things run

6 Making links

7 How the home feels to residents

Each topic is explored with two questions:

Can you describe... [the topic]

How much do think needs to be different?

Figure 14.4 Seven general topics

IQA is about considering the residential culture so that, over time, residents and those around them become more and more free to comment on things that affect their day-to-day lives.

IQA is about establishing a continuing self-evaluation process, made up of a description, a 'measurement' and setting of a 'standard'. This is a process about life and work in homes, and making available, as appropriate, details of both the achievements and difficulties.

So, IQA aims to give people their voice – about everyday things – particularly by establishing a safe place where people's comments can be lodged, to gradually establish new habits and to legitimate communication between residents and workers. The crucial question is, however, does IQA do this, or anything else, in homes and how lasting is its impact?

In order to develop IQA it was necessary to undertake continuous evaluation of its effectiveness. Since it is a gradual and relatively unobtrusive process, it is not easy to see its consequences over short periods. Nonetheless, it is possible to give an account of what people who have participated in its development have reported. At some future time it will be possible to draw upon evaluations which take account of longer lapses of time than is possible now (IQA Accreditation – forthcoming development work).

IQA: What It Does

One issue of concern is the possibility of user information arising through IQA that is not representative or reliable. The point is sometimes made that only the more vocal people may speak up, so that the user viewpoint will be a biased one. Further anxieties centre around the observation that people may not feel safe enough to make the criticisms they would like to make, and that they are often inconsistent, making comments and criticisms and then later saying something completely different. The evidence from IQA suggests that where information is collected in a brief one-to-one personal interview, even the most reticent residents can express a view, as can those with a cognitive impairment if they are given extra help. The issue of consistency is discussed later.

What Do Users Say?

The IQA approach generates data within which resident preferences can be detected. Unsurprisingly, residents and staff are circumspect in their comments, but the following points can be made about the character of the information they provide:

- Users say quite a lot. In response to the invitation to describe, in their own ways, their experiences under a few broad headings, people across the client groups had plenty to say. Even quite frail people, and those with cognitive difficulties, could be drawn to suggest their ideas and preferences.
- People make observations about the detail of day-to-day experiences of care.
- Users are frequently well able to focus their remarks on the service under question, the routines and the organisation of service allocation and delivery.

- People make suggestions for changes which generally tend to have low resource implications.
- People say things over and over again, but in different ways.
- Users do not say many surprising things, and yet staff – front line staff especially – are surprised and, sometimes, shocked and 'thrown' by confronting user comment in a collected form.
- Very occasionally there is a hint that something serious may be being said and may need further airing and exploration.

How Do Users Say Things?
- They make comments rather than criticisms:

  ...there's a bit of wall-paper torn off and I'm hoping they will be able to fix it...
- When people 'criticise' they compensate or balance with appreciative comment:

  ...They work very hard, they are very busy, it would be nice to chat a bit...
- Users – older people, children, people with learning difficulties and other groups – say things 'inside out', they hint, they are allusive rather than direct:

  ...the staff go home at two o'clock... (in describing bathing arrangements)

  ...the food is all right I suppose...

  ...they can be a bit rough...

  ...some funny things go on...
- Staff are much more critical than residents.

The form in which people describe and explain their experiences is an apparently fragmented one. It is not a form with which researchers are necessarily familiar, nor is it readily transformed into facts which the administrator or – perhaps – external inspector will have time to process. However, the Quality Groups which have had the task of sorting through and interpreting people's comments have demonstrated a facility in pulling out thematic content. It is interesting that inconsistencies among and within individuals do not appear to have presented insurmountable difficulties for Quality Groups.

What Do People Mean?
Nevertheless, the question remains, can we justify making interpretations about what people say, importing meaning, filling gaps? One response may be to argue that we – as outsiders – may have difficulty justifying such analytic leaps; for insiders the task and the accomplishment is a much more grounded one and as a consequence a more legitimate one.

What About Confidentiality?

There is a concern that, without guarantees of confidentiality, residents will not make the criticisms about the service that managers need to hear. The complex distinction between a formal complaints system and something like IQA emerges here. With IQA the framework is one which allows comment and which means that trust is not threatened in the way that a complaint may imply. However, reservations might be expressed about the likelihood of informants' comments and criticisms being identified by management, with the attendant risk of 'reprisal'. IQA can only go so far in dealing with these dilemmas and individual Quality Groups have to establish the ground rules appropriate for the setting. Firstly, it aims to be a process which opens up the residential setting, so that things can be organised differently. It aims to get the collective viewpoint by taking account of the main themes arising out of individuals' comments. People are reminded that others may well be able to guess who has said what and advised to say what they think can safely be brought into the open for discussion.

At the same time, those running IQA are alert for coded messages and hints that something may be seriously amiss. One difference between IQA and a formal complaints procedure is that IQA can pick up practice which, although habitual and entrenched, is on reflection judged borderline or unacceptable by insiders who understand existing dynamics and arrangements. And outsiders can take a fresh look at patterns of practice and people's reactions. In this way questionable practice can be corrected before the complaint stage is reached. This approach, however, serves to highlight a crucial difference between a managerial formulation of 'complaint' and a user idea of something that needs to be different, and which might be amenable to negotiation.

Has IQA Made a Difference to...?

Ultimately what matters is the extent to which a process such as IQA can help to establish the kind of climate – referred to earlier – in which individuals have good chances to be themselves, whatever that self is: a child, an old person, someone with a physical disability, a person from a disadvantaged group. The following questions were put to a range of participants in the IQA trials. The respondents were generally the non-residents, i.e. the staff and professional people on the IQA groups.

Has IQA Made a Difference to the Home as a Whole?

Speaking about the impact of IQA on the home as a whole a lot of very interesting observations were made.

The issue of quality has now been clearly flagged up and is difficult to ignore. The introduction of outsiders on a formal basis has opened up the home to the community.

It appears to have created interest from all in the home about future plans.

Has IQA Made a Difference to Residents?

> ...the opportunity to allow clients to express thoughts, opinions, individuality and self-worth.

> ...they enjoyed participating and hopefully are now enjoying some of the alterations to their lifestyles.

> ...it has given them a voice they did not have before, but this is still to be developed. It has made them all feel represented rather than just the vocal few at residents' meetings.

Has it Meant that People Have Better Chances to be Themselves?

> Once the residents' confidence in the IQA system has been developed, I feel that IQA should enhance individuals' chances to be themselves.

> I think IQA will make it more possible, but it is only the beginning of a long process.

> It is likely to make this more possible as the IQA provides a safe setting for people to state their views and feelings.

Reservations were expressed, as these extracts show, but generally, the following trends are emerging:

> I think IQA gave a good insight into some aspects of care in the home. It was accepted by staff and residents more readily than I would have expected. It was limited as regards results as I feel the home – residents and staff – felt it unusual to be asked their opinion and residents in particular did not think they were in a position to suggest change. However, this in itself is valuable to know.

> It was good to have guidelines to give ideas for new things to do in the future. It has given us an awareness of what is being provided. No impact yet, but a lot of hope for the future.

A more comprehensive evaluation which includes comments on residents' reflections on IQA is contained in *Raising Voices*, the account of Brunel University's Evaluation of the Caring in Homes Initiative (McCourt-Perring and Youll 1993). Particularly the observation is made that:

> What the system sets in place, therefore, is not a series of standards or definitions of quality but the people and constituencies of interest who are able to debate, define and implement these in relation to a particular home. (McCourt, Perring and Youll 1993, 61)

IQA: How it is Being Used

In the final trials in which around 100 homes participated, there was a spread across the client groups and sectors. But this spread was weighted in the following directions.

There was a high proportion of establishments for older people and a paucity of children's homes. The latter deficit was corrected by concentrating special efforts on two homes. In terms of sector participation:

68% public sector homes participated

19% private sector homes participated

13% voluntary sector homes participated

(n = 94)

After publication of the IQA Action Pack, aimed at residential homes of more or less 'traditional' character, the method has been adapted and adopted in non-traditional settings such as: refuges, hostels, sheltered housing and day centres. The principles which underpin IQA may well, in the future, be translated to the quality assurance of domiciliary care provision.

As an internal review, IQA appears to fulfil its goal of opening up the home, first of all to itself, and then to others, who have an interest and concern as 'outsiders'.

IQA: Where it Fits in with Other Frameworks and Approaches

While the researcher talks of quality of life, the terms 'quality control' and 'quality assurance' now find greater currency in everyday practice. Such terms derive from the worlds of business, management and economics rather than the socio-psychological disciplines which generated the paradigms used previously in consumer studies of welfare services. *Quality control* implies quality at a certain level and focuses attention on standards: objective criteria which may be imposed and which outsiders can use to take a 'snapshot' of what is happening.

Quality assurance, on the other hand, implies that the recipients of a service, and the 'public' at large, should in some way be assured of a certain quality of product which meets their needs. It is a continuous process and, consequently, insiders – 'those who really know' – have to be involved. Both systems should be complementary and feed into each other. The value base which underpins 'quality of life' studies, with its emphasis on personal need for dignity, choice, autonomy, privacy, self-determination – still remains at the heart of both quality control and quality assurance mechanisms – though it may be argued that other values such as 'value for money' and 'service efficiency' are now included (Pfeffer and Coote 1991).

In Figure 14.5 a number of systems for demonstrating quality in residential settings can be seen to have emerged in recent years.

Historically, we have sought to understand services through their administration and organisation rather than from the experiential viewpoint of the user. Today, regulatory bodies, be it the local authority inspection unit or the private long-term care sector itself through its professional associations, initiate quality control from the outside. At the other extreme a programme like Inside Quality Assurance starts at the centre with those who experience care 24 hours a day.

Two other programmes shown in Figure 14.5, BS 5750 and Homes Are For Living In (HAFLI), occupy the middle ground. They involve an understanding

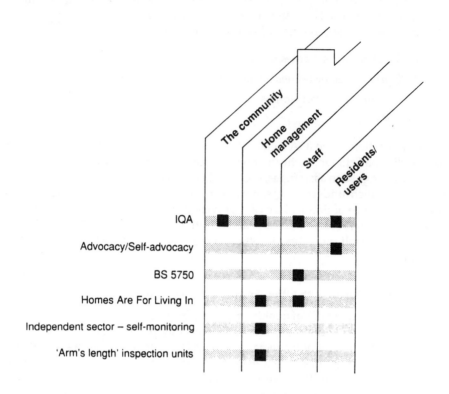

Figure 14.5 New perspectives on quality care

of residential life which is organised around staff and inspection officers' perspectives. The distinguishing feature of IQA is that it cannot proceed unless residents are involved. Other systems such as BS 5750 often involve residents, but they do not have to do so.

IQA: The Advantages and Disadvantages

Whilst it may be acknowledged that users often have quite a lot to say, there may be reservations about the 'softness' of the kind of data which IQA generates. Even if it were interpreted efficiently and with sensitivity, would it be a sound base for decision-making? How would different and perhaps opposing ideas be dealt with? What about demands which would be too expensive or otherwise impossible to implement? There are increasing numbers of people who have had experience of negotiating their way around at least some of these questions and who believe that it is possible to make headway, and important to do so. There are others who are doubtful as to whether user comment, collected through a system such as IQA, is a sound or even a possible basis for managerial or organisational action.

The important issue of standard-setting arises here. IQA can often reveal approaches to the task of setting standards which are different. Within IQA, user comment is likely to lead to a form of standard-setting which goes something like the following:

> If we can be convinced that the inside picture these users build up and present is one that suggests, in the main, that the organisation of the home produces an environment in which most people, most of the time, have good chances to be themselves, we might rest assured – for the time being.

At the same time, some will be sceptical or doubtful about this kind of formula for standard-setting. There is the danger that, left to themselves, users may opt for standards which are too low, that they would not have an overview of standards as a whole, and that a loose standard formula will make difficulties for regulation as an exercise which must continue to complement internal quality assurance. As information, this kind of user information is likely, it is sometimes argued, to be too diffuse and mutable. The common denominator which might link these two positions is probably the view that user information needs to be treated – that is, recorded and interpreted – more systematically if it is to have real legitimacy and be taken seriously as the basis for action in the future.

IQA: Evaluating Quality

IQA, as just one system built upon the user view, shows that useful and new approaches to care are to be generated this way. The value of user input lies in the new and different perspective it offers. But this perspective is frequently expressed in forms which may be unfamiliar to those with managerial and organising roles and responsibilities. It is important that user opinion and ideas are built into the management of social care provision in ways which preserve the uniqueness of the perspective, and do not convert it to the bureaucratic or administrative form. This means that sensitive interpretation rather than crude translation of the user viewpoint must be the goal, so that both managerial and user aspirations are, at least in part, achieved.

Summary of Discussion

(This covered the presentation by Alison Kerruish, Chapter 13, as well as that by Leonie Kellaher.)

Issues covered were whether IQA could take into account the wishes of people from different backgrounds who might enter a residential establishment in the future; how IQA would deal with serious complaints; staff attitudes to IQA; and whether allowances needed to be made for people who had lived in institutions for a long time and lacked confidence.

Taking into Account the Wishes of Future Residents

A delegate wondered how the views of people who had been traditionally excluded from an establishment might be taken into account, i.e. how people from different backgrounds might be attracted towards an establishment that had traditionally been for white middle-class people. Leonie Kellaher said that the goal in IQA was to set up a climate where individuals could be themselves, where the organisational influence does not overwhelm the individual influence. People who have not yet contributed their particular views might not find the climate in detail one that allows them freedom, but were they to come into it, the quality of talking and listening should be sufficiently established to allow them to put forward other ways of doing things.

Dealing with Serious Complaints
A delegate asked if IQA had a complaints procedure to respond to serious complaints. LK said that the manual advised that IQA should not be started unless the complaints procedure in the setting is in place and working. The manual also gives guidelines of what to do if something worrying is encountered – they must go to the chairperson who decides whether immediate action must be taken or whether the issue can be dealt with in the course of IQA.

Staff Attitudes
A delegate wondered whether staff, who were used to being in full charge, might be hostile to disempowered people expressing their opinions. Alison Kerruish said that in her work they had learned that there was a particular point in the feedback where staff felt vulnerable. They added a guideline into the manual that where an issue was likely to be sensitive to staff, staff and residents would be given information separately about it before coming to a big meeting. This avoided hurtful acrimonious confrontation. And once this is out of the way staff become invigorated – it is as if they are allowed not to be perfect – and real discussion can take place.

Are Allowances Necessary for Some Residents to Take Part in Quality Evaluation?
AK said that they had never had to make allowances. Some people did have awful side-effects from medication when they had been in institutions for a number of years, and it was difficult, and they had to relearn skills and build up confidence. But they found that people were able to do quite complicated things, and things that they were not used to doing. Some people they talked to were not used to having their views valued in any way at all. But people could choose whether they wanted to be involved in group discussions and, on the whole, they did choose to get involved. Some people who had spent up to forty years in hospital were involved in summarising and categorising information, pulling out the main points, which is usually regarded as a very skilled task that only a trained researcher can do.

References

Booth, T. (1985) *Home Truths: Old People's Homes and the Outcome of Care.* Aldershot: Gower.

Davies, B. and Knapp, M. (1981) *Old People's Homes and the Production of Welfare.* London: Routledge and Kegan Paul.

Kellaher, L. (1982) *The Essence of the Home.* Unpublished.

Kellaher, L., Peace, S., Weaver, T. and Willcocks, D. (1988) *Coming to Terms with the Private Sector*. London: Polytechnic of North London Press (now University of North London).

McCourt-Perring, C. and Youll, P. (1993) *Raising Voices, Ensuring Quality in Residential Care*. London: HMSO.

Peace, S. and Kellaher, L. (1990) *Making Sense of Inspection*. London: HMSO.

Peace, S., Kellaher, L. and Willcocks, D. (1982) *A Balanced Life*. London: Polytechnic of North London Press (now University of North London).

Pfeffer, N. and Coote, A. (1991) *Is Quality Good For You?* Social Policy Paper 5. London: Institute for Public Policy Research.

Wagner, G. (1988) *Residential Care: A Positive Choice*. London: HMSO

Willcocks, D., Peace, S. and Kellaher, L. (1987) *Private Lives in Public Place*. London: Tavistock.

Chapter 15

Framework for Accomplishment

Alan Tyne

I have been asked to talk with you about Framework for Accomplishment, but for a moment I shall return to my earlier theme (see Chapter 2) and the place where I have learnt many things that are important to me – the boat builder's shed by the side of the river in Wivenhoe. Several years ago I was lucky enough to acquire a boat and took it with pride to show my friend George, perhaps to boast a little. He was working on a piece of wood in his favourite place – the furthest dark corner of the shed. The conversation ran along the lines of:

'Your boat? How do you know it's your boat?'

'Well, I've paid for it.'

'Ah, you've only bought it but it ain't your boat yet nor it won't be, not till you've worked on it a couple of years. When there is some of you in it then that will be yours.'

Around him were things he has made, of grace, beauty, craftsmanship, elegance and utility. Throughout his life he has made such things with some tools, a saw, a plane, a brace and bit and very little else besides. The best tools are the simplest ones. What makes the difference is the commitment of their user to learn their use and to dedicate themselves to learning it again and again and again every day that they use them. I am deeply impressed by the learning I have seen going on in conferences and courses but George did not learn very much of the gift he has for creating beautiful and graceful things in books or in hearing about it from other people who had done it. There is really no alternative to doing it in order to understand things.

Framework for Accomplishment was designed as something to be done rather than something to be read. It is not an evaluation instrument, nor is it a training method. (Perhaps it was a bit of a fraud being at the conference at all!) It is designed for people who want to find a more effective way to improve services, to practically use, and consists of a set of loose-leaf pages written by John O'Brien and Connie Lyle O'Brien.[1] It is in this form because many people have made a

---

1   The Framework for Accomplishment manual is obtainable by attending Framework workshops. Information can be obtained about these in this country from: Constructive Options, 17 Belle Vue Road, Wivenhoe, Colchester, Essex CO7 9LD; or in the United States from: John and Connie O'Brien, 58 Willowick Drive, Lithonia, Georgia 30038, USA.

contribution to it. As they get new contributions based on people's practical experience, pages are taken out and fresh ones added. It is not 'done' yet – they keep finding new things to add. Also, as they use it people are encouraged to write in their own additional materials, to be with them for the next time they use it. It is a thing to be worked on – a design for a workshop in the sense that George's workshop is a workshop, a place where there are unfinished projects, work in progress, and materials and tools to hand. You will not necessarily use all of them for every job and a certain amount of space is taken up by things that are there because they 'just might come in again one day'.

To understand Framework for Accomplishment you need to understand two words: 'Framework' and 'Accomplishment'. I am assuming you have got the 'for' already.

'Framework' is the supporting frame of a building or other construction or the basic structure of an idea. Using PASS and PASSING maybe a hundred or more times we had the feeling that even then we had only begun to scratch the surface of what potential there was for learning with it. (In much the same way as George's chisels have been used hundreds and hundreds of times and he still seems to find new things to do with them.) But in using it we found that there was an awkward divide in public service bureaucracies around training and service development – a division between two activities seen as if they were quite separate. We also noticed that a lot of the organisations that seem to spend the most on training and service development actually seemed to be the organisations that were the most stuck. There is a condition described by the organisational theorist, Donald Schon (Argyris and Schon 1978), called 'Dynamic Conservatism', which essentially means that people run around very fast in order to remain still. It is the condition that enabled people in the 1950s to invent the notion of the therapeutic community (an idea which is fundamentally challenging to the very essence of the institution of the large psychiatric hospital, and attacked its very roots). Yet probably within months, certainly years, virtually every institution in the land declared itself to be a therapeutic community. They had absorbed the idea and had taken it on board. It is the practice that enables a revolutionary idea like normalisation to be 'taken on board' by organisations all over the country without significant change in what they do – Dynamic Conservatism.

There is a kind of a trap when processes and procedures become owned by the organisations that they were designed to change. One of the dangers that we have always found with PASS and PASSING is that it can become sucked into the 'training-and-service-development-conference round'. Although there is nothing inherently wrong with meeting and working with others on shared problems and issues, the round can become an activity-trap – an alternative to real change. Fashionable courses are something to put on the Curriculum Vitae – 'Have you done your PASSING yet?' It can become an unthinking 'part of the way we do things around here'. So one part of what we were doing was to step outside that. Framework was designed as an approach to changing services which could come from outside the standard organisational processes of 'training' and 'service-development'.

(Incidentally, the way that people have tried to safeguard PASS and PASSING against being colonised by the service system, is that the organisation – CHMERA – which co-ordinates PASS and PASSING in this country does not belong to any service organisation; it is completely independent. The second thing is that nobody who does the teaching of PASS and PASSING relies just on that for their living, in this country at least. It is done by people who stand outside the service-system in important ways.)

The notion of accomplishments may seem a little strange at first. The story begins[2] with a group of community politicians, people who had come together primarily on the basis that they voted the funds for services in the communities they represented and therefore had an interest in quality and in services. They responded to questions like: 'Why do you do this?', 'What are you working for here?', 'What kind of Community do you seek to build?' in some interesting ways. After about a day and a half of debate and discussion the list of things that they thought were really important in their picture of the Community that they aspired to build was narrowed down to five things:

- First, they said that they had a Community in which they were reasonably good at dealing with the people who were independent, you just ignored them, and you were pretty good at dealing with the people who were very dependent, you chucked them out or you put them away somewhere. What they were not really very good at was generating some kind of interdependence between people and fostering those things that build interdependence.

- Second, they said that there were a lot of human resources in their Communities that got wasted. There were a lot of people who could do stuff that they never got a chance to do. There were a lot of people whose lives were just spoiled, and that seems sad. There was a lot of waste going on.

- Third, they said there were conflicts in their Communities. People had different interests, some people needed to move fast about the place, others needed to take more time. Some people learned quickly, others took more time. People came from different segments and sectors, different ways of life, different patterns of life and these were a potential basis of conflict and strain in their Communities. What they needed was a way of resolving those conflicting interests creatively and in such a way that it did not damage anybody.

- Fourth, they said their Community did not value everybody equally, there were many people who were despised and who were rejected, people who did not gain respect of other citizens on the basis of characteristics that they had which they could do very little about.

- Finally, they said there were a lot of people who got shoved to the side, who did not share the same places that the rest of us do. People we do

2 John and Connie were meeting with community politicians in connection with helping people think about their community services supporting disabled children and their families in one part of the USA.

not see a lot, they get sent away, they are not here amongst us a lot of the time.

Those were five challenges – about as many as it is convenient to remember in one go. They then considered a response to the question: 'If you had a Community that was addressing those challenges in a creative and constructive way, what kinds of lives would people lead?' They said in essence:

Well, they would lead valued lives, and their valued lives would look like this. If we promoted interdependence between people then people would genuinely grow in their relationships, people would have growing sets of relationships which had greater and deeper meaning to them over time. Second, you would find that people discover and develop their gifts, people would make contributions to their Community, people would discover the capacities that they had. Third, if conflicts would be resolved in constructive and creative ways then lots more people would have power over their own lives and would be able to manage their own lives a great deal better and there would be many more choices available to people. Fourth, that if we offered valued roles to everybody then everybody would be respected and would have dignity and, finally, that if we included everyone in our Community then they would all get to share the same ordinary places and activities with one another.

Several days later they took up a challenge to meet some disabled people and find out what their lives were like, see how they measured up to the five ideas they had just created. Some time before, John had been associated with a group which developed a small manual called *Getting to Know You* (Brost, Johnson, Wagner and Deprey 1982). Essentially it said that before you begin to design services around people, it is not a bad idea to get to know them. The little manual taught people how to get to know somebody and had some suggestions and guidelines about how you make a sensitive, authentic, responsible profile of a person which genuinely does help you to understand what are some of the key circumstances in their life. The community representatives used this process.

- They found that commonly people had very few and very restricted relationships. Most of the people in their lives were people who were paid to be there, not people who had chosen to be there. A lot of the valued relationships in their lives had been lost and had been substituted with paid, bought relationships from service agencies. Their lives were surrounded by rented people.
- They found that people had a very low level of contribution to their Community, not much was expected of them, not many opportunities were given for people to make a contribution to their Community life. People did not expect much of themselves either.
- They found that people had a very limited voice, they did not have much choice because there were no options, there was no way out of where they currently were. Mostly, the place where they now were was the one game in town, that was the place where you would be if you

were disabled or if you have a learning difficulty, if you have mental health problems or if you are old.

- They found that disabled people where they lived had a negative reputation, they met prejudiced and inappropriate limited responses from the citizenry of the town. Other people held negative and self-fulfilling notions, 'well, you can't expect those people to do any more', and so those people never did – vicious circles that people get trapped in, of low expectation and low achievement.

- Finally, they found that a lot of disabled people were, quite literally, separated out, physically, geographically separated out from the rest of the town, did not take any part, the places provided for disabled people were not where everybody else was, and the buildings that were there for everybody else physically disabled people literally could not get in and out of anyway, so there were a lot of barriers too. There were other, less visible barriers too.

Some new questions began to occupy their attention. 'How much of this is it reasonable for paid human services to tackle? What is it reasonable for social services and health agencies to take on? What could we reasonably hold services accountable for? What should they be working towards?' The five key ideas were used to define worthy accomplishments ('outcomes that give meaning and worth to activity') of services.

Earlier, John had been asked to write a chapter about how you would use the normalisation ideas to plan the curriculum in developmental programmes for youth and young adults (O'Brien 1987). A version of those same five accomplishments was there used to describe the intended outcomes of designing services around the normalisation principle. This is an often-quoted reference

In fact Framework for Accomplishment is a somewhat different, a larger, idea. For instance, the notion of 'social role valorisation' occurs in just one of the accomplishments out of the five. Further, whereas the notions of social role valorisation and normalisation are based in the theory of devaluation and the response of revaluing people, 'Framework' looks to some of those other strands in the rope, the notions of empowering people and the notion of including people (see Chapter 2). It is different in another sense, too, in that it does not have the same weight of theory underlying it. It actually grows out of some attempts to learn from what people thought. It grew out from the ground rather than growing down from the University of Somewhere. So it is a different kind of idea and has a different source, although it seems to be quite compatible with normalisation. It does not seem to contradict or be in any way antagonistic towards some of its main ideas. It does have a somewhat different focus, and it is worth paying attention to the differences and learning from them.

The idea of 'accomplishment' is itself a slightly unfamiliar one. Bureaucratic organisations love rules, standards and principles because these express their sense of hierarchy and order and structure. They become the basis from which you can judge the loyalty and performance of employees. From them you can decide where information goes, what information is valid and who shall have what information. Second, rules, standards and principles express our sense of what we know now, our current state of knowledge. They are our best stab at trying to set out in abstract form what we currently know about what it is possible to do and how it is reasonable to try and do that. Now, that works well with organisations operating in a fixed, firm and steady environment. But we actually live in a very turbulent service world where change is endemic and often pointless; simply trying to understand which changes make sense and which do not is a major problem. A lot of people doing the most important things in serving people with disabilities are often having to work right out on the very very edge of their organisations. They are almost having to work without the protection of the rules, standards and principles. They are also having to discover new knowledge that lies beyond the ken of the organisation that formulated those standards. So we need to think in terms of things that will draw people on rather than pushing them from behind. The problems with rules, standards and principles is they are things that are used to push people. The interesting thing about an accomplishment is that it is out there; we are yet to get there – it draws us towards it. It is not just a chance that we use the word 'accomplishment' rather than talking about objectives, principles, standards or rules. It is a very different conceptualisation of the nature of the task.

To focus on accomplishments does a number of things. It fixes our attention on the people, because it asks us quite clearly to say, 'What are the experiences in people's lives; and of these, what are the accomplishments of the services that help them?'

Second, it draws our attention to real outcomes. One problem with principles, standards and rules is that organisations get used to cheating and lying about them. They adapt and counterfeit results to show that what they are doing fits with the principles, rules and the standards. That is why you will find all kinds of things being done in the name of normalisation up and down the country. A rule, a principle, a standard is reshaped to justify some bizarre things done in its name. Focusing on accomplishments is a helpful way of valuing the knowledge that grows out of experience rather than down from theory. So these are some reasons to think in terms of accomplishments.

The manual 'Framework for Accomplishment' is a basic supporting structure for a workshop. Although it grew from earlier experience its main resemblance to PASS and PASSING is that it takes about five and a half days. The manual structures people's work by drawing their attention to capacity. A problem of most evaluation systems is they tend to focus on deficiency. They lead us into a search for things that are going wrong. Framework directs people's attention to seek out capacity – capacity in the people served, capacity in the unused skills and qualities of the staff and the communities round about – all of the gifts that they have. Second, Framework directs people to strategies for problem-solving. It purposefully sets out to encourage innovation and creativity. Third, it directs attention towards Community and relationships. (PASS and PASSING did both of those things, but somewhat inadequately.) Framework directs attention to look for sources of natural support in people's lives that services may seek to encourage and enhance.

As a process Framework is again somewhat different. It purposefully sets out to be a collaborative process. Typically we invite a group of local services in one area each to offer themselves as focal services in the workshop. They receive a visit from people keen to learn how you provide services. We often seek out services that are themselves small, new, fragile, innovative and struggling – already moving towards change. One exciting thing about a Framework workshop is that people get the chance to look at some of the most advanced projects of their kind that currently exist, and that in itself builds a special potential for learning.

Those services are not just the subject of the workshop to help us learn, we also invite them to have people come and be learners too. They visit other local services that like themselves are small, struggling, innovative and fragile. From this, collaboration grows between services in one locality. This has led us to look again at standard processes commonly used in workshops of this kind. In much evaluation people feel vulnerable because they have been very open and have invited a stranger to come in and look at what they are doing. One safeguard has been to offer a guarantee of confidentiality around the whole process. We set some rules about who can talk about what and when. One unintended consequence is that it seals off a flow of information, and may make it very difficult to learn certain things. It cuts off possibilities for collaboration between people. So we do not operate with a 'confidentiality rule' in the Framework workshop. We encourage teams to collaborate with one another during the process of the workshop, and to build a collaborative relationship with the people in the service they are visiting. We remind them there is a problem with information about things which are sensitive in people's lives and we counsel them to be thoughtful and aware about who they have permission to share what they have learnt with. So the issue ceases to be about confidentiality (protecting the organisation) and becomes one of responsibility to seek permission and that responsibility is placed on individual participants and on teams.

Framework is the result of an effort to create the very lightest structure – the simplest form that will work. It was tempting to use all of that experience from hundreds of PASS and PASSING workshops – to try and build in what was known about structuring people's learning in thoughtful and productive ways. We tried to see what of that it was necessary to use – it seems very little. Instead of experienced team leaders there are some fairly detailed written agendas for team meetings. There are frequent instructions to 'Check with the workshop leader now'. We have found it works well. People stay up late at nights (about as often as they do at more structured PASS workshops), and generally work more hours than you would ever reasonably expect them to. Putting people alongside others who use services and saying, 'Have a think about this person's position, see if you can invent some creative ideas, in that person's life' places a strong responsibility on them to work hard.

The accounts people give of the nature and conditions of people's lives are as incisive, as sharp and as perceptive as those seen in any other kind of evaluation. Perhaps the accounts of service structures lack some of the precision and sharpness you would get from a PASS or a PASSING analysis. But they are good enough – people seem able to learn enough about service systems using Framework to be able to get done the job they are there to do.

The workshop invites participants to engage with two simultaneous streams of work. One asks them to focus on people and the community of which they would naturally be a part. The team goes and finds that community and the resources that are there to begin to build community lives for the people who rely on it. There are a number of tools in the manual and also in the form of some separate workbooks with blank pages and questions by them. They guide curiosity and jog the memory. Like George's tools, we don't expect them all to be used for every job. Participants pick out those that seem to make some sense and are helpful and they write in the book. (This is not one of those events where you try to keep the pages clean so that you can take them home and photocopy them free for all your colleagues back at work – we can give participants blank copies to take home if they really want.)

At the same time we ask people to go and visit a service user, to be introduced to somebody and to spend time over three days, getting to know something of that person's life. They will never 'know' that person, any more than you can ever know anybody, but you can know a good deal about them in three days, about the major circumstances in their life. They will not be that person's friend (and we counsel people not to promise that), but they will know enough to gain some sense of where services need to be making a major contribution in people's lives. So that is one whole piece of work we ask people to undertake.

In parallel with that task Framework supports them in making a description of the service that is provided, in several different forms. Worksheets direct attention to the five service accomplishments, and invite participants to construct measures of how much the service supports each of them. The Manual invites them to analyse the strategy the service is currently using. The service has some resources, buildings and settings, some people grouped in various ways, a lot of time, and its own personal behaviour and demeanour – these are all things that the service can manage. They may not have as many staff, as much money as they would like and there may be all kinds of outside constraints, but how are they using what they do have? What, specifically, are they investing in these five valued experiences in people's lives? What is their strategy for increasing their support of the five accomplishments?

After a couple of days participants are ready to make two crucial statements about:

- What's most important now, in the life of the person that I met, or in the lives of the five or six people that our team met?
- What are the key service development issues for this service now – in terms of how it is doing what it is doing?

At that point we ask people to make an imaginative leap:

this service is responsible for some important things in people's lives – it may not be able to do everything – but it can act constructively. Think of a constructive action that would both address that situation in people's lives, and would also address those key things this service needs to learn in order to develop and grow.

So teams are challenged to use all their creative skills. The manual has some useful prompts (which I will not spend time on here) to encourage people to think in the most creative ways they can.

A constructive action is defined in Framework by these three criteria:

- It will be action that focuses on capacity – of people, of communities, of services themselves, by redirecting resources that are already available. This is not quite the same as saying, 'See if you can find a service you can do in that building' (a common enough 'planning' strategy). Rather, it is about trying to use all of the capacities currently available including many we may not even recognise – for instance when we were looking for a family for Christopher who did not have one, we failed to notice that right next to him was a staff person who had worked with him for many years and had a family that needed somebody like Christopher to make it complete. Only when we realised staff people are members of the community too, did we see their skills, capacities and resources. We began to understand how we could unlock unused capacity if we started thinking differently about the people we paid. So that is one thing a constructive action does.

- Second, it will be an action that requires the service to learn by doing – by trying something out.

- It will be an action that will increase valued experiences for at least one person. You may think that is a small criterion, though mostly people find it the hardest test of all to administer. It asks you to try doing for one person what you may not be able to do for everybody. Sometimes people have grown used to doing nothing for anyone. Mostly, we only make progress by making exceptions.

So that, briefly, is Framework for Accomplishment. It is not designed to replace PASS or PASSING, any more than George's plane was designed to replace his chisels. They are simply different tools, and they do a different job. Framework for Accomplishment seems to give people a permission they did not think they had. It gives a creative focus to work, that they thought before was simply a matter of conforming to rules, standards and principles. It encourages people to take small initiatives around individuals – initiatives that often make a big difference in their life.

It is a different strategy for service change. It is not an alternative to some kind of social revolution, but is something we can be getting on and doing, that will make real differences. It engages the attention of many people who wish to make small but significant changes in people's lives, including their own, and at the same time to invest in organisational learning.

Summary of Discussion

Discussion covered questions of using the material appropriately, its accessibility, and over-servicing.

Preventing Inappropriate Usage of Framework

A delegate asked Alan Tyne how you could prevent people taking on board these ideas and using them inappropriately. AT replied that he thought that a lot of the safeguards for the processes that had been under discussion relied on techniques which forced people to work alongside and with people and to struggle together around the problems they faced. He thought that many perversions of the ideas resulted from wanting to package the whole thing and do it at a distance from people. Debate and personal contact were the most important guarantees.

Accessibility

A delegate said that Framework was difficult to get hold of. AT said that this was partly because one of the strategies in using Framework was to use it for services that asked for it to be used with them. It had not been made available for use by inviting professionals from all over the country to workshops to come and learn it and take it away and do it. That way it would have become just another of the things that gets packaged and used in strange ways. They had handed it on to a lot of people who have actually worked with it, and now used it as service development practice in their particular areas.

The delegate then asked if AT was saying that the safeguard was not to make the manual very accessible to people. AT said that this was a sad and unfortunate consequence, although he could not see why in time it would not get more accessible. The way to get it was by working on it. There were packaged versions available. He had recently been asked to review an Irish version. These people had taken a whole chunk of the material out and copyrighted it in their name. There was very good stuff about analysing the structure of services, but it seemed to miss out a great chunk about getting alongside people and understanding what their lives were like.

Another delegate said she had not come across the five accomplishments before, and was not sure if she had understood. Were they five things that services can aim to accomplish? AT said that they were like five useful projects for services to work on.

Dangers of Over-Servicing

A delegate asked if there was a danger of over-servicing, of trying to accomplish everything through services. AT said that one of the big dilemmas for services was the in-built assumption that the answer to every problem in a person's life was a member of staff. Dependency upon paid staff had been encouraged, to do things which were within the natural remit of friends and relatives. One of the interesting things that they had used Framework for a great deal was trying to think how scarce service resources might be used to support and enable people to do things that they might not otherwise have been able to do. They had asked Denis what they would have to do for him to be able to look after Christopher, and he had said he would not be able to come in (to work) every day. They said that was fine, they would arrange for him to go on getting his salary and not come in. A lot of Framework was about using existing resources in innovative ways which unlock other resources.

Resources were wasted by over-helping people. A person might need twenty minutes help a week to get to and from Brownies. What they were given was a Brownie pack inside an institution that nobody else wanted to go to. It was horrendously costly in every way.

A delegate said she could imagine the obstacles that would be raised if she brought the Denis/Christopher story into her organisation. AT said that you could not expect things to be easy. You needed a strong guiding model, like Framework, and you needed to give permission to use the creativity that lies in all of us and to provide people with tools to do this. For a lot of the time organisations did the reverse: they provided muddled models, and they did not allow people to do things without permission.

References

Argyris, C. and Schon, D. (1978) *Organizational Learning*. Reading, Massachusetts: Addison-Wesley.

Brost, M. Johnson, T.Z., Wagner, L. and Deprey, R.K. (1982) *Getting to Know You: One Approach to Service Planning and Assessment for People with Disabilities*. Madison, WI: Wisconsin Coalition for Advocacy.

O'Brien, J. (1987) A guide to life style planning: using the Activities Catalog to integrate services and natural support systems. In B.W. Wilcox and G.T. Bellamy (eds) *The Activities Catalog: An Alternative Curriculum for Youths and Adults with Severe Disabilities*. Baltimore: Paul H. Brookes.

Part 4

Workshops
What Are Evaluations for, and How Should They Be Carried Out?

Chapter 16

Service Evaluation by People with Learning Difficulties[1]

Simon Gardner and Andrea Whittaker

Simon Gardner (People First): We had to evaluate two houses. We went with the people who lived in them to their day centres and to their clubs to see how they lived their lives. One house had been open for about a year and one for only a few months.

We met people at the Regional Health Authority in Paddington in 1990. We had to work out what we were going to do. We met John Spargo, who works at Hillingdon, and the other people from the health authority and social services and found out what they wanted us to do. It was the first evaluation of its type to be done by people with a learning difficulty. My learning difficulty is that I am dyslexic, so it is very difficult sometimes to read a lot of things in one lump. But that did not stop me doing the evaluation.

We interviewed managers and key workers, and spent time with people who were living in the houses to see what they did. I found it a bit hard at the beginning because we had only two weeks to do it in. We had to almost be 'on their shoulders' and see it through their eyes. We did get quite friendly with a lot of them and this helped. Could you go out and interview somebody you do

1 The evaluation discussed in this workshop is reported in: Whittaker, A., Gardner, S. and Kershaw, J. (1991) *Service Evaluation by People with Learning Difficulties*. London: King's Fund Centre.

not know at all and not have your knees going nineteen to the dozen? That itself is quite nerve-racking.

The people in the houses went to clubs – most were only for people with learning difficulties, but one was mixed – they had non-disabled people and disabled people, and that was great, the integrated club.

Joyce Kershaw (also from People First) from Huddersfield and I worked together as a team. When she was interviewing, she wrote things down on paper; through being dyslexic, I found it a bit hard reading the questions, but I did memorise a lot of the questions so it was all in my head. When I did my bits of putting the report together, I would rush out of the room that we did the interview in and go and sit in Andrea's car and put it all on to a dictaphone while it was fresh in my memory; then it was typed up and put into the report. Sometimes I would go into one of their bedrooms and sit on the floor and put it all on to the dictaphone. I had not used a dictaphone before doing this work, so that was an experience; and even today I use a dictaphone quite a lot for other work that I do. I learned that skill very quickly – it is a useful skill.

Why Was it Important to do the Evaluation?

Evaluations have always been done by non-disabled people; they have gone into hospitals, hostels or whatever and evaluated services. When I was asked to do the evaluation, I jumped at it. Through working with elderly and disabled people in Wandsworth, I understood a lot of the issues around independent living, the problems that the people are having living in the community, and so on. I felt that, because of my experiences being a disabled person and because I had lived in hostels and a group home for about six months, I could relate to a lot of the problems that these people were going through in the two houses that we had to evaluate. Because I did not go in wearing a 'whistle and flute' (that is, a suit), they felt comfortable; I went in wearing jeans and T-shirts and that sort of thing. In a way, most people feel more relaxed then; if you go in wearing a suit, people feel threatened by it – because you are 'official' and you are 'up here', and they feel very uncomfortable.

Andrea Whittaker (King's Fund): A key factor in this work was that senior people in Hillingdon were already convinced about the need for user involvement. They had already done a lot of work in trying to involve users in services in Hillingdon and the regional health authority was prepared to back up this conviction with funding for the evaluation. Joyce and Simon were the consultants, and I was there in a supporting role. Another important point was that we started by asking People First members what they felt was important about living in the community, started by getting the users' opinions about what they want.

SG: Our very first meeting was at the King's Fund Centre in Camden. Members of People First came and talked about all their experiences of their lives; that is how we drew up the questionnaires for the interviews. We put up loads of flip-chart paper all over the walls in quite a lot of the rooms, and we drew up the questionnaires – how we were going to ask the questions and what questions we were going to ask. To help people tell us how good or bad things were compared to where they lived before, we used the faces shown in Figure 16.1.

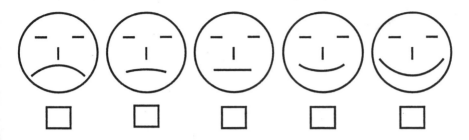

Figure 16.1

We had to understand how these people were feeling and what they were going through, moving from a group home or a hostel into a house in the community. Some were pleased that they were there, and so a lot of the time they did go for the happy face; they got enough support from their link workers or key workers in the house.

One of the houses had four men in it, and the other had three people, two ladies and a gentleman. In the second house, the three people needed minimal support: staff were only there at certain times during the week. The other house, staff were there on a 24 hour basis. In the house where more support was needed, staff prepared the meals and the residents would help. At the other house, people did their own shopping and cooked their own meals.

When they moved into the houses, they chose the furniture: that was good. It was paid for by social services, but the people went out and chose the decor – which was brilliant because, when you go to an establishment that is run by social services, you have always got the same fittings. But in their bedrooms they had their own personal touch.

One of the houses was in a cul-de-sac. I thought, 'Why is it right down at the end of the cul-de-sac – because there is nobody next door?' I would have thought it would be more in the middle of the road, not right down the end, away from everybody else. But they were not very far from the shops, which was good. They could go out the back gate of the garden to the high street and get stuff like milk with a member of staff if they needed help to get it. They would go and buy things for themselves in that way, using the shops in the community.

AW: Simon and Joyce used John O'Brien's five accomplishments (see Alan Tyne, Chapter 15, for more information about these) to help judge the services. These are: community presence, choice, competence, relationships, respect. The last one is about respect and links with the community. Simon and Joyce decided they could not really judge that one because they had not seen enough examples of people actually being linked in the community nor reactions of local people. So they used the first four only.

To summarise, they used a system of pluses and minuses. Where there is a plus and a minus, that was Joyce and Simon's way of saying they did not think it was all bad or all good but was in between: it was average. It was just an overall way of making a very summarised judgement (see Table 16.1).

Table 16.1

	House 1			House 2		
	At home (the houses)	Daytime (working hours)	Leisure	At home (the houses)	Daytime (working hours)	Leisure
Community presence	+	-	-	+	±	-
Relationships	-	-	-	-	-	-
Choice	+	-	-	+	-	+
Competence	+	-	-	+	-	±

The score on relationships was low because there was not very much yet about relationships with people outside the house. It was OK within the house; people's connections were mostly with the staff in the house or with the family where the family was involved. But outside there was pretty well nothing. The fact that people were still using very segregated day services did not help.

SG: The day centre was all the people's life. They would go from home to the day centre, come back home again, have their evening meal and then be taken out in the car to their clubs – and that was their life. They had not been living there long; they knew each other through living in the group home and in the hostel previously, but they had not made links with the neighbours – they were just getting to know the neighbours. It all takes time to move into a new area and to get to know the shops and to know who they can trust and who they cannot trust.

SG: Planning and timing was quite complicated. We had to be in many different places at different times – like Joyce and I would be separately going to different places: I was dropped off, Joyce would be dropped off. With club visiting, sometimes we would stay at the club. We had to fit in meals when and wherever we could. I have never eaten so much junk food!

AW: Getting on with the residents and staff went very well. As Simon has already said, there was a very friendly atmosphere in the houses. That was partly because the staff were so positive about the evaluation and there already was this ethos of users being involved. The staff were very willing for us to come in, and we worked very well together; that was really good.

SG: We supported each other as well, which was a good thing. Joyce's accent was hard, coming from Huddersfield – you can imagine! At first it was quite hard for me to understand what she was talking about; but, by the end of the fortnight, she could say something in her own way and I would understand it.

AW: Recording information worked well – the questionnaires and using the dictaphone and so on. Helping people understand the questions was good too. However, some of the questions were difficult for people to understand, even though they had been phrased in the way that People First members wanted.

SG: Sometimes we had to change the question, so the people understood it.

AW: We had a special office at Hillingdon put at our disposal. It was very important to have this to just relax or do some of the work, as well as using my house or the King's Fund Centre. Although it was very hard work, we all enjoyed it.

SG: Yes, we were shattered by the end of the fortnight, I can tell you.

AW: Another lesson we learned was that we needed more time to get to know people. We did have half a day in each house, getting to know the people, but that was not really enough time, particularly for the people who did not communicate through words. At the end, we talked about that and we doubt whether, in the scope of the evaluation and the resources we had, it really would have been possible to get to know the people well; it would have taken a very long time.

SG: In the house with four men, two in particular had severe communication problems. One person could only answer 'Yes' and 'No'. That was very hard when you had to ask, say, ten questions. With the other person, the key worker sat in because she understood his nods and his dislikes and so forth, and that was helpful. But she would not put any words into his mouth or speak for him. It was only what he felt following the questions that she asked him, interpreted by sign language.

AW: An interesting point about that person, who only 'spoke' with sign language, was during the interview he said he was not happy in the house. His key worker was very surprised as it was the first time that he had said that. She did not know, and it was obviously genuine. We felt that this was at least partly due to the fact that he was being interviewed by someone who shared some of his life experience and so he felt understood how he was feeling.

SG: Andrea was 'the taxi'. Sometimes we would not get home till 11 o'clock at night; that was the killer – especially if you had to go to the day centre and interview the manager or anybody else on the next day at 9 o'clock in the morning and you had only had a couple of hours' kip. It is hard to get to sleep, your brain is so much in gear, thinking about what you have done that day and making sure that you put it down on paper or, in my case, on to the dictaphone, and seeing that you have not missed out anything. That was the hard thing.

A Delegate: Would you just say something about how the evaluation was presented back to the homes – and what was the reaction?

SG: The report back to the homes was very positive. They were very impressed with what we had done for them, and they realised how good things really were. With staff working there and the people living there, they take things for granted.

AW: We had half a day reporting back in each house. Particularly for the four men, we did a poster with lots of pictures about what Simon and Joyce had thought. The staff were very positive about that. We also had another meeting with more senior people in the Borough. There were one or two of the middle managers who were a bit defensive on that occasion, but on the whole they were pretty positive. The biggest change was that they closed a day centre.

SG: Yes, they closed it – because we condemned it. When we went in there, it was a dump. All it was was Army-type cabins, all put together and holes knocked through and door frames put in and so on.

A Delegate: Did you find the homes over-supervised or under-supervised?

SG: Where the four men lived, I felt that there was enough support for the people who were living there. The staff were tuned in to their individual needs and knew what they wanted; the people would say what they wanted or did not want. They did go out and buy the food, choosing what they were going to have – which was good. They were in control of that side of their lives – which was good.

A Delegate: After purchasing the food, they were supervised in preparing...

SG: Yes. The staff would do the cooking, but they...

The Delegate: Oh, the staff did the cooking? I do not think that was a very good idea.

SG: The people had not long moved out of a hostel where the food was all prepared for them, and it had been opened for only six months; so there was a lot of work to do. Some people take a long time to learn to prepare a meal or open a tin and put the baked beans into a saucepan; this is a slow process. So, in six months, the people had achieved a lot. If we went back there today, there would be a big difference.

AW: There was a big difference in the second house. The people there were older and had a lot of skills. For me, one of the sad things about one of the two ladies in the second house (both were approaching retiring age) was that she had lived with her family until she went into the hostel; she was describing all the things she used to do when she was with the family – and had lost all those skills when she had been in the hostel and was now just relearning them in the house; it was such a waste.

A Delegate: Did you have any agreement up front of the evaluation that your findings would be acted upon?

SG: A lot of the things that we recommended in the report were acted on anyway. They did not really question what Joyce and I said. They looked at our judgement and our experiences and what people had said to us as 'gospel' really – because they wanted the whole project to work. They wanted to prove to the managers in the various departments of social services that this could work.

AW: We did not have any formal contract in the sense of it being written down in black and white. But the initial meeting that Simon was talking about with the Region and in the other preparatory meetings definitely gave us the impression that they were going to be very open to change. Of course, the day centre was the best example. I do not think that Simon and People First would claim that it was only just because of People First that the day centre was closed – because people were aware that there were things wrong with it. But the senior managers definitely said that it was People First's opinion – the very telling account from both him and Joyce about that centre – that tipped the balance into making the decision that it should be closed down. This is a quote from what John Spargo, one of the senior people in Hillingdon, said:

> Most if not all of the practical steps recommended in the evaluation have been taken, and the world and lives of the people directly involved in the study have moved on, as one would expect. But the model of the evaluation is positive and the successful outcome has given Hillingdon a range of insights which are being built into the thinking about service inspection and standard settings.

He then says:

> Actual examples are a user–carer forum playing a part in the future shape of daytime services, user groups working alongside inspectors in the arms-length inspection of residential homes, a user group working alongside officers to look at the way respite services are provided.

Although we have not gone back formally, we have been in touch from time to time. Some of the practical things have happened – like getting more volunteer drivers so that people can go to more activities in the community.

Delegate: I ask that because I think it is enormously important that you got the Hillingdon senior management on your side to carry that through. Two user consultants did a similar exercise in two different boroughs and, where they got senior management support, the recommendations from the evaluation were carried through; training and various other changes in the day centre actually occurred. In the other case, where there was antagonism from senior managers, nothing actually changed.

AW: I am sure that is extremely important. As Simon said, People First is going to do another evaluation, this time funded by Rowntree, which follows on from this work and is going to be much bigger. It will be in two London boroughs; they have not been chosen yet. We are very aware that, with the Hillingdon project, Hillingdon approached People First; they were already convinced about what they wanted to happen. In the next, People First is going to have to do that work about agreeing what is going to happen afterwards – which they did not have to do before.

A Delegate: I was wondering about the man who said he did not like where he lived. What happened to him?

AW: He has moved. I think to his own flat or sharing with someone else

Delegate: One of the places that we went into as consultants, interviewing people, was a community house where people were living and there were some staff living in. When we spent time there when the staff were around, we got one set of views; when the staff were not there, we got a very different set of views from the users. However, the users said, 'Please don't tell what we're saying because we're in fear of reprisal.' That put us in a really difficult position. Do we actually say how it is – and worry the life out of these users, and some of them were putting up with some really uncomfortable practices – or do we not? It is one of those dilemmas that you have to think through first – and almost put it to the staff and users before you go in. That was something we found difficult. We get all this information and then we have to make some very delicate choices. In this instance, we persuaded the users that it was in their interests to say what they were actually feeling.

AW: All the interviews in our work were done without staff being present – except the one that Simon mentioned where we needed help to understand what one man was saying.

A Delegate: Were all the people living in the houses willing to participate in the project? How was that sounded out before the project was started?

SG: The people in the bungalow were more open to being interviewed and to tell us about their lives. But the people in the other house were not so happy about being asked questions – because they had different abilities and they did not want to share it as openly as the other people. But it was all to do with trust; they trusted us. As I said earlier on, I did not go in there with a collar and tie on and nicely polished shoes; they did not feel threatened.

A Delegate: Simon brought out one good thing about the evaluation – that the authority closed down the day centre. Did the authority replace that with a better service?

AW: What they were aiming to do was to have several small 'bases' in different areas from where people could go out to use ordinary facilities in the community. I do not know how far they got with this plan: there have been a tremendous lot of cuts in Hillingdon (as there have been in other places). Some of the things they would ideally like to have done they have not been able to do.

A Delegate: Is not that the problem? With resources for larger numbers of people, such as day centres that are set up for people with learning difficulties or with mental health problems, how can you provide a service like that for a group with such a vast range of difficulties all together. You inevitably get the lowest common denominator. In the centre where I work, if you ask some people who have been in hospital or in an institution for a long time, they actually wanted the staff to wear uniforms again. They felt more comfortable with that...

SG: It is a slow process for people to adjust to coming back into the community. A lot of them have not known anything different. That is all they know...

A Delegate: If one of the users said to you they would like the staff to wear uniforms, would your recommendation be that the staff should wear uniforms or that they should not? Is it your recommendation or is it your users' recommendation?

SG: When we were asking the question – whatever the question might have been at the time, we would have gone by what they said; it would have been wrong if we had put down on the paper what we felt they had said. The evaluation was to evaluate their quality of life and their life – not my quality of life and my life. So you had to be impartial about what they were saying, be in tune with what they were saying.

A Delegate: Would you have said what you have just said to us as well – about how with time that will change?

SG: This is the first time that this question has ever come up while I have been doing this. My personal opinion would be that the staff could wear uniforms and eventually do away with the uniforms gradually so that they would adjust to it. In that way, in time, they would adjust; so you would wear the uniform regularly for, say, six months, and every so often you would go in your new clothes. You would not go and change into a uniform; you would wear your uniform for, say, three hours a day, depending on circumstances for the people who are in the house, and eventually you cut down the hours you wear that uniform, and eventually they would adjust to seeing you in your clothes. That is my personal opinion on how I would deal with it.

AW: To finish off with, some issues for the future. We have already talked about the need for users to be involved from the top to the bottom. The commitment of staff at all levels in the service is going to be essential for user involvement to be effective and for this type of work to be effective. One of the great things about Hillingdon was that the service users – members of People First – were involved right from the beginning and they had control over the work. It was all built on what they said; it was not professionals deciding first of all what the questions were and then involving users afterward.

Providing appropriate support is essential; getting the balance right between the support being appropriate but not actually taking away from the people who are doing the work – their actual ideas, their opinions and their way of doing it and letting them be in control.

We need to work out how much help from professional researchers is appropriate – for example, training for the consultants and help with developing questionnaires. We felt it was better for this first time that there was not much involvement because it meant that the control did stay with People First members. On the other hand, we have to consider for the future what training would be helpful to enable people to do the job even better – without turning them into quasi-professionals or quasi-researchers; that is important.

SG: I personally would not let myself go that way. Once you get into that trap, then the whole process changes; people will not open up to you and talk to you on their level, because they will see an image of a professional person who is up there and they are down here, and they are looking up to you.

I mentioned earlier that, since the evaluation, I joined my Community Health Council and now I go around in my two boroughs (Merton and Sutton Health Authority) and monitor with other members the quality of life in the hospitals and the hostels that are run by the health authority in our district. So the skills that I learnt from doing the evaluation I use every day when I am involved in my Community Health Council. As far as I know, I am the only person with a learning difficulty on a community health council in the whole country. Doing the evaluation helped me and naturally made me decide to go on to my Community Health Council.

Chapter 17

Aiming for Objectivity and Balance in the Evaluation of the Quality of Life Experienced by Service Users with Learning Disabilities

David Hughes

Introduction

The aim of this workshop was to explore issues around objectivity in evaluating services for people with learning disabilities.

The workshop had the following format:

1. A presentation by the workshop leader on objectivity in evaluation, using three measurement tools that are commonly employed by the Tizard Centre, which is based at the University of Kent at Canterbury, to illustrate some of the issues.

2. Exercises in small groups with feedback reported to workshop participants as a whole.

Presentation

Non-Participant Observation, Using the MTS Programme

This involves taking a momentary time sample of an individual's (or group of individuals') level of activity and participation, social behaviour, level of contact received from staff/carers and problem behaviour using a Psion hand-held microcomputer loaded with the MTS software, developed by staff at the Tizard Centre.

At the end of each 20 second interval of the observation session, the observer records the activity and behaviour of an individual using the codes in Table 17.1 (taken from Beasley, Hewson, Mansell, Hughes and Stein 1993).

At the end of the observation, the observer will probably end up with data somewhat like that in Table 17.2 which indicate the amount of time (in percentage terms) of the observation period that the individual spent in each type of activity/behaviour.

Table 17.1

	Activity		*Staff contact*
A	No activity	M	None
B	Leisure/recreational/	N	Positive
	unstructured educational	O	Negative
C	Personal/self care	P	Neutral/indeterminate
D	Practical tasks using electrical/	Q	Assistance
	gas equipment	R	Contact from other client
E	Other practical tasks		
F	Work/formal education		
L	Out walking		

	Social behaviour by client		*Problem behaviour*
G	No social act by client	S	None
H	Clear social act by client	T	Self stimulation/stereotypies
I	Unclear social act by client	U	Self-injury
J	To observer	V	Aggression to others
		W	Damage to property

()%\ 4 additional keys

K	In seclusion	Z	Reminder key	Y	Missed observation

Table 17.2 Data collected during an observation session using MTS programme

A = 55%	G = 86%	M = 75%	S = 94%
B = 10%	H = 12%	N = 5%	T = 3%
C = 15%	I = 1%	O = 5%	U = 1%
D = 15%	J = 1%	P = 15%	V = 2%
E = 0%		Q = 0%	W = 0%
F = 0%		R = 0%	(= 0%
L = 5%			) = 0%
			% = 0%
			\ = 0%

Thus, if we look at the activity data, we can see that this individual spent 55% of his/her time engaged in no activity, 10% engaged in leisure activities, 15% engaged in personal care, 15% engaged in a domestic task involving electrical equipment and 5% out walking.

And, if we look at the staff contact data, we can see that he/she received no contact for 75% of the time observed, positive contact for 5% of the time, negative contact for 5% of the time and neutral contact for 15% of the time.

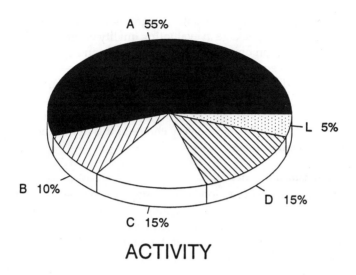

ACTIVITY

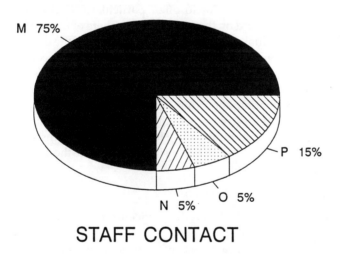

STAFF CONTACT

Figure 17.1

For analysis purposes, these data can be effectively presented in the form of pie charts (Figure 17.1).

I have highlighted these two data categories because they highlight the primary use of the MTS package in evaluating quality of service. It is an accurate and, to a high degree, an objective measure of levels and types of participation and of contact received. However, in recent evaluations, a small proportion of staff have suggested that this non-participant type of observation feels intrusive and has had an effect on their behaviour.

If one equates quality of service with levels of participation and contact received, one will use MTS. *But* the very choice of it is dependent on the values of those who make the choice.

Participant Observation

Essentially, participant observation is a method whereby the researcher is placed within the study setting to observe the activities, people and physical aspects of the situation. In effect, this means that the evaluator him/herself is the recording instrument and it is always the case that the information collected will be based on his or her own interpretation of what is witnessed. In many situations, it is impossible to record information as events happen and so much can depend on a good memory.

Having just cast doubts upon its objectivity and reliability, I have to say that participant observation has a lot to offer, particularly if one wants data on carer–user relationships and on the general atmosphere of the service. It can also be useful both in the initial stages of an evaluation to help the evaluator develop an insight into the service and in the latter stages to verify data collected by other methods. A further advantage, from my experience, is that staff appear to find this method far less intrusive than non-participant observation, and I have acquired more information about how they feel about aspects of the service casually from staff and service users in this stage of an evaluation than when I have interviewed them more formally. However, it still seems to me to be the case that using participant observation by itself to evaluate the quality of a service will provide inadequate data.

Service User Interviews

The final method I want to look at is the service-user interview. This is intended to measure user satisfaction.

However, in services that have users who are non-verbal/non-signing, as well as those who are verbal/signing, this method biases the evaluation by excluding all those who are unable to communicate verbally or through signing. The involvement of relatives, key workers and/or advocates is an option, but is not entirely satisfactory.

Another difficulty when using this method is legislating for the acquiescence phenomenon – the tendency to answer 'Yes' to any yes/no questions which are not clear; for the nay-saying phenomenon – the opposite of acquiescence; and for the phenomenon of recency – i.e. choosing the most recently heard option.

From such interviews that I have conducted, it is often the case that service users are most concerned with the physical amenities provided – the size of their bedrooms, the decor, whether they have own bathroom facilities – rather than their participation levels, the amount of staff contact, the number of training programmes, etc.

Whilst hotel services offered may be approved of by service users, it seems rather a narrow set of criteria upon which to judge the quality of the service. There is, however, an immediate parallel with hospital patients who also express their opinions of the service received in terms of the hotel services, because they have insufficient knowledge to judge the standards of the medical treatment they have been given.

Conclusion

It seems that individual measurement methods used in isolation will be insufficient to give us an objective and balanced picture of the overall quality of any service. From my own experience, I would recommend all three of the above methods be used in combination, and with other measures as appropriate.

Group Exercises

Workshop participants were divided into three groups, each discussing the same two questions, with feedback to the workshop as a whole.

Question 1: Given that users' views are an important factor in measuring the quality of a service, how do you/might you collect these views when the user has difficulties with verbal communication?
The groups suggested observation and consultation with people who knew the users with communication difficulties well as ways of collecting their views. One group suggested getting to know the person well, so that the observer would see how they react and could get to know what pleases and upsets them. It was mentioned that PASS/ING evaluations try to do this, following one service user through their day. Another group suggested using video recording, or MTS, perhaps carried out by other users. Various people were mentioned by the groups as possibly being able to communicate the views of those with communication problems. Advocates were suggested by one group, although they had worries about how these were chosen. Other possibilities mentioned by the groups were: carers; friends, relatives and significant others; other service users who can communicate.

Question 2: How does/might your service involve its users more fully in the whole of its evaluation process?
The groups seemed to concur on the need to avoid tokenism. One group thought that users should be involved in all aspects of evaluation. For there to be communication, jargon had to be avoided. Evaluation should involve working together with users, sharing information with them, and sharing writing any report that might result. This group also considered, though, that there could be too much evaluation, 'for its own sake'. It was also necessary to be clear (and honest) and spell out what can and cannot be changed. A somewhat different viewpoint was expressed by another group, who said that some user groups

might not want to be involved with the management, but would prefer to campaign from the outside.

Reference

Beasley, F., Hewson, S., Mansell, J., Hughes, D. and Stein, J. (1993) *MTS: Handbook for Observers*. Canterbury: Tizard Centre, University of Kent at Canterbury.

Chapter 18

Who Should Evaluations be Carried Out for?

Charles Ritchie

(The views and opinions expressed in this workshop report do not necessarily reflect those of the author. Apart from a minimal amount of interpretation, all the material presented was provided by participants in the workshop.)

There are many different 'stakeholders' concerned with any organisation or project – users, funders, staff, etc. – all of whom have a legitimate interest in any evaluation activities. The aim of this workshop was to consider the different interests and requirements of the various stakeholders and to see how possible it might be to reconcile their requirements.

The workshop was organised around a participatory exercise based on a hypothetical local health project. It was hoped that the exercise would allow people to explore general theoretical aspects of evaluation, as well as looking at practical processes and measures. The following briefing material was given:

> Following a local 'health week' in an inner-city ward of a large industrial city, local health and community workers have managed to set up a community health project attached to a local GP surgery. The project has managed to raise sufficient money to employ a worker for a period of 3 years: she is actually employed by the surgery, with a proportion of her wages being reimbursed by the local Family Health Services Authority (FHSA). The remainder of the money for the project has been raised through a number of sources including the local authority, area health authority, the local healthy city initiative and charitable sources. In addition the Project has been able to apply for 'one-off' funding relating to specific events or campaigns.
>
> The Project works on community development principles and a number of groups (such as Agewell, Women's Health, Food Issues) have been established. A weekly 'drop-in' session is held. In addition a number of courses, some funded through the local branch of the Workers Education Association (WEA), have been run on a variety of topics (such as herbal health, healthy cooking, stress management). The Project also attempts to hold special events focusing on particular topics.

The focus of this session is to consider evaluation aspects of the Project. We will consider these in four stages:

1. Who might be interested in the evaluation? (Stakeholders)
2. What aims might each stakeholder have for the Project and what sort of information will each be interested in?
3. How might information be collected and analysed for each stakeholder? Who should collect it?
4. Are these evaluation requirements different? If so, can they be reconciled?

The first stage of the workshop was to consider who were the main stakeholders. The following list was drawn up by the group working as a whole:

- Local community – users of the health project

    – non-users

- Funders – various
- Management Committee
- Project worker(s)
- Other local workers
- Other communities – not local
- Researchers (with interest in health)
- Local politicians
- Evaluation group (professionals)
- Other GP practices
- Disabled (and other) groups
- Businesses – local

    – relevant national e.g. drug companies

After some discussion it was decided to cluster the different stakeholders into four groups:

1. Recipients (of health project activities).
2. Providers (workers and management committee).
3. Financial stakeholders (actual and potential funders).
4. Other vested interests (mainly groups who are not closely involved with the project such as other communities, researchers, other practices, etc.).

Members of the workshop were split into four groups corresponding to each of the stakeholder groups. Each group was asked to consider the attitude towards the Health Project and its evaluation from the perspective of the group of stakeholders which they represented. Specifically they were asked to consider:

1. the aims that the group might have for the Project
2. the decisions that they might wish to make based on the results of the evaluation
3. the information that they would need in order to be able to make those decisions (and how it could be collected and by whom).

Each group was given (a woefully inadequate) time to explore each of these issues and was then asked to record the main points of their discussions on 'Post-its' – each group using a different colour pen. Each group appointed a member to report back by sticking their 'Post-its' on the wall and supplying any necessary commentary. The intention had been that this exercise would be followed by a session to cluster the main issues raised by the different stakeholder groups and then to look at the similarities and differences to see how 'fundamental' these were. Based on these findings it might then be possible to explore the possibility of a single evaluation exercise being able to satisfy all groups.

As ever, time was the enemy and the exercise did not get through to the later stages. However, each individual group had valuable discussions and the report-back session produced some lively debate. The following represents a summary of some of the discussions which were had. A complete record is not possible because of the failure of the recording equipment, so that the following represents the results of the report back plus 'snippets' overheard as I sat in on each group.

Recipients

The group were clear that 'recipients' would have a clear, though complex, set of aims for the Project. Essentially these focused around whether the project was of 'Direct Benefit to Individuals' and of 'Benefit to the Wider Community'. These were expanded, in the context of the purpose of the evaluation, to asking, 'Do Activities Reflect Need?', questioning the 'Quality and Relevance' of Project activities and establishing 'Information and Access' provided by the Project.

Interestingly, the group rapidly moved onto issues of scope, ownership and control of the Project, highlighting issues such as: 'Who Decides On Activities' and 'Who was Consulted – Users and Non-Users'. A whole area of discussion for 'recipients' focused on process and power rather than outcomes and activities: the decision-making process was deemed to be an element of the quality of the Project.

This concern was reflected in the group's attitude towards the conduct and content of the evaluation. It was seen to be important that the evaluation was carried out by a 'User/Local Person' who was 'Trained and Sensitive'. There was no reference to 'objectivity' or an 'independent/outside evaluator'. The content of the evaluation should focus on 'Questions to Users and Non-Users – about Project Activities/Alternatives, Satisfaction and Outcomes. The main vehicles for gathering information were through 'Questionnaires' and 'Interviews'.

Providers

This group spent less time considering what aims the providers might have for the Project, but concentrated on their hopes (and fears) of evaluation. This may have been of significance in itself.

For the evaluation, the group began by focusing on the high-level objectives of 'Does it Work' and 'Do we Change'. It was interesting that the group's public presentation of their thoughts reflected a professionalism, noting factors such as 'Quality', 'Costs', 'Profile' and 'Values', e.g. 'confidentiality'. However, this masked their internal discussions and notes which clearly demonstrated their wariness about evaluation, noting the following: 'a good accurate evaluation which doesn't cause TROUBLE', 'Confidential (highly)', 'Justify [sic] what we are doing', 'Unmet needs not shown outside', 'cheap, practical and easy' and 'good profile – glossy brochure'. There were clearly positive motives behind these comments as well as more cynical reasons.

In terms of the conduct and content of the evaluation, the group noted the need for 'Qualitative' measures such as 'User accounts', Questionnaires' and 'Surveys', and 'Quantitative' measures such as 'number of visits to/from/by...' and 'local statistics'. They also noted the benefit of having the survey as 'a measure of success – before and after'. As for the 'recipients', the 'providers' saw the evaluation as being carried out by a 'Worker' or 'User'.

Financial Stakeholders

This group noted that different 'financial stakeholders' might have quite different aims for the Project and the evaluation and spent some time exploring these. Objectives for the Project included a number of broad (and difficult to define) measures such as 'Value for Money' and 'Quality of Service' and more specific factors such as the surgery's aim to 'Cut Down On Medical Use'. The evaluation was seen as answering the question of 'Has It Met Its Objectives?' – always assuming that objectives had been defined in the first place. The evaluation should aim to aid 'Planning for the Future'. Charities might ask, 'Has It Met Unmet Needs?' while other funders (more cynically) might want the evaluation to show 'We're Being Seen to be Doing Something'.

Crucially, the results of the evaluation would contribute to the decision of 'Whether to Carry On Funding or Not'. Subsequently there was a good deal of debate as to what impact most evaluations had in determining future funding: a common perception being that funding decisions are made and subsequently evaluations are used to justify the decisions.

The type of information was felt to include 'Statistical', 'Number of Users', 'Charities – Users' views' and 'Authorities – Full Reports'. Throughout charities were seen as focusing more on users' views and involvements.

Finally, and a major difference to the previous two groups, was that this group saw the need for an 'Independent Reviewer', albeit with 'Charities – User Involvement'.

Other Vested Interests

Perhaps unsurprisingly, this group found most difficulty in addressing any of the questions raised (and failed to produce any 'Post-its') in that they were unlikely to have any aims for the Project but would perhaps want to learn from the experience. Therefore, they would be interested in anecdotal stories of success and failure, how the Project was set up, sources of finance and financial viability. They would be interested in the 'rich' stories which could be told rather than too many facts and figures. Maybe an evaluation report would not be highly relevant (other than to show to potential funders for a new project) but an open and honest talk with people who had been closely involved.

Final Discussion

As noted earlier, time prevented much further analysis taking place though a number of topics emerged in the final discussion. Firstly it was felt that the only people who would really know what was going on in a project were those who were involved – as workers or users. However, neither group would have the complete picture or be able to state that the project had been a success. There would inevitably be a diversity of views and opinions. However, this should not be regarded as failure, and indeed any other result would be highly suspect.

No one felt that the full nature of the impact of this type of activity could be captured in facts, figures and data alone. Even written accounts, however anecdotal, do not manage to capture everything. However, facts, figures and data were seen as being an important element.

Mutual trust is a major issue in evaluation. As soon as outside bodies are involved in any evaluation, either actively or as readers of reports, issues of trust, responsibility and confidentiality arise. The only way there will be truly satisfactory evaluation is when all those involved are able to live with (and not be negatively affected by) the consequences of the results of the evaluation. This situation was felt to be approached only when the evaluation was focused internally in a project where there was clear coincidence in the values of workers and users (or where these concepts were not important).

Overall it was felt that it was difficult to reconcile the competing needs of different stakeholder groups in the evaluation process. The information which is gathered needs to be wide and varied, and making the process of evaluation an integral part of the overall running of a project is vital. Perhaps cynically, people felt that projects needed to carry out their own internal evaluations on a continuous basis, gathering sufficient information for presentation to outside bodies after suitable censorship. External evaluations will continue to be fraught with difficulty.

In summary, the workshop session was able to explore a number of the problems which arise because of the different stakeholder interests. The nature of the case study did not reveal the differences between users and workers ('the experts') which was evident elsewhere in the conference. No one in the workshop would claim that any startling new material was revealed or innovative solutions found. However, the process was able to confirm a number of factors about evaluation which need to continue to be addressed. The results of the workshop could constitute a useful starting point for a more detailed exploration at a similar future event.

Chapter 19

Summing Up – Safeguarding Quality

David Felce

It seems to me that we have addressed some wide-ranging issues over the two days. Three themes have been introduced: social role valorisation (SRV), user empowerment and quality of life. My first summary comment is that these three themes are distinct. However, because they appear to overlap, I think that it has sometimes been hard for us to keep the issues separate. Clearly, the starting point for the Conference was a focus on PASS and PASSING and, in particular, on the research project that Doria Pilling has undertaken at City University looking at both instruments as evaluation tools. Other types of evaluation, quality assurance and the issue of user involvement have then been added to this initial focus.

The first theme concerned SRV, which Alan Tyne (see Chapter 2) introduced yesterday morning. He emphasised its status as a theory more than as an ideology. I am not sure if I am recalling what he said exactly, but he seemed to be saying that, whereas many people would view SRV as a set of values, it is important to see it as a theory concerned with social devaluation. PASS and PASSING are instruments that relate to that theory. There are implicit values written into them as a consequence of adopting the stance of equality of value for all, but the remit or purview of the instruments is set by the theory. This seems to me to be an important point. Neither instrument can be legitimately criticised for failing to serve another purpose, such as to reflect user views or to measure quality of life.

A second theme has been the user voice and user empowerment. It is a separate and distinct issue. PASS and PASSING take a particular stance in relation to representing user interests, both in the short and longer term, but it is one which does not simply equate to eliciting user views and holding them as paramount. Some people have been critical of this. However, I think that a more useful way of thinking about the issue is to understand that an SRV analysis and a survey of user views provide two distinct perspectives. They may have some elements of overlap, but they also reflect different purposes. One example of user empowerment may be when service design or service action is determined by user views. Similarly, service design may be said to be consistent with SRV when it scores well against the criteria set by PASS or PASSING.

The third term that we have talked about is quality of life, again a related but distinct perspective. It would be wrong to say that PASS and PASSING took no account of issues commonly included as part of quality of life. But PASS and PASSING are not themselves quality of life assessment instruments. Nor is the user view definitionally synonymous with quality of life. Individual perspectives have an important place in the assessment of quality of life, but so too might a range of objective indicators. For, not only are individual views important but so too are the factors which have shaped those views. What people think does not drop out of the sky, nor does it simply well up from inside of them without reference to the events which have helped to form preferences, aspirations, expectations and beliefs. I think we are widely agreed that people learn out of their experience. The views people express are, therefore, also a product of their experience. We have to recognise that this may complicate the matter of assessing quality of life among people whose experience may systematically differ from that of typical members of society.

A second point in summing up is that, for better or worse, in one way or another, the importance of all three of these themes seems to be more established now than ten or twenty years ago. It is easy to be pessimistic about the direction in which we are heading and there is much to concern one about the nature of our society and the role and place of services within it. But it seems to me that one should avoid the cynical view that these positive developments are just palliatives which allow us to live with the more concrete and perhaps more damaging developments in services. Actually there are grounds for optimism. There is a greater willingness to put user experience at the centre of the frame of reference – either by close identification with their experiences as people in danger of being devalued, or by responding more to their views and preferences; or by responding to the challenge of a decent quality of life using criteria applicable to the general population. There has been movement and I feel that it is unlikely to be reversed. Commitment is greater than in the past and is held across a broader group of people this decade than in the last or the one before. Services tend to be criticised and service professionals often feel under pressure. However, most of the people at this Conference are service professionals and I feel that there is a broad acceptance of solidarity with user values here. I can speak from personal experience that there was considerably more defensive cross-questioning and anger in the air when values-driven work began than we have witnessed in the last two days.

I am sure that the people involved in PASS and PASSING do not feel that they need external legitimation. However, the notion of external evaluation brings with it the healthy aspect of scrutiny by those not already deeply committed and involved in spreading the word. Done well and free of bias, such an exercise can be extremely useful. For example, it would be easier to mount a defence of the criticism that PASS is just one of those things that is passed around a group of adherents who are somehow brainwashed during the training (or conversion) process if it emerges with credit from a dispassionate review. What I heard yesterday suggested that PASS and PASSING did receive broad support. So the approach may be now seen as carrying greater weight to the extent that this has been done.

Finally, I would like to end by commenting on one further issue which I would like to highlight. It was noticeable that a group or team perspective was common across everything being talked about. The team is an essential part of the process in PASS and PASSING. This is also true of QUARTZ. The quality assurance mechanisms described again brought groups together to formulate a collective view. It seems to me that the team approach contributes to a fundamental purpose: the provision of protection and safeguards. One of its strengths is in gaining a broadly-based perspective, one which reflects a wide range of key stakeholder and other vested interests. Rather than seeking a single path to putting quality safeguards in place, it might be better to exploit all three approaches we have been discussing in the last two days in order to make sure that the quality of life and place in our society – and the future quality of life and place in society – of people who are vulnerable are protected.

An important reason for looking for complementary approaches is that each one has its weaknesses. User views may set low standards. People may have low expectations. In the interesting discussion in the Workshop that Andrea Whittaker and Simon Gardner led, somebody asked: 'Our users said that they liked it when staff wore uniforms: what would you do?' Simon replied that he had never had such a difficult question put to him before, but that his inclination was to say that staff should go back into uniforms because there should be respect for the views of users. But he made a second point: perhaps in six months' time, after the users have become used to being 'in the community', certain things will influence them to choose the 'correct' solution – for the staff to come out of uniform. This illustrates that perspectives other than immediate user views are being applied to what is considered desirable for the general good.

Similarly, the quality of life concept has been misused. Paul Williams mentioned yesterday that a major problem may arise if people are considered as not being able to have a decent quality of life. That can lead to greater segregation or to worse. We have all heard arguments which 'justify' the withholding of life-preserving treatment for people with considerable disabilities on the basis that they could not have a reasonable quality of life. We, therefore, have to strive constantly to make sure that the application of well thought out concepts is positive.

In this respect, SRV can provide a very strong basis for looking at the protection of people who are in danger of being devalued. This is precisely because it relates to this purpose. The ruler for assessment embodied within PASS and PASSING provides an absolute standard, one of equality with the typical culture, which acts as a strength against low expectations and an obstacle to common attempts to develop separate and lower criteria by which to assess the welfare of people with disability. In conclusion, then, my hope is that a greater appreciation and application of SRV theory, together with increased user empowerment and a heightened concern for quality of life, will lead to better protection and safeguard for the welfare of vulnerable people in our society.

Contributors

Peter Allen works as Head of Psychology Services in Newham, East London, where he has been since 1984. Prior to this he was employed by Barnardos and Social Service Departments. He has always worked either with children and their families or people with learning disabilities. He works nationally as an Associate Consultant for the N.D.T. (National Development Team) and lives in South London.

Jim Band and **Dale Walker** are both members of the Medway Users Forum where they are actively involved in promoting the users' perspective. They are currently involved in quality reviews of a number of local day and residential services. Jim is also chair of Medway MIND and Dale is a member of the council of management of the United Kingdom Advocacy Network. They were both founder members of the South East Training and Consultancy Co-operative.

David Felce is Professor of Research in Learning Disabilities and Director of the Welsh Centre for Learning Disabilities Applied Research Unit. He has spent twenty years researching in the field, much of which has been dedicated to looking at quality of life issues in the course of evaluating residential services for people with severe learning disabilities.

Simon Gardner is a member of People First and was one of the two consultants who carried out the evaluation of services in the London Borough of Hillingdon. He is a freelance trainer working with staff and people with learning difficulties on self-advocacy and related subjects. He is a member of the Merton and Sutton Community Health Council.

Kath Gillespie Sells has a background in health and education. She was a ward sister and college lecturer prior to her disablement. She has worked continually in the field of disability equality training and social policy for the last ten years. She is currently undertaking research into disabled women and sexuality, and further developing her work in the area of HIV/AIDS and disability.

Bill Gorf and **Margaret Guerrero** are members of the Lewisham Users Forum. In addition to campaigning for better services the Forum provides consultancy and advice to Lewisham and North Southwark Health Authority. Its members also provide training sessions for medical and nursing students. They were both founder members of the South East Training and Consultancy Co-operative.

David Hughes is Lecturer in the Applied Psychology of Learning Disability at the Tizard Centre, University of Kent at Canterbury. In addition to teaching, he has worked as Service Development Consultant with the Special Development Team and is manager of the Tizard Centre's quality assurance and enhancement projects. David is a qualified and experienced teacher of children who have special educational needs and has extensive experience in a wide range of services for people with learning disabilities. His publications include (with Beasley, F., Hewson, S., Mansell, J. and Stein, J.) (1993) *MTS: Handbook for Observers*. Canterbury: Tizard Centre.

Leonie Kellaher is the Director of the Centre for Environmental and Social Studies in Ageing (CESSA) at the University of North London. At CESSA, with colleagues, her work has focused upon the regulatory environments which affect people – notably but not exclusively older people – in residential settings. Most recently, in developing IQA, her work has been concerned with the importance of the influence which can be exerted by those who are recipients of services, and the ways the regulation of services can be improved by taking account of user viewpoints.

Alison Kerruish is a Project Manager for the Care Programming Approach Development Project at the Ravensbourne NHS Trust, Bromley. At the time of the Evaluating Quality Conference she was a Research Fellow/Project Manager for the Centre for Applied Psychology of Social Care (CAPSE, now the Tizard Centre), University of Kent. She has carried out action-oriented research on quality assurance in health and social care over a number of years. This has included five years as a Research Analyst with CAPSE Research developing a satisfaction system for acute health services and two years working on a King's Fund project developing methods of monitoring the quality of residential services for people with long-term mental health problems.

Peter Lindley works in the Training and Development section at the Sainsbury centre for Mental Health. Formerly he was a Service Development Consultant and worked at the Tizard Centre at the University of Kent. He has worked all his career in mental health services and has extensive experience of management, teaching and research. His work includes the Consultative Development Programme, a course for current and ex-users of mental health services, facilitating the patients' Council at Broadmoor Hospital and collaborative work with users on their role in commissioning services.

Gerald Midgley worked as a Research Assistant in the Rehabilitation Resource Centre at City University for two years, conducted research independently for another four, and then took a Research Fellowship in the Centre for Systems Studies at the University of Hull. He is now Deputy Director at the Centre. Gerald's main research interests are community systems studies and systems philosophy. On the theoretical side he has written extensively about the need for a critically reflective research practice that places the exploration of values at its heart. On the practical side, he has been involved in numerous projects, including several evaluations of services for people with disabilities. He has a particular interest in the development of methods to facilitate user involvement in the design and management of services. He has many publications, aimed at both academics and practitioners working in the community.

Doria Pilling was the Co-ordinator of the Evaluating Quality Conference. At the Rehabilitation Resource Centre at City University, she has carried out a number of evaluations of innovative services for people with disabilities, as well as the evaluation of PASS and PASSING. Previously, at the National Children's Bureau, she carried out studies using data from the National Child Development Study, and wrote a number of literature reviews, mainly concerned with children with disabilities and their families. She is the author of several books, including: *Approaches to Case Management for People with Disabilities*, Jessica Kingsley Publications (1992) and *Escape from Disadvantage*, Falmer Press (1990).

Stephen Pilling is a Clinical Psychologist who is Head of Mental Health Psychology Services for Camden and Islington Community Health Services Trust. He has long experience and interest in rehabilitation, and for the past six years been involved in the developing of the QUARTZ system.

Judy Renshaw is a Project Manager at the Audit Commission. She is currently working on a national review of mental health services as well as the joint Welsh Office/Audit Commission quality measurement project. She was previously the Director of Good Practices in Mental Health and, before that, a Research Fellow at University of Kent, monitoring hospital resettlement teams.

Charles Ritchie is the Director of the Community Operational Research Unit at the Northern College. He has been involved in Operational Research in a variety of contexts since 1977 and in the community OR Unit since 1989. The Unit works with community and voluntary sector groups on a wide range of issues such as financial and strategic planning, group work and team building and evaluation. He has recently co-edited a book of case studies showing how OR can assist community and voluntary sector organisations, called *Community Works*, which is available from the Community OR Unit.

Alan Tyne taught in schools before joining 'Campaign for the Mentally Handicapped' (now VIA – 'Values into Action') as research and information officer. In 1979, with Paul Williams and Morag Plank, he founded the sister-organisation, CMHERA, to develop a programme of normalisation-based training and service-evaluation in the United Kingdom. Since 1988 he has developed an independent programme of work called 'Constructive Options'. Through this he works alongside handicapped people, their families and friends, co-operating with services and community organisations to seek better futures in ordinary communities.

Dale Walker – see Jim Band, above.

Andrea Whittaker is Project Manger, Building Inclusive Communities, which is part of the Community Care Group at the King's Fund Centre. Her work covers user participation and self-advocacy, particularly with people with learning difficulties. She has had a major involvement in the King's Fund Ordinary Life initiative and is now developing work related to community participation. Andrea Whittaker has been closely associated with the self-advocacy organisation People First since it began in 1984 and was its Adviser until October 1988, when People First set up its own independent office.

Paul Williams has worked in the field of learning disabilities for thirty years. He was a member of the Wessex Health Care Evaluation Research Team in the 1960s, has experience of residential work with people with severe disabilities, and was a tutor at Castle Priory College, the staff training centre of the Spastics Society, for ten years. He was one of the founders of the Community and Mental Handicap Educational and Research Association, set up in 1979, to bring training in the use of PASS and PASSING to Britain. He became assistant director of CMHERA in 1983 and has been Director since 1988. He is co-author of a book on self-advocacy by people with learning disabilities. He has a part-time post in the Department of Community Studies at Reading University, where he teaches on work with people with learning disabilities, on research, and on anti-racist and anti-discriminatory practice.

Paul Wolfson is a psychiatrist at Bexley Hospital with a special interest in rehabilitation, and an honorary lecturer at the United Medical and Dental Schools, University of London. He has done research on the removal of elderly people from their homes, under Section 47 of the National Assistance Act. He was a member of the team at RDP (Research and Development in Psychiatry – now Sainsbury Centre for Mental Health), which evaluated the closure of Cane Hill Hospital, and with Paul Clifford devised ACE (formerly FACE, a Functional Assessment of Care Environments), which was used in the project. Other interests include comedy script writing, and making training videos.

Subject Index

References in italic indicate figures or tables.

abuse issues 151–2, *151*
acceptability, as quality measure 156
accessibility, Framework for Accomplishment 189
accomplishment categories 160, *193*
development of 182–5
ACE (Assessment of Care Environments) 2, 5, 78–83, 84–105
PASS/ING compared 5, 86–105
four evaluations 96–100
residential home example 90–6, *92, 94*
procedure and practice 81–3, *82*
requirements and components 79–80
'activities' ratings 16
'activity level' data 201, *202, 202, 203*
administration ratings 14–15, 29
adult training centres 18
advocates 142
age-appropriateness rating 15
All-Wales Strategy 6, 126–33
evaluation methods 126–30

lessons learnt 130–1
new instrument 131–3
annual reports, Wales 127–8
appropriateness, as quality measure 156
appropriateness ratings 15, 95–6, 99–100, 156
ARC-ometer 111
Assessment of Care Environments *see* ACE
attitude change, and PASS/ING 58
Audit Commission project, Wales 126–33
autonomy ratings *94, 95,* 98–9

Barnardos research project 129
behaviour change, and PASS/ING 58
black minority groups 103–4
Bromley services project 158–63
aims 158–9
methods 159–62, *159, 161*
results 162–3
BS 5750 175–6, *176*

Cane Hill Hospital 79, 81–3, *82*
care environments, difficulties of assessing 78–9
carers 137, 144–5, 155
see also staff
Caring in Homes initiative 164–6
CESSA (Centre for Environmental and Social Studies in Ageing) 164–5
checklist approach 131, 156

children, adult's service quality compared 71, *71*
'choice' accomplishment 160, 183–4, 193, *194*
'client groupings' ratings 55, 95–6, 99–100
client individualization ratings *92, 93–4, 98*
coercion 35, 47
commissioners of services 160–1
communication systems evaluation 40–1
community, as key value 28
community integration (presence) accomplishment 160, 182, 183, 184, 193, *194*
Community and Mental Handicap Educational and Research Association (CMHERA) 17
competence (developing skills) accomplishment 160, 183, 193, *194*
competency enhancement, PASS/ING 16, 22, 51–2, 53–4, 141
complaints systems 152, 173, 178
complementarity of methods 33–47, 215
Critical Systems Thinking 34–7, *34*
four methods compared 37–45, *38*
'complex' contexts 34, 35
examples *38,* 40–1, 43–4
conference, *Evaluating Quality* 1–3
confidentiality 173, 186
'conservatism corollary' theme 22

consistency, PASS/ING
results 70, 70
Constructive Options 180
'contacts and
relationships' ratings
16
contexts, Critical Systems
Thinking 4, 34, 34–5,
37–44, 38
continuing care ward,
ACE example 81, 82
contracts, evaluation 31
creative methodology
design 36
Critical Systems Thinking
4, 34–7
critique, and evaluation
36–7
cultural values,
PASS/ING 20–1,
119–20
culture-appropriateness
rating 15

day centre closure 196,
197, 198
day services 18
Quality Action Group
example 108–12
QUARTZ day hospital
examples 142–3,
144–5
residential compared
73–4, 73
debate structuring
methods 41–4
de-institutionalisation
56–7, 115
devaluation, PASS/ING
theory 2, 4, 20, 27–9,
39, 213
black minority groups
103
and foundation
discussion 21
and normalisation 51–2
'development and activity'
domain 118, 119, 122

'developmental growth'
ratings 15
'developmental model'
theme 22
difference, tolerance of 56
dignity 157
disempowerment 4, 29
disruptions to people 130
drug 'side-effects' issues
153, 154
'Dynamic Conservatism'
181

East London, Quality
Action Group
example 108–12
Eastern Nebraska
Community Office of
Retardation (ENCOR)
19
ECT (electro-convulsive
therapy)
issues 152–3
effectiveness and
efficiency, as quality
measures 156
electro-convulsive therapy
(ECT)
issues 152–3
'emotional wellbeing'
domain 118, 119, 123
empowerment 9, 29, 159,
162, 184, 213–14
ENCOR (Eastern
Nebraska
Community Office of
Retardation) 19
environmental quality
ratings, ACE 80, 88
'equality' (respect)
accomplishment 160,
182, 184, 193
equity, as quality measure
156
ethnic identity, PASS/ING
4, 20–1, 103–4
Evaluating Quality
conference 1–3

exclusion issues 4, 29, 56
expectation theory 4, 51,
52–4
expectations, and
satisfaction 117
external evaluation 215
external influences, life
domains 118, 119
external research, Wales
130
external review, QUARTZ
137

'faces' rating scale 193, 193
Facility Review checklist
161, 162
feedback 4, 109, 130, 195–6
PASS/ING 31, 57, 58,
75–6, 142
'felicity' ratings 91, 92, 93–4
financial stakeholders
(purchasers) 107,
160–1
attitudes to evaluation
208, 210
flexibility ratings 92, 94, 98
follow-up see feedback
foundation discussion 4, 5,
21–2, 30, 74–5, 88
Framework for
Accomplishment 6–7,
8, 180–90
'accomplishments' 160,
182–5
'framework' 181–2

gender, and quality
assurance 151, 154
gender identity,
PASS/ING 4, 20–1
group-forming activities,
Quality Action Group
110
group homes, QUARTZ
review examples
143–4

grouping ratings, client 55, 95–6, 99–100

'halo effect' 66–7
handbooks, PASS/ING 13, 30
'health project' exercise 8–9, 207–11
Hillingdon project 191–200
homes
    community
        ACE example 81–3, 82
        Hillingdon examples 191–200
        housing projects 71–3, 72
        QUARTZ review examples 143–4
    day services compared 73–4, 73
    institutional
        ACE/PASS comparison 90–6, 92, 94
        large/small compared 70, 70–1, 71
Homes are for Living In (HAFLI) 133, 175–6, 176
hospitals
    day examples 142–3, 144–5
    residential examples 81, 82
House User Groups 161, 162
housing projects 71–3, 72, 115

ideals, and evaluation 99
identity issues, PASS/ING 20–1
image enhancement ratings 16, 51–2, 55–6, 91, 99, 133, 141

Image Juxtaposition rating 15
'imitation, power of' 22–3
inclusion issues 29, 184
individual plans, Wales 127
individual service review (ISR)
    checklist 161, 161
individualization ratings 92, 93–4, 98
information collection issues 151, 160–1
Inside Quality Assurance see IQA
'insiders' 1, 6, 7, 148–9
    see also staff; users
inspection processes 166–7, 175, 176
inspection units, Wales 129
integration ratings 15, 54, 91, 97, 100, 103
'integration' theme 23, 54, 56
intensity ratings 91, 94–6, 94, 99
interests, balancing different sets 166–7, 166
internal review, QUARTZ 137
interviewing 204–5
IQA (Inside Quality Assurance) 7–8, 164–79
    advantages and disadvantages 176–7
    conceptual basis 166–7, 166
    other approaches compared 175–6, 176
    process 167, 168, 169, 170
    purpose 169–71
    rationale 164–6
    results 171–5

junior training centres 18
justice, as key value 28

key values 28–9
King's Fund 50, 84, 158

labelling theory 53
language problems 123–4
large residences, small compared 70, 70–1, 71
learning disabilities, people with
    educability 53
    negative perceptions of 18–19
life conditions 115, 116, 117
life domains 118, 119, 121–3
Life-Enriching Interactions ratings 92, 93
lifeline exercise, Quality Action Group 110
low staff home, ACE example 81–3, 82

management involvement 130, 137
    Hillingdon 192, 197
    Quality Action Group 108, 112
management ratings 14–15
management systems evaluation 40–1
manuals, PASS/ING 13, 14, 17, 30
'material wellbeing' domain 118, 119, 121
medication issues 153–4, 153
mental health service users' views 7, 148–55
methods of assessing quality
    All-Wales Strategy 126–33
    Bromley project 158–63, 159, 161

complementarity 33–47, *34*, *38*, 215
observation and interviewing 201–5, *202*, *203*
see also ACE; Framework for Accomplishment; IQA; PASS/ING; QUARTZ
minority group view 58, 103–4
'model coherency' ratings 15
momentary time sample (MTS) 201–4, *202*, *203*
monitoring methods, Bromley project 158, 160–2, *161*
monitoring groups, Wales 128
MTS (momentary time sample) 201–4, *202*, *203*

needs of service users 74–5, 88, 96, 99, 160–1
see also foundation discussion
negative perceptions of people 18–19, 20, 55
'new genocide' 23
NIMROD service 71–3, *72*, 115
non-participant observation 201–4, *202*, *203*
non-verbal users, obtaining views 195, 204, 205
'normal' services, and PASS/ING 76
normalisation 2, 3, 9, 18, 19–20, 39, 50–2
integration into society 54, 56–7
PASS ratings 15, 120, *121–3*

and SRV 39, 52, 58
North Wiltshire Community Living Project (NWCLP) 71–3, *72*

objective life conditions 117, 118, *119*, 120
objectivity in evaluation 201
examples 201–5, *202*, *203*
QUARTZ 137
O'Brien, John and Connie 21, 180, 182–3
observation methods 201–4, *202*, *203*
Omaha, community-based services 19
outcome, as quality measure 85
over-servicing dangers 189–90
over-supervision observations 196

participant observation 204
'participation' (integration) theme 23, 54, 56
PASS/ING 1, 2, 3–5, 9, 213, 215, 216
ACE compared 5, 84–105, *92*, *94*
context 4, 11–12, 23, 25–7
description 13–24, 25–32
background 17–19
concepts underlying 19–22, 27–30
content 14–16, 27, 29, 30
core themes 22–3
instruments and process 13–14
in practice 17
critique 50–60

quality of life models compared 119–20, *121–3*, 124
QUARTZ compared 135–6, 137, 138, 141–2, 145
results 61–77
consistency 70, *70*
examples 70–4, *71*, *72*, *73*
reliability 64–8, *65–6*, *67*, *68*
scoring system 61–4
validity 68–70, *69*
use with other methods 37, *38*, 38–40, 41, 44–5, 46, 133
Pennhurst Longitudinal Study 115
People First, Hillingdon project 191–200
perceptions, negative 18–19, 20, 55
personal care ratings *94*, 95
personal competency enhancement, PASS/ING 16, 22, 51–2, 53–4, 141
personal values and aspirations 115, *116*, 117, 118, *119*
physical comfort ratings *92*, 93
'physical wellbeing' domain 118, *119*, *121*
physically disabled users views 7, 155–7
'pluralist' contexts *34*, 35
examples *38*, 42, 43–4
policy statements, principles from 131–2, 133
political change, and quality improvement 112–13
Population Profile, ACE 79, 87
'post-evaluative depression' 31

'post-primary production economy' 23
'power of imitation' theme 22–3
preparation for evaluation 31, 57
'prerequisites' emphasis, PASS/ING 98–9, 100
process, importance in evaluation 131
Program Analysis of Service Systems see PASS
Program Analysis of Service Systems Implementation of Normalization Goals see PASSING
providers 107, 160–1
    attitudes to evaluation 208, 209–10
Provision Ratings, ACE 80, 87–8
psychiatric day hospital, QUARTZ example 142–3
psychogeriatric day hospital, QUARTZ example 144–5
purchasers (financial stakeholders) 107, 160–1
    attitudes to evaluation 208, 210

QRT (Quality Review Teams) 138
qualitative methods, Systems of Systems Methodologies 35–6
Quality Action Groups East London 6, 108–13
Wales 129
quality assurance definitions 149, 150, 175
    system characteristics 137, 150, 175–6, 176

quality-collage activity 109–10
quality control 175
quality definitions 107, 109, 112, 136–7, 155–6
quality measurement principles 156
quality of life 6, 9, 114–25, 213, 214, 215
    conceptual models 115–17, 116, 119
    PASS/ING compared 119–20, 121–3
    relevant life domains 118
Quality of Life Questionnaire 123–4
quality of setting ratings 15, 92, 93
Quality Ratings, ACE 80, 88
Quality Review Teams (QRT) 138
quantitative methods, Systems of Systems Methodologies 35, 38
QUARTZ 6–7, 135–47, 215
    components 137–42, 139–40
    user involvement 142–5
questionnaires 161, 162, 192–3, 195

ratings
    ACE 79–80, 86–8
    ACE/PASS/ING compared 88–100, 92, 94
    PASS/ING 5, 13–16, 55–6, 57, 61–4
recipients of services see users
Registered Homes Working Group (RHWG) inspection documents 133
regulatory processes 166–7, 175, 176

rehabilitation ward, ACE example 81, 82
'relationships' accomplishment 160, 182, 183, 193, 194, 194
'relevance' ratings 91–3, 96, 99
reliability, PASS/ING 64–8, 65–6, 67, 68
reprisal fears 198
research units, Wales 130
researchers
    importance of style 130
    users as 131, 151, 191–200, 205–6
residential homes
    ACE/PASS/ING comparisons 90–6, 92, 94
    day services compared 73–4, 73
    large and small compared 70, 70–1, 71
    see also Bromley services project; IQA
residents see users
Residents' Associations 161, 162
residents' management practice scales 85–6
'respect' (equality) accomplishment 160, 182, 184, 193
revaluation 20, 29, 104
'rights' ratings 94, 95, 98
'role expectancy and circularity' theme 22
RRC (Rehabilitation Resource Centre) 2, 50, 84
rules, accomplishments compared 184–5

Sainsbury Centre for Mental Health 135

SAST (Strategic Assumption Surfacing and Testing) 37, 41–2, 44, 46

'satisfaction with life' (wellbeing) 115–17, 116, 118, 119, 121–3

schedules, QUARTZ 139–42, 139–40

scoring systems, PASS/ING 5, 14, 61–74
consistency 70, 70
reliability 64–8, 65–6, 67, 68
validity 68–70, 69

'scrapping' services 76, 196, 197, 198

Self-Assessment and Performance review, CESSA 164–6

self-evaluation 169–71

self-organised groups, role of 32

service provision ideology 4, 26

Service Review Package 133

service users see users

'setting' ratings 15, 16, 92, 93

'seven themes', PASS/ING 22

'side-effects' issues 153–4, 153

'simple' contexts 34, 35
examples 38, 39–40, 42

'skill development' (competence) accomplishment 160, 183, 193, 194

small residences, large compared 70, 70–1, 71

'snapshot' evaluation methods 100

'social care' ratings 87, 94, 95

'social devaluation' see devaluation

social image enhancement see image enhancement

'social imagery' theme 23

social integration see integration

'social relationships' ratings 87, 92, 93, 99

social role valorisation (SRV) 2, 3, 9, 20–2, 23, 213, 216
and normalisation 39, 52, 58

'social wellbeing' domain 118, 119, 122

Soft Systems Methodology (SSM) 37, 42–4, 45, 46

'softness' of user views data 176

South East Training and Consultancy Co-operative 148

SRV see social role valorisation

SSM see Soft Systems Methodology

'staff characteristics' ratings 55

'staff contact' data 202, 202–4, 203

staff involvement 199
attitudes to user involvement 178
QUARTZ 7, 137, 141, 142
in user interviews 198

staffed group homes, QUARTZ review examples 143–4

'stakeholders' 8–9, 207–11

standard-setting, IQA 177

stewardship, as key value 28

Strategic Assumption Surfacing and Testing (SAST) 37, 41–2, 44, 46

strategic quality action approaches, Wales 129

structured evaluations, Wales 129

subjective wellbeing 117, 118, 119

subscores, PASS/ING 63–4

survey work, Wales 128–9

System of Systems Methodologies 34–6, 34, 37–8
examples 38, 39–40, 40–1, 42, 43–4

teachers' expectations study 53

team perspective 215
PASS/ING team 14
see also Quality Action Groups; Quality Review Teams

telephones issue, Quality Action Group 110, 111, 112–13

theory basis of PASS/ING 27–9

time, studying change over 73

time-keeping issues, Quality Action Group 111

Time-Use Efficiency rating 94, 95, 99

training 30, 64–5, 163
users as trainers 157

tranquillisers issue 154

transport issues, Quality Action Group 110, 111

trust 7, 159, 173, 198, 211

'unconsciousness' in services 22

uniforms issue, community care 198–9, 215

'unitary' contexts 34, 35
examples 38, 39–40, 40–1

Update Associates 157

users 1, 6–8, 9, 213–14, 215, 216

attitudes to evaluation 208, 209
carers and families as 144–5, 155
consultant role 157
evaluator roles 131, 151, 191–200, 205–6
needs assessment 21, 74–5
obtaining views
   All-Wales Strategy 131, 132, 133
   Bromley project 158–63, *159*, *161*
   interviews 204–5
   IQA approach 165, 166, 169–73, 176–7, 177–8
   mental health service users 148–55, *150*, *151*, *152*
   PASS/ING 101–2
   physically disabled 155–7
   Quality Action Groups 107–11
   QUARTZ 139, 140, 141, 142–5

validity, PASS/ING 5, 68–70, *69*, 84, 100–1
values
   PASS/ING 4, 26, 27–8, 101–3
   QUARTZ 137–8, 145–6
Vanier, Jean 27
verbal communication difficulties, users with 195, 204, 205
Viable System Diagnosis (VSD) 37, *38*, 40–1, 45, 46

Wales, quality measurement 126–33
wards, ACE comparisons 81, 82

weightings, PASS/ING items 62–3
wellbeing (satisfaction with life) 115–17, *116*, 118, *119*, *121–3*
Welsh Office project 126–33
Wisconsin PASS workshop 25–6
Wolfensberger, Wolf 3–4, 17–21, 23
workshops
   PASS/ING 4, 25–6, 30
   SSM 43
'wounding people' analogy 27

Author Index

Alinsky, S.D. 157
Allen, H.M. 117
Aloia, G.F. 53
Andrews, F.M. 117
Argyris, C. 181

Baldwin, S. 53, 55
Banathy, B.H. 35
Bano, A. 20
Barnes, C. 54
Baxter, C. 20
Beasley, F. 201
Beer, S. 40
Bentler, P.M. 117
Blackstone, T. 53
Bollinger, M. 117
Booth, T. 165
Borthwick-Duffy, S.A. 115
Bradley, V.J. 115
Brechin, A. 55, 56
Breggin, P. 152
Brost, M. 183
Brown, H. 20, 22, 39, 50,
    55, 56
Brownlee, L. 115
Burrell, G. 34
Burton, M. 38, 56

Campbell, A. 117
Carmines, E.G. 84
Cataldo, M.F. 115
Chadsey-Rusch, J. 115
Chappell, A. 22
Checkland, P. 42
Clark, A.D.B. 53
Clark, A.M. 53
Clemson, B. 40

Clifford, P. 2, 70, 79, 86,
    135, 136, 137
Conroy, J.W. 115
Converse, P.E. 117
Coote, A. 175
Cummins, R.A. 114, 117

Dalley, G. 56
Davies, B. 165
Department of Health
    (DH) 133
Deprey, R.K. 183

Edgerton, R.B. 117
Edison, M.R. 54
Emerson, E. 142
Emshoff, J.R. 42
Espejo, R. 40
Evans, G. 133

Felce, D. 101, 114, 115, 118
Ferns, P. 56
Firth, H. 19
Fleiss, J. 64
Flood, R.L. 34, 35, 36, 37
Floyd, M. 40
Flynn, M. 117
Flynn, R. 63, 64, 70, 73, 74

Gardner, S. 191
Glenn, L. 1, 2, 11, 25, 27,
    33, 38, 50, 57, 61, 62,
    78, 84, 85, 115, 136
Goffman, E. 11, 85, 114
Goldsbury, T. 115
Gordon, R.A. 53
Grant, G. 127
Gray, P. 133
Gregory, W.J. 34
Grover, R. 142
Gullone, E. 114
Gutek, B.A. 117

Harnden, R. 40
Heal, L.W. 115
Herr, B. 117
Hewson, S. 201
Hill, R. 135, 145
Hodapp, R.M. 54
Hoffman, K. 117, 123
Holland, A. 117
Horrobin, J.M. 53
Hubbell, M. 115
Hughes, D. 201

Jackson, M.C. 33, 34, 35,
    36, 37, 42
Jacobsen, L. 53
Jensen, A. 53
Johnson, T.Z. 183
Jones, R.L. 53

Keith, K.D. 117, 123
Kellaher, L. 165, 166
Kendall, A. 19
Kershaw, J. 191
Kerruish, A. 163
Keys, P. 33, 34, 35
Kilmann, R.H. 42
King, R. 11, 12, 114
Knapp, M. 165
Kugel, R. 18
Kushlik, A. 114

Landesman-Dwyer, S. 115
LaPointe, N. 64
Lavender, T. 69, 135, 136,
    138, 139
Leiper, R. 69, 135, 136, 138,
    139, 145
Lindley, P. 2, 136, 138
Lowe, K. 114, 115

MacMillan, D.L. 53
Mansell, J. 201
Mason, R.O. 41, 42
McCabe, M.P. 114

McCourt-Perring, C. 174
McGill, P. 142
McGrath, M. 127
McKennell, A.C. 117
McLain, R.E. 115
Midgley, G. 34, 35, 36, 40
Mitroff, I.I. 41, 42
Moos, R. 115
Morgan, G. 34
Morris, P. 69
Mortimore, J. 53

Nadirshaw, Z. 20
Nirje, B. 39, 51

O'Brien, J. 160, 184
O'Connor, N. 18
Oliga, J.C. 35

Paiva, S. de 114, 115
Patton, M.Q. 33
Peace, S. 165
Perrin, B. 51
Perry, J. 101, 115, 118
Pfeffer, N. 175
Pickard, L. 79
Pilling, D. 53
Pilling, S. 69, 135, 136, 138, 139
Poonia, K. 20
Pringle, M.K. 53

Ramcharan, P. 127
Raynes, N. 11, 12, 85, 114
Registered Homes
    Working Group 133
Risley, T.R. 115
Robinson, T. 56
Rodgers, W.L. 117
Romeo, Y. 114
Rosenthal, R. 53
Rynders, J.E. 53

Sackett, G.P. 115
Schalock, R.L. 117, 123
Scholes, J. 42
Schon, D. 181
Shepherd, G. 136
Shrout, P. 64
Sigelman, C.K. 124
Silverstein, A.B. 115
Simons, K. 127
Smith, H. 20, 22, 39, 50, 55, 56, 163
Smith, J. 114
Stark, J.A. 115
Stein, J. 201
Stowers, C. 53
Swain, J. 55
Szivos, S. 54

Thomas, D. 19
Thomas, S. 1, 2, 26, 27, 33, 38, 39, 50, 52, 56, 61, 64, 84, 133, 135
Tizard, J. 11, 12, 18, 114
Towell, D. 69
Tsoukas, H. 34
Tullman, S. 51
Tyne, A. 75

Ulrich, W. 34, 37

Wagner, G. 164, 166
Wagner, L. 183
Wainwright, T. 2, 136, 138
Ward, L. 20
Weaver, T. 165
Welsh Office 127
Whitehead, S. 57
Whittaker, A. 191
Willcocks, D. 165
Williams, P. 20, 54, 64, 70, 75, 96
Wilson, B. 42
Wolfensberger, W. 18, 23, 51, 57, 64
    and Glenn, L. 1, 2, 11, 25, 27, 33, 38, 50,
        57, 61, 62, 78, 84, 85, 115, 136
    and Thomas, S. 1, 2, 26, 27, 33, 38, 39, 50, 52, 56, 61, 84, 133, 135
    1972 2, 19, 39, 56
    1980 2, 54
    1983 2, 13, 20, 21, 29, 30, 39, 56, 61, 64, 90
Wolfson, P. 2, 79, 86, 101

Youll, P. 174

Zauha, H. 23
Zeller, R.A. 84
Zigler, E. 54